S0-BLV-400

WARRIORS
Collector's Edition

by Joseph Hession

Foghorn Press
BOOKS BUILDING COMMUNITY.

51995 >

9 780935 701678

ISBN 0-935701-67-2

Copyright © 1993
by Joseph Hession

All rights reserved. This book may not be reproduced
in full or in part without the written permission of the
publisher, except for use by a reviewer in the context
of a review. Inquiries and excerpt requests should be
addressed to:

Foghorn Press
555 DeHaro Street #220
The Boiler Room
San Francisco, CA 94107
415-241-9550

Foghorn Press titles are distributed to the book trade
by Publishers Group West, Emeryville, California. To
contact your local representative, call 1-800-788-3123.

To order individual books, please call Foghorn Press
at 1-800-FOGHORN (364-4676).

Library of Congress
Cataloging-in-Publication Data

Hession, Joseph

Warriors — Collector's Edition/
by Joseph Hession.
p. cm.

Includes index.

ISBN 0-935701-67-2
1. Golden State Warriors (Basketball team) — History.
2. Golden State Warriors (Basketball team) — Chronology.
3. Basketball players — United States — Interviews.
I. Title.

GV885.52.C2H47   1993
796.323'64'097946 — dc20   93–32016
CIP

Printed in the United States of America.

WARRIORS
Collector's Edition

by Joseph Hession

Foghorn
Press
BOOKS BUILDING COMMUNITY™

PHOTO CREDITS

Cover Photo and all Color Photos: Sam Forencich

AP/Wide World Photos: pp. 14, 17, 21, 27, 30, 32, 33, 36, 37, 40, 41, 43, 47, 49, 52, 57, 58, 60, 63, 66, 69, 71, 76, 80, 81, 85, 86, 88, 89, 91, 93, 94, 95, 97, 101, 102 (bottom), 105, 108, 110 (top), 118, 120 (top), 123 (bottom), 126, 127, 130, 141 (bottom), 145

Golden State Warriors Photo File: pp. iv, v, viii, xii, 45, 55, 61, 65, 67, 75, 83, 92, 99, 102 (top), 103, 106, 110 (bottom), 111, 113, 115, 117, 119, 120 (bottom), 121, 123 (top), 125, 129, 132, 134, 135, 137, 138, 139, 141 (top), 142, 143

Naismith Memorial Basketball Hall of Fame: pp. x, 19, 20, 23, 25, 35, 39, 54, 73

BOOK CREDITS

Managing Editor: Ann-Marie Brown
Cover Design: I. Magnus
Book Design and Layout: Michele Thomas
Copyediting: Howard Rabinowitz and Samantha Trautman
Research Assistants: Josh Bertetta, Peter Gallagher and Erik Mattias

Special thanks to the Golden State Warriors for their cooperation in providing photographs and historical information.

For Sam, a seven-pound, 12-ounce screaming Warriors fan.

Page IV: Victor Alexander (52), nicknamed "Smoothie" by his teammates, holds his ground against the Houston Rockets.

Page V: Chris Mullin (17) tosses a shot over the outstretched arm of Miami's Pearl Washington during action in a 1989 contest.

CONTENTS

FOREWORD *by Al Attles*

In any professional sports organization, there will inevitably be periods of euphoria and disappointment. The Golden State Warriors have certainly been no exception. But through the vicissitudes of joy and despair, one constant has always distinguished the Warriors and their rich history: a strong sense of family.

In my 34 years with the organization, many players have left for one reason or another, only to return later to tell me how much they miss the Warriors. Ever since Franklin Mieuli bought the team from Eddie Gottlieb and moved Wilt Chamberlain, Tom Meschery, head coach Bob Feerick and the rest of the team from Philadelphia in 1962, through Franklin's years and right up to the present ownership team of Jim Fitzgerald and Dan Finnane, the Warriors have always been more than just a group of players on a basketball court.

Of course it is a business first, and no event was more illustrative of that fact than the gut-wrenching trade of Nate Thurmond prior to the 1974-1975 season. Nate's emergence as one of the league's premier players in the mid-1960s made it possible for us to trade away Wilt in one of the league's true blockbuster deals, but a few years later it was Nate who we traded. It was one of the most difficult decisions that Franklin, general manager Dick Vertlieb and I ever had to make, but a year later we stunned the basketball world and won the championship. I struggle with the term "destiny," but that year was a rare experience.

Clearly the NBA Championship was a high watermark for the organization, Franklin and for me, but I think it was the way it happened that made it so special. Having lost three-fifths of our starting line-up from the year before to free agency, our expectations were understandably tempered. We had a true superstar in Rick Barry, but I believe we never would have achieved such success without the hard work of others such as Clifford Ray, Keith Wilkes, Phil Smith, George Johnson, Jeff Mullins, Charles Johnson and assistant coach Joe Roberts. The season provided a perfect example of what a team can do when it collectively works together. It was just one of those years that won't be matched.

We suffered through some down years in the late 1970s and mid-1980s, but what we lacked in wins, we more than made up for in rich, diverse personalities. Bernard King, World B. Free, Larry Smith, Manute Bol and Mitch Richmond all helped to make up the fertile fabric of the Warriors. They are gone now, but each one will remain an important member of our extended family.

While I join the rest of you in looking forward to the years ahead with NBA All-Stars Chris Mullin and Tim Hardaway and future star Chris Webber, I still find it comforting every now and then to sit back and take a few minutes to reminisce about the wonderful history of the Golden State Warriors.

INTRODUCTION

Few professional basketball teams have a history as rich as the Golden State Warriors.

Long before Chris Mullin and Tim Hardaway were putting up jump shots for Golden State, the Philadelphia Warriors established themselves as one of the premier professional teams in the country.

Under the leadership of basketball pioneer Eddie Gottlieb, the Philadelphia Warriors won the Basketball Association of America Championship in 1946-47. Soon after, they joined the National Basketball Association as one of the league's original teams.

For the next 16 years, the Warriors thrilled basketball-mad Philadelphia fans with players like Joe Fulks, Howie Dallmar, Paul Arizin, Tom Gola and Wilt Chamberlain.

Always the enterprising franchise, the Warriors continued to break new ground in 1962 when they packed up and moved west to the promised land — California. The San Francisco Warriors joined the Los Angeles Lakers as the only professional basketball teams west of the Mississippi.

Within a year of moving to the San Francisco Bay Area, center Wilt Chamberlain was rewriting the NBA record book, and the Warriors were playing the Boston Celtics for the league championship.

It took time for the club to build a solid fan base but eventually the Warriors put together one of the most entertaining teams in the league. Then in 1974-75, with Rick Barry, Jamaal Wilkes and a cast of players unknown outside of the Bay Area, the Warriors won the NBA title over the Washington Bullets in one of the great playoff upsets of all time.

Don Nelson brought his basketball expertise to the franchise in 1987 and has patiently put together a team on the verge of another championship.

Warriors Collector's Edition is the first historical account of the Warriors ever produced. It recounts every season in Warriors history from Eddie Gottlieb's original Warriors club that won a championship in 1946-47 to Don Nelson's current team.

This book has captured the essence of the Warriors' fine history but is probably not without blunders or oversights. We encourage readers to contribute information that may help us improve upon our effort in future publications. After all, history is a constantly evolving process.

Page X: Forwards Paul Arizin and Joe Fulks (10) teamed in 1950-51 to give the Warriors the best scoring tandem in the NBA. Fulks averaged 18.7 points that season while Arizin chipped in with 17.2 points.

Page XII: Tom Meschery (14) was the first native San Franciscan to play for the San Francisco Warriors. The Lowell High School graduate averaged 12.9 points during his six years with the club.

1945–1950

CHAPTER ONE
1945-1950

Long before the appearance of millionaire athletes with mythical names like "Air" Jordan, "Magic" Johnson and "the Mailman," professional basketball was a struggling enterprise. There was no such thing as a shot clock. Dribbling with two hands was accepted and courts in many gymnasiums were surrounded by a rope or wire cage.

Professional basketball was played in factory towns then, and largely sponsored by local companies eager to promote their products. The players often worked regular nine-to-five jobs and picked up spending money shooting hoops for the firm on winter evenings. The National Basketball League of the 1930s and '40s, a predecessor to the National Basketball Association, included the Chicago American Gears, Fort Wayne Zollner Pistons, Akron Goodyear Wingfoots, Toledo Jim White Chevrolets and Cleveland Chase Brass, all company-sponsored professional teams.

But there were also a number of barnstorming clubs made up of paid professionals with marquee names. Many of these teams were distinguished by their ethnic or racial group. Among the most popular were the original Celtics of New York City; two all-black clubs, the Harlem Globetrotters and the New York Rens; and the Philadelphia S.P.H.A.s (South Philadelphia Hebrew Association). The S.P.H.A.s were organized and coached by Eddie Gottlieb, who later became part owner and the original coach of the Philadelphia Warriors.

Many of the barnstorming teams found it difficult to find places to play. Professional basketball had de-

veloped an unsavory reputation and was banned from Y.M.C.A. gyms because of the overly aggressive nature of the sport and the rowdy characters who often came to watch the contests.

As a result, these early clubs were forced to rent high school and college gyms, ballroom dance floors, convention halls, armories or renovated auditoriums in order to stage games. The players could be found setting up folding chairs before the action started, while the coach and general manager sold tickets. Often a professional basketball game was simply a side-show held prior to a dance, concert or circus.

In some gyms in the Northeast, a rope net or cage surrounded the playing court. The cage kept the ball inbounds where it was playable off the net. More importantly, it kept the unruly fans off the court and for good reason. The crowds in Brooklyn had become notorious for throwing chairs at opposing players. And in the rough coal mining regions of Pennsylvania, a visiting player who tumbled into the seats might get a quick beating before being thrown back onto the court.

With the end of World War II, a group of professional hockey promoters who owned their own teams and arenas in the Northeast began to see the potential in professional basketball. These men were looking for a new way to attract fans to their arenas when their hockey clubs were out of town. Collegiate basketball had grown increasingly popular and the National Basketball League was surviving financially, so they gambled on the idea that a new professional basketball league with teams in the Northeast's largest cities could add additional income to their bank accounts.

Among the group leaders were Eddie Gottlieb, the future coach and owner of the Warriors, Walter Brown, who would become owner of the Boston

OPPOSITE: Joe Fulks (11) was one of the NBA's first superstars. In 1949 he fired in 63 points against Indianapolis, a single-game scoring record that stood until Wilt Chamberlain broke it 12 years later.

Celtics, and sports writer-turned-promoter Ned Irish, who would later run the New York Knickerbockers. With the help of the Arena Managers Association of America, they organized the Basketball Association of America and persuaded American Hockey League president Maurice Podoloff to run the new basketball league.

The Basketball Association of America began play in the winter of 1946. It was divided into the Western Division, which consisted of teams from Chicago, St. Louis, Pittsburgh, Detroit and Cleveland, and the Eastern Division, which was made up of Boston, Toronto, Providence, New York, Washington and Philadelphia.

1946-47

Philadelphia was hungry for professional basketball in 1946 when Eddie Gottlieb was hired by the Philadelphia Arena management group to organize and coach a professional basketball team to be called the Philadelphia Warriors.

Gottlieb was already something of a legend in Philadelphia basketball circles. He had spent most of his life in the hoops game, and had coached the highly-acclaimed Philadelphia S.P.H.A.s in the early 1920s. In 1926, he organized a new barnstorming team known as the Philadelphia Warriors which included Stretch Meehan and Chick Passon. The original Warriors played for two years, from 1926 to 1928. The American Basketball League then folded. It was from that team that the 1946 Philadelphia Warriors of the B.A.A. took their name.

Gottlieb originally joined the Warriors as coach and general manager, but in 1952 he purchased the club for $25,000. One of his first chores was to find players who could compete at the professional level. He scoured local playgrounds and college gymnasiums and found Philadelphia teeming with eager young talent. But his most promising players were veterans returning from World War II who had honed their skills on the courts of Philadelphia and surrounding areas.

Gottlieb's prize catch was 6-foot-5 forward Joe Fulks, who had starred at Murray State before joining the Marines during World War II. Fulks was the only player on the original team not from the East Coast. Using a one-handed jump shot, the Kentucky native developed into the B.A.A.'s first superstar.

"Eddie signed Joe Fulks without ever seeing him play," said Harvey Pollack, a public relations man for the original Warriors and now the director of statistics for the Philadelphia 76ers. "Some of the guys coming back from the war told Eddie about this guy in the Marines who they saw shooting hoops in Okinawa. They told Eddie he should try to sign him. It turned out to be Joe Fulks."

Guard George Senesky signed with Philadelphia after a four-year military stint and was named captain of the first Warriors team. Senesky was a well-known local commodity, having played collegiate ball at Philadelphia's St. Joseph's College, where he led the nation in scoring before going off to war.

"I was 24 years old and hadn't played much because I'd just spent 40 months in the service," Senesky said. "But I was still about the youngest guy on the team. We had guys in their thirties playing who had just come back from World War II. They were considered rookies, I guess."

Senesky was joined in the backcourt by 5-foot-9 set-shooter Angelo Musi, a graduate of Philadelphia's Temple University. Musi found himself in the middle of a bidding war between Gottlieb and Washington Capitols coach Red Auerbach.

"I was all ready to play for Auerbach," Musi said. "Then I got a call from Eddie Gottlieb who wanted me to play for Philadelphia. Money wasn't a consideration. I decided to play for Philadelphia because it was my home town."

Center Art Hillhouse was one of the club's 30-year-old rookies. The 6-foot-7 Hillhouse supplied muscle under the boards. He averaged six points and was the club's leading rebounder. Hillhouse got rebounding help from 6-foot-4 forward Howie Dallmar, a collegiate star at Stanford. Dallmar also averaged 8.8 points.

Ralph Kaplowitz and Jerry Fleishman, a pair of

ANGELO MUSI
1946-49

Angelo Musi is a living testament to the evolution of basketball. In 1946, nearly 50 years ago, Musi, at 5-foot-9 and 140 pounds, was the undisputed floor leader of the world champion Philadelphia Warriors.

A graceful playmaker and flawless ballhandler, Musi understands he would have no place in today's fast-paced NBA.

"Basketball was quite different back then," Musi said. "The players were much smaller and it was more of a team game that involved five players passing and working off one another. There was much more team involvement. It was important that you moved the ball around. You watch guys like Michael Jordan now. He just goes one-on-one and does it himself."

Musi took enormous pride in his fancy passing and dribbling skills. Although he had an accurate set shot in his arsenal of weapons, his forte was setting up his teammates. Losing the ball on a turnover or steal was an egregious error.

"Turnovers were sacrilegious," Musi said. "There was no game clock so if you had a lead then ball control took over. It was important to be able to handle the ball well. You could literally run out the clock without allowing the other team to get the ball.

"I was a good outside shooter, though. I had a two-handed set shot that I threw from well beyond what is now the three-point line. Of course, there was no three-point shot then. Most set shots in my day were taken from maybe 30 feet or beyond."

During the 1946 championship season, Musi averaged nearly 10 points, second best on the team. But his main job was to get the ball to the club's scoring machine, Joe Fulks.

"Joe Fulks was our impact player," Musi recalled. "He was a heck of an outside shooter. He used a jump shot but it was different than the jump shot you see today. It was a one-handed jump shot off the pivot. It was very effective. Not many other people had an effective jump shot then. I don't know where he got it from. It was pretty unique."

"Joe was probably the best player in the league but there were some other big stars. Max Zaslofsky, Bobby Davies and Red Holzman are a couple of the names that come to mind. Later when George Mikan came into the league, he was the most dominant player around."

Davies, known as "the Harrisburg Houdini" because of his brilliant passes and behind-the-back dribbles, spent 10 years with the Rochester Royals where he averaged 14 points and five assists a game. Holzman teamed with Davies at Rochester before going on to an illustrious coaching career.

Zaslofsky was a 6-foot-2 guard who averaged 14 points to lead the Chicago Stags to the B.A.A. Finals against the Warriors in 1946.

Mikan single-handedly revolutionized the game. At 6-foot-10, Mikan was the first big man to effectively control the action on the court. He averaged 23 points per game during his 12-year career.

Like most of the early Warriors, Musi made a name for himself as a local collegiate player. A graduate of Philadelphia's Temple University, Musi found himself in the armed forces in the midst of World War II.

But professional basketball had been a part of the Eastern sporting scene since Dr. James Naismith nailed a peach basket to the wall of a Springfield, Massachusetts Y.M.C.A. in 1891. After his discharge, Musi considered a professional basketball career and began playing for Wilmington in the Eastern League. When the Basketball Association of America started in 1946, Musi found himself in the middle of a bidding war. When it came time to settle on a team, money wasn't his prime consideration.

"I got a call from Red Auerbach who was with the Washington Capitols then, and he wanted me to play for them," Musi said. "I was all set to sign with Auerbach when I got a call from Eddie Gottlieb, the Philadelphia coach, and he asked me if I'd play for them. I wasn't concerned about the money. There wasn't that much difference, so when I had a chance to play for Philadelphia, my hometown, I took it. That's the only reason I chose Philly over Washington. Money had nothing to do with it."

The nucleus of the 1946 team was made up of returning war veterans, many of whom were a bit rusty on the court after their stint in the military. Musi was joined on the original team by longtime pal George Senesky. The two had played together in the armed forces and against one another in college when Senesky starred at St. Joseph's College in Philadelphia. It was just a matter of time before they returned to form.

"We weren't that great of a team until about the middle of the season when we really started to jell," Musi recalled of the 1946 club. "Then we started to play together. It turned out to be a pretty scrappy team."

Once they got the kinks out, the 1946

Warriors became the team to beat in the B.A.A. They posted a 35-25 record and won the league championship from the Chicago Stags in five games.

"Winning the championship was the most exciting part of my career," Musi said. "The Warriors were the first Philadelphia-based team to win a championship since the old Philadelphia Athletics under Connie Mack. We were very proud of what we accomplished."

In the club's initial season, Eddie Gottlieb did a little of everything. In addition to coaching his club to a title, he functioned as general manager and was part owner. Sometimes he could be found taping ankles and washing jock straps. He took pride in his organizational skills and went to great lengths to ensure his team had the best travel arrangements. The Warriors became one of the first professional sports franchises to travel by plane on a regular basis, but it led to some nerve-wracking experiences for the club.

"Traveling always seemed to be an adventure for us," Musi said. "The Warriors traveled by air most of the time. Once we played against the Chicago Stags and we were flying to Chicago in a TWA Constellation. It was a new plane and the airline was very proud of it. We weren't in the air for two minutes when the plane started filling with smoke. It accumulated in the cabin and we could hardly see the people next to us. The navigator came out and looked around and, before we knew it, we were back on the ground at the airport. We were getting out of the plane and (teammate) Jerry Russo turned to me and said, 'That's it. I'm not flying anymore.' He ended up taking the train to Chicago."

Musi retired from basketball in 1949, after just three seasons with the Warriors, to try his hand in business. At 31, he was just reaching the prime of his career.

"When I left the team," Musi said. "I went back to Trenton where I played and coached for awhile. Then I got involved in the vending and food service

business which all stemmed from me playing basketball. I made some friends in basketball that helped me get started in that business.

"It was an exciting time. We were there when basketball got started, but I don't think of myself as a pioneer. I just happened be in the right place at the right time. If I didn't play, someone else would have come along to play and pro basketball still would have taken off like it did."

George Senesky (left) and a Chicago Stags player battle for the ball during the 1946-47 Basketball Association of America Championship series. Senesky averaged 10.9 points during the 1946-47 playoffs.

forwards who starred at New York University, provided bench help. Kaplowicz started the year with the New York Knickerbockers and joined the Warriors midway through the season. He provided seven points per game. Fleishman averaged 4.5 points.

A number of other Philadelphia natives filled out the original Warriors roster, including Matt Goukas, Jerry Rullo and Petey Rosenberg.

"Our original home was at the Philadelphia Arena," Rullo recalled. "It held about 8,500 capacity. They had an ice hockey team that played there, too. During Christmas, the Ice Capades would come to town and we had to play somewhere else, usually the Philadelphia Convention Hall where LaSalle plays now."

Coach Gottlieb's game plan was simple. Feed the ball to Fulks and let him shoot. Fulks excited the league's new-found fans with his revolutionary jump shot. At a time when most players were scoring in single digits and teams averaged 65 to 70 points per game, Fulks set the league on fire. He led the B.A.A. in scoring, averaging 23.2 points, eight points per game more than the league's second leading scorer. Midway through the season, he thrilled Philadelphia fans when he poured in 41 points against Toronto to set a B.A.A. single-game high.

Despite Fulks' generally accurate shooting, the Warriors set a team low late in the season when they shot .160 from the floor against the Boston Celtics. Philadelphia hit 17 of 106 shots to set a franchise single-game record for ineptitude.

Philadelphia finished the season with a 35-25 record, 14 games behind the Washington Capitols in the Eastern Division. The Capitols, coached by dy-

The 1946-47 Philadelphia Warriors won the Basketball Association of America Championship. Standing left to right are Assistant Coach Cy Kaselman, George Senesky, Ralph Kaplowitz, Howie Dallmar, Art Hillhouse, Joe Fulks, Matt Goukas, Coach and General Manager Eddie Gottlieb. Seated left to right are Jerry Rullo, Angelo Musi, Warriors co-owner Peter Tyrell, Petey Rosenberg and Jerry Fleishman.

namic 29-year-old Red Auerbach, were the class of the league. Former Santa Clara star Bob Feerick was the club's floor leader.

A practitioner of the revolutionary one-handed shot pioneered by ex-Stanford star Hank Luisetti, Feerick averaged 16 points per game and shot .400 from the field to lead the league in field goal accuracy. He later became head coach and general manager of the San Francisco Warriors.

The B.A.A. instituted an unusual playoff system in which the first place teams in the two divisions faced each other, as did the second place teams and the third place teams. In the first round of the playoffs, Washington was knocked off by the Western Division Champion Chicago Stags. Meanwhile, the Warriors defeated the St. Louis Bombers and then the New York Knickerbockers to set up a showdown with Chicago for the B.A.A. Championship.

Chicago, coached by Ole Olsen, won the Western Division title with Max Zaslofsky and Swede Carlson

at guard, Tony Jaros and Jim Seminoff at forward, and Chick Halbert in the middle.

The first game of the seven-game series was played at Philadelphia before 7,918 fans who saw "Jumping Joe" Fulks put on a one-man scoring show. He dropped in 37 points as the Warriors won, 84-71.

Center Art Hillhouse led Philadelphia to an 85-74 win in the second game. In game three, Fulks took over again, scoring 26 points as Philadelphia squeaked by Chicago, 75-72, to build a 3-0 lead in the series.

In game four, Chicago's Zaslofsky and Carlson combined for 23 first-half points to help the Stags build a 15-point lead. The Warriors made a run at the Stags in the final quarter when Fulks, who had been riding the pine in the third period after getting into foul trouble, came off the bench to score eight quick points. Fulks fouled out after tallying 24 points, but not before bringing the Warriors to within one. The comeback bid ended there and Chicago snatched a 74-73 win to send the series to a fifth game.

JERRY RULLO
1946-50

Long before the National Basketball Association was dominated by seven-foot centers, tractor-sized power forwards, and guards built like tight ends, the hardwood courts were run by average-sized men who considered dribbling a fine and noble art.

Jerry Rullo was one of those pioneer guards. He walked into a tryout for the original Philadelphia Warriors back in 1946, confident that at 5-foot-10 and 165 pounds he would become a

professional basketball player. He was right. He used his ballhandling and defensive skills to carve a niche for himself with the Warriors during professional basketball's infancy. He averaged three points between 1946 and 1950 as he witnessed the birth of one of the NBA's most celebrated franchises.

"I was a good ball handler and defensive player," Rullo said. "I really wasn't a scorer. Back then the game was

a little more defense-oriented than what you see today. It was a rougher game, too. You took it as a personal insult if someone scored on you. And then you worked twice as hard to stop your man the next time."

In 1946, their first year of play, the Warriors were made up of veterans returning from World War II and a handful of local college graduates with names familiar to Philadelphia basketball fans. Rullo had just finished his military stint and decided to give professional basketball a try. At the age of 23, he was one of the youngest men on the team and found himself competing for a job alongside a number of 30-year-old "rookies."

"I had given a little bit of thought to playing professional basketball while in college," Rullo said. "It was new then. But when I was a senior, I went into the service and missed a whole year of college ball so I kind of forgot about it. When I returned home, I thought I'd give it one more shot."

Most of the Warriors' early players attended college at Pennsylvania institutions like St. Joseph's, LaSalle, University of Pennsylvania, Duquesne and Temple. A few graduated from New York universities. Rullo had been a scrappy guard at Philadelphia's Temple University before World War II interrupted his studies.

"In those days everybody played for the pro team in their area," Rullo said. "If you played college basketball in Philadelphia, then you played pro ball for Philadelphia. It gave the teams a local flavor and attracted more fans."

Although money was a consideration, it wasn't the most pressing concern among Rullo and his teammates. Players were motivated by hometown pride. It was more important to represent your city of birth and perform well for the local fans. Bringing home a championship trophy ensured the highest form of community respect. In 1946, the Warriors rewarded Philadelphia with a title.

"The year we won the B.A.A.

Championship (1946), my salary was $3,500 for the entire year," Rullo said. "We got an additional $2,000 for winning the championship. It wasn't the money that was important to us. It was the knowledge that we were the best."

During their initial season, Eddie Gottlieb was ringmaster for an ongoing circus. He served as coach, general manager, travel agent, and part-owner of the Warriors, as well as a promoter and scheduling guru for the Basketball Association of America. Gottlieb was the glue that kept the struggling franchise from falling to pieces.

"A lot of credit should go to Eddie Gottlieb," Rullo said. "He was a real promoter and great for basketball. No matter where we played, he would make sure that we signed autographs for all the kids. He said, 'These are the future fans. These are the people that will be buying tickets someday.' He was always promoting the game.

"During that first season, he did a good job keeping everything together. We all got along well. There was a lot of companionship. No one complained if they didn't get enough playing time. You just sat on the bench and rooted for the guys in the game. We always cheered for one another."

One of Gottlieb's most important duties was to make travel arrangements for his new club. He insisted on traveling first class as a means of providing comfort for his players, but also to promote the idea that the B.A.A. was not a fly-by-night league as many professional basketball leagues of the past had been.

"We traveled in what was considered first class back then, in propeller-driven planes," Rullo said. "Unfortunately, they had some problems. We had fires on these little planes and there were times we got lost in storms. By the end of the season I didn't want to fly anymore. I developed a phobia about flying."

Rullo's harrowing travel experiences caused him to leave the team after that first season. He returned in 1948 because he missed the camaraderie he found with the early Warriors.

"We had a good team relationship," Rullo said. "It was like a big family. We did everything together. After a game, we all went to the movies or to a restaurant. I still get together out here in Philadelphia with some of the guys who are left."

When the Warriors returned to "The City of Brotherly Love," they called the Philadelphia Arena home. It had a seating capacity of about 8,500 and was also home to the local ice hockey team. Hockey had first priority. One of Gottlieb's duties was to schedule Warriors games to coincide with hockey's off days.

During the Christmas holidays, Gottlieb faced an even bigger problem. The Ice Capades came to town for several weeks and forced the Warriors to find another arena altogether, usually the Philadelphia Convention Hall. Despite juggling its home games between different sites, Philadelphia averaged about 4,500 fans during its first two seasons before attendance began to taper off.

"Just about everywhere we went, we played in ice hockey arenas because most of the team owners also owned the hockey arenas," Rullo said. "When the hockey team was out of town, they would lay down the hardwood floor over the ice. On hot days, the ice would start to melt and sweat and make the floor really slippery. They had a box of resin on the sideline and you'd put your sneakers in there to get better traction."

The Warriors' family atmosphere and collective spirit carried over to the club's manner of play. Although the Warriors had one of the league's biggest individual stars in Joe Fulks, Coach Gottlieb stressed teamwork over individual heroics.

"We played a very team-oriented game," Rullo said. "It was much different than the style you see now. We called it the New York style. You used the screen-and-set shot, the give-and-go. There was much more team play. Now you watch the NBA and you see a lot of one-on-one action."

Not every game was devoted to team play, however. The Warriors had two of the league's most exciting stars, and Rullo enjoyed watching them in action.

"Howie Dallmar, who was from Stanford, was a great player, no doubt about it," Rullo said. "He had this little drive to the basket and underhand layup that was effective. Joe Fulks was in a class by himself, though. He was the Babe Ruth of basketball. The other team would put two or three guys on him and he'd still be the leading scorer. I saw him score 63 points in a game once, which was a tremendous number for those days."

Rullo retired in 1950, a year after the Warriors joined the NBA. He missed the league's rise to prominence and the big money that came with it.

"I got a championship ring and had a lot of fun doing it," Rullo said. "That's all that mattered, having a good time and meeting nice people."

The two clubs returned to Philadelphia where 8,221 screaming Warriors fans saw Fulks explode for 34 points in game five. But it was Howie Dallmar's field goal with less than a minute to play and Ralph Kaplowitz's free throw that provided the winning margin as the Warriors captured their first championship with an 83-80 win.

The club split $14,000 for winning the B.A.A. championship and another $10,000 for its playoff victories.

"I always felt the Chicago Stags were probably a better team," Senesky recalled. "But they got the shaft as far as the home court goes. Even though they won the Western Division, we got the extra home game because they had something going on at their home court in Chicago, probably a hockey game. It worked out for us."

Fulks averaged 22.2 points in the playoffs and was named to the first B.A.A. All-Star Team. His offensive prowess attracted an average of 4,300 fans to the Warriors' 30 regular season home games and another 7,400 to each playoff contest.

1947–48

The Basketball Association of America started its second season on shaky ground when the Cleveland, Detroit, Pittsburgh and Toronto franchises folded. In order to keep the league functioning, B.A.A. president Maurice Podoloff recruited the Baltimore Bullets from the American Basketball League, a minor league, then restructured the divisions. The newly formed Western Division was made up of Baltimore, Washington, Chicago and St. Louis while the Eastern Division embraced Philadelphia, New York, Boston and Providence. To save money on travel costs, the schedule was shortened from 60 to 48 games.

The rival National Basketball League flourished and expanded to the cities of Flint and Minneapolis. Professional basketball's biggest star, 6-foot-10 George Mikan, signed with the Minneapolis Lakers, joining former Stanford great Jim Pollard. With Mikan and Pollard, the Lakers were the best team in basketball and attracted large crowds wherever they played. The

George Senesky left the coal mines of Pennsylvania to try out for the Philadelphia Warriors in 1946. He played eight seasons with the club then coached the Warriors to an NBA title in 1955-56.

Lakers easily won the N.B.L. championship in their first season.

The Warriors experienced tragedy in the off-season when reserve guard Matt Goukas was involved in a serious auto accident that resulted in the loss of a leg. To bolster the backcourt, the Warriors picked University of Pennsylvania guard Francis "Chink" Crossin in the 1947 college draft. Crossin was a slick ballhandler and playmaker who added quickness to the club.

The starting lineup for coach Eddie Gottlieb's Warriors remained largely untouched from the championship team of 1946-47. George Senesky and Angelo Musi started at the guard spots, while Howie Dallmar and Joe Fulks were at forward. Art Hillhouse began the season at center once again, but after 11 games decided to retire. To strengthen their inside game the Warriors made a deal with Chicago to acquire 6-foot-9 center Charles "Chick" Halbert.

As the reigning B.A.A. Champions, Philadelphia was considered the team to beat in the Eastern Division. The Warriors played strong defense and got plenty of scoring from Fulks, who led the league with a 22-point average. He got help from Dallmar, who averaged 12.2 points and three assists, Halbert, who averaged 10 points, Senesky, who averaged 8.8 points, and Musi, who chipped in 7.5 points per game.

The title race ultimately came down to a struggle between Philadelphia and the New York Knickerbockers, led by Sid Tannenbaum and Bud Palmer. The Warriors won the Eastern Division championship with a 27-21 record, one game ahead of the Knickerbockers.

In the playoffs, Philadelphia was matched with the St. Louis Bombers, winners of the Western Division. The Bombers, behind the scoring of stars Red Rocha and Johnny Logan, won three of the first five games and were on the verge of eliminating the Warriors when the series returned to Philadelphia for games six and seven. Before the home fans, Philadelphia won the final two games decisively, 84-61 and 85-46, to advance to the finals against the Baltimore Bullets.

Baltimore, led by player/coach Buddy Jeannette, defeated the powerful New York Knickerbockers to advance to the finals. It was a small and quick team that relied on finesse and the outside shooting of Paul Hoffman and Chick Reiser.

Philadelphia defeated Baltimore in the first game, 71-60, and held a 41-20 lead at halftime of game two before falling apart. Baltimore forwards Connie Simmons and Paul Hoffman fired away in the second half as the Bullets rallied to a 66-63 win.

Baltimore won the next two games at home to build a 3-1 playoff edge, but the Warriors recovered to capture game five, 91-82, and send the series back to Baltimore for the sixth game.

Philadelphia dominated the first quarter of game six, but with four minutes left in the half, the momentum suddenly switched. Baltimore took the lead for the first time and never looked back. The Bullets outscored the Warriors, 26-17, in the third period and cruised to an 88-73 win for their first B.A.A. Championship.

Once again the fans were happy with their new professional team. Attendance increased to an average of 4,546 for the regular season games and 6,462 for the six playoff contests.

1948–49

The Basketball Association of America got an enormous boost during the summer when league president Maurice Podoloff convinced several teams from the National Basketball League that it would be more lucrative for their franchises to play in the larger arenas and cities found in the B.A.A. The owners of the Rochester Royals, Indianapolis Kautskys, Minneapolis-Lakers and Fort Wayne Pistons agreed and left the N.B.L. to join the B.A.A. The new teams brought with them a number of established stars who had become major attractions, most significantly George Mikan and Jim Pollard of the Lakers and Bob Davies of the Royals.

The N.B.L. scrambled to find replacement teams for its fading league and brought in the New York Rens, an all-black barnstorming team, midway through the season. The Rens relocated to Dayton where they showcased Pop Gates, Hank DeZonie and George Crowe. They became the first all-black franchise to be admitted to a major sports league and opened the way for the integration of professional basketball.

With the new additions to the B.A.A., the Warriors were no longer one of the top teams in the league. The Lakers now became the team to beat. Coach Eddie Gottlieb was determined to keep the Warriors among the top echelon of the B.A.A. and tried to bring in fresh new talent. One of the young players he counted on was Phil Farbman from City College of New York. Gottlieb picked Farbman on the first round

Warriors forward Joe Fulks (10) has a shot blocked during the final game of the 1946-47 Basketball Association of America Championship series. The Warriors defeated the Chicago Stags in the Finals four games to one.

of the college draft, but the 6-foot-1 guard proved disappointing, averaging only 3.2 points a game before being traded to the Boston Celtics late in the year.

Gottlieb went searching for a center again and brought in a succession of big men. Seven-foot Elmore Morganthaler had a short stay with the club, playing 20 games, and 6-foot-6 Roy Pugh appeared in 23 contests, but it was Big Ed Sadowski who filled the middle for most of the season.

At 31, the 6-foot-5, 275-pound Sadowski was a bit of a wanderer. He had already played with six different professional teams when he showed up on the Warriors' doorstep. Big Ed was well known for his overly aggressive defensive tactics, a style that could get him arrested for assault in more timid communities, but in

1948-49 he turned into one of the league's most reliable point scorers. He averaged 15.3 points and 2.8 assists when he wasn't fouling out of games.

Forward Howie Dallmar missed nearly half the season with injuries, but in his absence Gale Bishop chipped in 8.3 points per game. Guard George Senesky averaged four assists and 6.5 points.

Joe Fulks led the club in scoring again. He averaged 26 points and had his greatest game as a professional late in the season. Against the Indianapolis Jets, Fulks connected on everything he put into the air, threading the nets for 63 points. His scoring outburst set a team record that stood for 14 years until Wilt Chamberlain came along to break it.

"When Fulks scored 63 points it was simply unbelievable," remembered Jerry Rullo, a reserve guard for the early Warriors teams. "It was like Babe Ruth hitting 60 homers. It was an incredible feat."

Fulks was the league's second leading scorer behind George Mikan, who had a 28.3 point average. He was named All-League for the third consecutive year.

Philadelphia finished the year with a disappointing 28-32 record and met the Washington Capitols in the playoffs. With Joe Fulks out of action due to an injury, Chink Crossin picked up the scoring slack. He averaged 15.5 points during the playoffs but it wasn't enough. The Capitols handed the Warriors a quick exit, beating them in the first two games of the best of three series.

The Lakers, with George Mikan at center, went on to win the B.A.A. Championship, defeating the Washington Capitols four games to two. Mikan played the final two games of the series with his wrist in a cast after breaking it in game four.

1949–50

The National Basketball Association (NBA) was formed in 1949 when the Basketball Association of America and the National Basketball League merged after three years of financial warfare. Maurice Podoloff, who had headed the B.A.A., was named president of the NBA.

The NBA's first season was chaotic at times. A total of 17 clubs joined the NBA as a result of the merger and many of them were on the verge of bankruptcy. Scheduling was a nightmare. Travel was uncomfortable and often unreliable because of the harsh Northeastern winters.

"The Warriors were one of the first professional teams to travel by plane on a regular basis," recalled George Senesky. "But if the weather was bad or even too cloudy, we didn't fly and had to catch a train. If we were going to St. Louis, a train ride took about 24 hours."

Admitted to the new league from the B.A.A. were the New York Knickerbockers, Boston Celtics, Philadelphia Warriors, Washington Capitols, Baltimore Bullets, Rochester Royals, Minneapolis Lakers, Chicago Stags, St. Louis Bombers and Fort Wayne Pistons. From the N.B.L., the NBA took the Syracuse Nationals, Anderson Packers, Tri-Cities Blackhawks, Waterloo Hawks, Sheboygan Redskins, Denver Nug-

gets and Indianapolis Olympians. The teams from the B.A.A. had a distinct advantage over their brethren from the N.B.L. because they played in larger arenas in bigger cities.

The NBA was divided into the Eastern, Central and Western Divisions. The Warriors were assigned to the Eastern Division along with Syracuse, New York, Baltimore, Boston and Washington.

Despite Big Ed Sadowski's fine season in 1948-49, the Warriors selected a pair of centers in the annual draft. Utah's 6-foot-5 center Vern Gardner was the club's first selection and Jim Nolan of Georgia Tech was picked in the second round.

Sadowski opened the season at center, but Gardner quickly proved he could play in the NBA so Sadowski was traded to Baltimore for 6-foot-10 Ron Livingstone. Livingstone gave the Warriors scoring and rebounding help off the bench, averaging 8.3 points.

As the starting center, Gardner averaged 13.5 points to take some of the scoring pressure off Joe Fulks, who put in 14.5 per game and was named to the first ever All-NBA Team. Guard George Senesky was the team ball handler and playmaker, averaging four assists and nine points per game. Forward Leo Mogus and guard Chink Crossin rounded out the starting five.

Coach Gottlieb guided the Warriors to a 26-42 record and a place in the playoffs against the Syracuse Nationals. The Warriors found they were severely overmatched against the Nationals and their star forwards Alex Hannum and Dolph Schayes. Syracuse swept the best of three series, two games to none. Rookie Vern Gardner paced the Warriors in the playoffs with an 18-point average.

Playing in the NBA actually hurt the Warriors at the gate. Attendance dropped to an average of 2,109, the lowest in franchise history.

GEORGE SENESKY
1946-58

In the coal mining regions of northern Pennsylvania, basketball has always been viewed as an escape, a way to forget about the day's backbreaking labor. For a lucky few, it was a way out, a chance to get a college education and land a safer job.

George Senesky had been a pretty good high school basketball player but he didn't figure he would be going anywhere. He was prepared to spend his life in Mahanoy City, 100 miles

northwest of Philadelphia, shoveling coal like his father and enjoying a couple of cold beers at the end of a hard day. But the funniest things happen when you least expect them.

"Some guy phoned from St. Joe's in Philly and offered me a basketball scholarship," Senesky said. "It was completely out of the blue. I didn't even know where St. Joe's was. I'd never seen the place. I guess another kid must have declined a scholarship at the last minute

and I was the next guy on the list."

That was it. There were no sweet-talking scouts involved. No promises of cars or money. Not even a second offer from another school. A simple unexpected phone call was Senesky's ticket out of the coal mines.

He made his way to the big city, found St. Joseph's College and eventually led the nation in scoring. As a senior, he was voted the country's outstanding collegiate player. Senesky began thinking of a career in professional basketball. But there was a war on and as soon as his collegiate days were over, Senesky was whisked off to military duty.

"I just got out of college, maybe a couple of months, and I was taken into the service," Senesky said. "I spent 40 months in the service. By the time I got out of it, I lost a lot of valuable time. I wasn't sure how well I could play."

The 6-foot-2 Senesky headed back to Philadelphia and wandered into one of Coach Eddie Gottlieb's tryouts for the Warriors. He made the team, won a starting spot at guard, and averaged 6.5 points in his first season. The team's top gun and the league's leading scorer with a 23-point average was Joe Fulks. The Warriors went on to win the B.A.A. title.

Due to an odd playoff system devised by the league office, the Eastern and Western Divisions' first place teams, second place teams and third place teams played each other. As a result, one of the first place teams was eliminated in the first round. The system benefited the Warriors, however, who finished in second place in the East. They defeated the St. Louis Bombers and then the New York Knickerbockers before meeting the Chicago Stags in the Finals.

"I don't think we were the best team in the league that season," Senesky said. "It was probably the Chicago Stags. They got the shaft in the playoffs. They came in first in the Western Division but we got to play an extra game at home during the Finals. I remember they had something going on in Chicago, probably a hockey game, so we couldn't play there. It ended up working out for us. The extra home game was important."

Despite the championship, players' wages were small. Professional basketball was a fledgling endeavor operated on a shoestring. Attendance was sparse and press coverage was almost nonexistent. Four teams folded at the end of the 1946-47 season.

"I made $5,000 that year," Senesky said with a laugh. "People say that was good money for back then. My reply is how many Cadillacs could you buy with that money in 1947? Maybe two. Today an average player gets $1 million. How many Cadillacs can you buy with that?

"I couldn't afford a car until I was 27, my third year of pro ball. After the 1946 season, I hitchhiked home with a championship ring on my finger. I put my luggage on the train. We all had these big foot lockers from being in the service, and I had mine shipped home while I hitchhiked. I saved money and it was actually faster than the train. I got a ride pretty quickly.

"After 13 years in the pros, I was making $7,000. I worked in the off-season. We all did. We always thought the pay was going to get better. We said to ourselves, 'Next year. I'll make more next year. I'll play better and they'll raise my salary.'

"One season I missed nine games and they docked me $1,000. I complained that I got hurt while playing and they said 'You still missed nine games.' But you've got to look at it this way. The owners didn't make much money either. The top ticket was $2.50. A lot of times the owners would sell players just to make ends meet. We drafted Gene Shue as the number one pick in 1954, then sold him to New York because the team needed money. He was a bigger draw in New York."

Although the salaries were minimal when compared with today's million dollar contracts, coach and general manager Gottlieb tried to do the best for his players. One area in which he didn't cut corners was in travel costs. The Warriors always flew in style.

"The Warriors were the first professional team in any sport to travel by plane on a regular basis," Senesky recalled. "We flew on props but they were so much better than the train. To St. Louis it was about a 24-hour train ride. Of course, flying wasn't like it is now. If the weather was bad, or even if it was too cloudy, we didn't fly. We took the train."

The Warriors battled their way to the B.A.A. Championship Series again in 1947 but succumbed to the Baltimore Bullets in six games. Although the Warriors made the playoffs for six consecutive years, it wasn't until 1956 that they were able to duplicate their championship season. By then, they were playing in the National Basketball Association and George Senesky was the club's head coach.

"I took over as coach in 1955," Senesky said. "I had no experience whatsoever, unless you want to count the time Eddie Gottlieb had a gall bladder attack and I had to take over for a month. Nowadays you see guys coaching for years in college before they go to the pros."

Lack of experience didn't seem to deter Senesky. In his first season at the helm, the Warriors won the NBA Championship. With a starting five of Paul Arizin, Neil Johnston, Tom Gola, Joe Graboski and Jack George, the Warriors posted a 45-27 record, the best in basketball. Philadelphia defeated first Syracuse, then Fort Wayne in the championship series. Senesky followed up the NBA title by leading Philadelphia to the playoffs the next two seasons. But it wasn't enough for the championship-hungry Philadelphia fans and the front office.

"They kept saying 'We should be winning the championship,'" Senesky said. "I'm not making excuses but this was when Boston was unbeatable. Bill Russell and Tommy Heinsohn just came into the league, and we lost Tommy Gola, who went into the service in 1956. I didn't last long. I got fired after my third year."

In his three seasons as Philadelphia's head coach, Senesky compiled a 119-97 record. He led the team to three straight playoff appearances and an NBA Championship. His .551 winning percentage is third highest among all Warriors coaches, behind Neil Johnston and Frank McGuire.

"I got the chance to play with some of the best players of all time," Senesky said. "The 1951 team was the best we ever had. I played with four guys who are in the Hall of Fame: Joe Fulks, Paul Arizin, Neil Johnston and Andy Phillip. I'm the only starter not in the Hall of Fame."

During his eight-year playing career with the Warriors, Senesky averaged 7.2 points, three assists and two rebounds. But basketball meant more to Senesky than just statistics.

"Basketball was a way for me to improve my life and get ahead a little bit," Senesky said. "I got a scholarship and college education at St. Joe's. Then, when I started making money, I was able to buy some things for my parents. They never had a refrigerator until I had enough money to buy them one. If it wasn't for basketball, I would have been working in a hole like my father."

1950–1960

CHAPTER TWO
1950–1960

1950–51

Controversy swirled around collegiate basketball in 1950 as rumors of gambling, bribes and point shaving turned into reality. The New York District Attorney's office determined that several players for New York colleges, including City College of New York, Long Island University and New York University, had been involved in illegal gambling activity. Several collegiate stars were arrested, among them Sherman White and Floyd Lane, considered two of the country's top players. However, the professional ranks were not tainted by the gambling allegations.

The NBA, which offered an entertaining alternative to collegiate basketball, consolidated into 10 teams and realigned into two divisions. The Eastern Division consisted of the Philadelphia Warriors, Boston Celtics, New York Knickerbockers, Syracuse Nationals, Washington Capitols and Baltimore Bullets. The Western Division included the Minneapolis Lakers, Rochester Royals, Fort Wayne Pistons, Indianapolis Olympians and Tri-Cities Blackhawks.

Six of the league's original teams folded and the remaining clubs scrambled to claim the players who were cut loose. The Warriors signed former Chicago Stags playmaker Andy Phillip. The Boston Celtics signed a little known guard by the name of Bob Cousy.

For the first time, black players were allowed to compete in the NBA. Among the early black stars were Chuck Cooper, Earl Lloyd, Harold Hunter and Nat "Sweetwater" Clifton, who had spent several years as

OPPOSITE: Philadelphia Warriors guard Tom Gola (15) grabs a rebound against the Boston Celtics as Tom Heinsohn (15) and Bill Sharman (21) close in. At 6-foot-6, Gola was the NBA's first "big guard."

the center and leading scorer of the Harlem Globetrotters.

The Warriors selected Villanova's Paul Arizin in the first round of the college draft and Ed Dahler of Duquesne in the second round. In his junior year, Arizin set a collegiate scoring record when he pumped in 85 points in a single game. The 6-foot-4 forward was one of the early practitioners of the jump shot and made an immediate impact on the Warriors. He quickly turned into one of the club's leading scorers and rebounders, and teamed with Joe Fulks and Andy Phillip to lead the Warriors to a first place finish in the Eastern Division with a 40-26 record.

Bill Closs began the year at center, but gave way to 6-foot-8 Ed Mikan toward the end of the season. Mikan contributed 5.6 rebounds and nine points per game. Phillip ended the season as the league's leading assist man, dishing out 6.3 per game to go with 11.2 points. Fulks continued as one of the NBA's most accurate shooters. He led the club with 18.7 points per game while Arizin added 17.2 points and 10 rebounds.

The Syracuse Nationals, who finished the regular season with a 32-34 record, traveled to Philadelphia to meet the Warriors in the first round of the playoffs. The Warriors had been virtually unbeatable at home during the regular season, posting a 29-3 record on their own court. In game one, Syracuse played like a team possessed. Behind the incomparable Dolph Schayes, who scored 26 points, the Nationals defeated Philadelphia, 91-89, in overtime. Then, in game two, the Warriors' title hopes were dashed when they were defeated soundly by the Nats, 90-78.

Arizin averaged 26 points in the playoffs, shooting 52 percent from the field, while Fulks contributed 21.5 per game. Fulks finished the season as the NBA's top

Warriors forward Paul Arizin (11) snags a rebound as Mel Hutchins (9) of the Fort Wayne Pistons watches. Warriors guard Jack George (17) waits under the hoop.

free throw shooter, hitting 86 percent from the line. He was selected to play in the NBA's first All-Star Game, alongside teammates Paul Arizin and Andy Phillip.

1951–52

The college basketball scandals of 1950 reached the professional ranks in 1951 when it was disclosed that Indianapolis Olympians stars Alex Groza and Ralph Beard had fixed games while playing for the University of Kentucky. Both men played on the gold medal-winning U.S. Olympic basketball team in 1948. Groza was the NBA's second leading scorer in 1950-51, averaging 21.7 points. Beard had a 17-point average. They were banned for life from the NBA.

Only one of the Warriors' collegiate draft picks

made the final roster in 1951-52. Second round selection Mel Payton of Tulane contributed three points per game as a rookie and lasted just one season with the club.

Philadelphia opened the season with the same starting lineup that took it to the playoffs a year earlier. George Senesky and Andy Phillip started at guard, Paul Arizin and Joe Fulks at forward, and Ed Mikan at center.

In his second NBA season, Arizin took over as the club's catalyst. He led the league in minutes played, averaging 45 per game, was the team's top rebounder with 11.5 per game, and scored 25.4 points per game, the best in the NBA. Arizin got plenty of help from playmaker Andy Phillip, who averaged 8.2 assists to lead the league in that category. Joe Fulks contributed 15 points per game.

Despite the individual heroics of Arizin, Phillip and Fulks, the Warriors plummeted in the standings,

PAUL ARIZIN
1950-62

basketball player was an idea that never entered his mind.

"I played intramural basketball in high school, but that was it," Arizin said. "I enjoyed the academic side of school. I chose Villanova strictly for academic reasons and I paid my own way there. I didn't even think of playing sports. When I was a freshman, I decided to try out for the basketball team and made it, so in my sophomore year they gave me a scholarship. But I went to college as a student, not an athlete. Academics came first. I never dreamed I'd be a professional athlete."

By his senior year, Arizin was a full-fledged star and set a collegiate scoring record by pouring in 85 points in a single game. In 1950, the Philadelphia Warriors made him their first round pick, the third overall selection in the draft. At Philadelphia he teamed with Joe Fulks to give the Warriors the best scoring duo in the league. Fulks was the NBA's fourth leading scorer with an 18.7 average. Arizin was right behind him with a 17.2 average. Together they led the Warriors to a first place finish in the Eastern Division.

"It's funny," Arizin said. "Most people will say I was a good outside jump shooter, but in reality I liked to drive. If the defense dropped off me, naturally I'd shoot from the outside, but if they played close, I'd drive to the hoop. I could do a lot of different things."

In his second season, Arizin blossomed into one of the NBA's brightest stars. He led the league in scoring and accuracy, with a 25.4 average and a .448 field goal percentage. Then, just when Arizin was preparing to set the NBA on fire, he was taken into military service and lost two years of his professional career. When he returned to the Warriors in 1954, it was as if he never missed a beat. He averaged 21 points, third best in the league, and 10 rebounds. Teammate Neil Johnston was the league's top scorer by then with a 22.7 average. The Warriors, however, languished in last place in the Eastern Division.

Back in the age of the set shot and the four-corner offense, Paul Arizin came along to help usher in the NBA's modern era. Arizin was not the first man to leave his feet in order to put up an eccentric shot, commonly known as a jumper, but he was one of the first to use it with accuracy. In an era when shooting 35 percent from the field was top notch, Arizin hit the jump shot nearly 45 percent of the time.

"Paul Arizin was one of the first great jump shooters," former teammate Al Attles said. "There were others who used a jump shot—Joe Fulks is one person who comes to mind—but his was a little different. Paul was the first to be really effective with it."

Arizin became a basketball star almost by accident. He never played the game in high school and was a walk-on at Villanova. To someday make a living as a

"There were only eight or nine teams in the league back then and none of them were easy," Arizin recalled. "We played 72 games a year so we played the same teams about 10 to 12 times each. You became very familiar with them and it led to big rivalries. One year we played Boston 19 times because we faced them in the playoffs. That turned into a big rivalry. The fans in Philly were tough on the Celtics."

The early Warriors developed a fierce rivalry with the Syracuse Nationals and their stars Dolph Schayes, Paul Seymour and later, Johnny Kerr. Between 1950 and 1962, the Warriors met the Nationals nine times in the first round of the playoffs. On five occasions Syracuse advanced to the next round. There was bad blood between the clubs.

"Syracuse was a rough team, very physical," Arizin remembered. "They had the worst fans in the league. They'd really get on you. We had to have six or eight cops around our bench whenever we played there."

Eddie Gottlieb was the coach and part owner of the Warriors in the early years. He was known as an excitable coach who looked after his players. But occasionally he lost his temper.

"Eddie Gottlieb was a screamer," Arizin said. "If you didn't like being yelled at, you couldn't play for Eddie. One time we lost a close game and he took us all into the men's room. There were 12 of us big guys all standing around and Eddie was screaming at us. Then some poor guy comes in. He had to use the facilities. Eddie looked at him and yelled, 'What the hell are you doing in here?' We had a hard time to keep from laughing."

In 1955, Gottlieb turned the coaching duties over to longtime Warrior player George Senesky. Under Senesky the Warriors began to jell. Arizin and Johnston finished second and third in the scoring race and rookie Tom Gola gave the team added spark. Philadelphia captured the Eastern Division title with a 45-27 record, the best in the league, then swept through the playoffs defeating the Fort Wayne Pistons for

the NBA Championship.

"Winning the championship was the highlight of my career," Arizin said. "We got a championship ring, which I still treasure. It was kind of a low-budget ring but the sentimental value is more important. I made the Hall of Fame in 1977 but the championship was more important to me."

Not long after the Warriors won the league title, Wilt Chamberlain came along to make his mark on professional basketball. When he joined the Warriors in 1959, he changed the face of the NBA, not just as a player but in terms of salary.

"We heard Wilt was making about $60,000 to $70,000 a year, which was phenomenal money for that time," Arizin said. "$30,000 was my top salary and I thought that was pretty good. Plus you got $5 a day for meal money. You have to take into consideration that a regular job back then would pay about $5,000 a year. Wilt was an amazing player though. He intimidated people and could score at will. Any time he wanted he could score.

"Before Wilt, George Mikan was dominant. There were some other good centers. Nowadays you look at the NBA and most of the centers playing the game are stealing their team's money. They don't even belong out there. All they do is dunk. That's one of the big changes you see in the game. There was no dunking in our day. There were plenty of people who could do it. But if someone tried a slam dunk, he'd get floored. You just didn't do it. You'd get put right on the deck."

Arizin has noticed a number of other changes in the game, but one of the most irritating to him is the way the rules are now ignored.

"What ever happened to the walking call?" Arizin asked. "They never call it anymore. That makes a tremendous difference. I would have liked to see what Elgin Baylor could have done if there was no walking."

In 1961-62, Arizin averaged 22 points while Chamberlain put together the

most remarkable individual season in NBA history, averaging over 50 points and 25 rebounds. Almost as astonishing, Chamberlain played virtually every minute of every game, averaging 48 minutes a night. But for the 33-year-old Arizin it was his last hurrah. At the end of the season, the Warriors moved to San Francisco and Arizin decided to retire.

"I was thinking of retirement and when the team announced it was moving, that kind of settled it," Arizin said. "I didn't want to leave Philly. It's my home.

"I was caught by surprise though. Eddie Gottlieb was always a Philadelphia person. He must have thought that it was a good time to get out of pro basketball. People were upset about it in Philly. He went out to San Francisco with the Warriors but I think he realized that it was a mistake to sell the team. I think he regretted it later."

In 10 seasons with the Warriors, Arizin averaged 23 points, 8.5 rebounds and 2.4 assists. He made the All-Star Team every season he played in the NBA, and is the third highest scorer in Warriors history behind Chamberlain and Rick Barry.

The NBA recognized his contribution to the game on its 25th anniversary when it named Arizin one of the four best forwards during the league's first 25 years of play.

"The awards are nice," Arizin said. "But I hoped over the years I did the ethical things that needed to be done. The things that are important are the people you meet and associate with. I'm happy. I've had a good life and a lot of that is because of basketball."

finishing with a 33-33 record. Philadelphia was unstoppable at home, winning 24 and losing seven, but on the road they posted a 6-25 record. The Warriors still managed a fourth place finish in the Eastern Division and a spot in the playoffs, but their problems on the road continued. In the playoffs, Philadelphia beat Syracuse at home, 100-95, but was eliminated from the series when it dropped the next two games on the road.

1952–53

Philadelphia lost the services of star forward Paul Arizin for the year when he was inducted into the armed forces, so coach Eddie Gottlieb juggled players in an effort to find an effective starting lineup. Andy Phillip was traded to Fort Wayne and Ed Mikan was sent to Indianapolis, and the Warriors looked to the college draft for assistance. They selected Temple forward Bill Mlkvy with their first round pick but he wasn't the answer. Mlkvy saw limited action and averaged six points per game.

The surprise of the team was second-year center Neil "Gabby" Johnston, who became the Warriors' top scorer and averaged a league-leading 22.3 points. As a Warriors rookie, Johnston saw limited action behind Mikan and was good for just six points per game. His sophomore performance earned him a spot on the NBA All-Star Team.

Johnston had little help around him, though. Joe Fulks, in his final campaign as a regular, was a little slower but still able to give the team 12 points per game. Guard Danny Finn joined the team at midseason and added another 12 points per game, but the Warriors were clearly among the weakest teams in the NBA. They suffered through one of the most dismal seasons in club history, winning just 12 of 69 games and finishing with the worst record in the league.

1953–54

Professional basketball had become an increasingly popular spectator sport by 1953, but concerns were raised about the aggressive and overly physical style of some of the NBA's players. Referees were in-

Center Neil Johnston (6) was a five-time NBA All Star for the Philadelphia Warriors and is eighth on the club's all-time scoring list.

structed to curb the "hockey-like atmosphere" on the court by whistling more fouls. When referees obeyed the league's edict, a new problem developed. Fans grumbled that all the foul calls were changing the sport into an endless march to the free throw line.

The NBA was reduced to nine teams before the season began when the Indianapolis Olympians folded their operation. The Warriors benefited from Indianapolis' misfortune by signing the Olympians' leading scorer, 6-foot-8 forward Joe Graboski.

The Warriors' first round draft pick was Ernie Beck, a 6-foot-4 forward from Pennsylvania. He was good for 7.5 points per game before being taken into military service after appearing in just 15 contests. The Warriors also played the season without Paul Arizin and Jim Mooney, who were on active duty in the armed forces.

Tom Gola (15) and Neil Johnston (6) battle Fort Wayne Pistons forward Larry Foust (16) for a loose ball. Johnston averaged 19.4 points in his eight seasons with the Warriors.

Once again, center Neil Johnston carried the load for the Warriors. He averaged 24.4 points to top the NBA and set a team single-game high against Syracuse late in the season when he hit for 50 points. Johnston also dragged down 11 rebounds per game and was selected to the All-Star Team for the second year in a row.

Johnston got scoring help from Graboski, who added 13 points per game, while guard Jack George averaged six assists.

The Warriors improved their record to 29-43, good for fourth place in the Eastern Division, behind New York, Boston and Syracuse. But for the second straight season, Philadelphia finished out of the playoff picture.

Joe Fulks, one of the original Philadelphia Warriors, retired at the end of the year after averaging nearly 17 points a game during his eight seasons with the club.

1954–55

The NBA enacted two new rules in 1954. The 24-second clock was introduced to stop the stall tactics used by some coaches as a way of neutralizing more powerful offensive teams and to add more excitement to the game. In addition, each club was allowed only five fouls per period so that a sixth foul would produce a penalty shot. This limited the intentional fouling that often slowed the games.

The return of forward Paul Arizin after a stint in the military promised a resurgence for the Warriors. He teamed with center Neil Johnston to give Philadelphia one of the top scoring tandems in the league.

WILT CHAMBERLAIN
1959-1965

Certain players define specific sports because of their dominance in a given era. Babe Ruth epitomized baseball in the 1920s. Jim Brown personified football in the 1950s and early 1960s. But Wilt Chamberlain may have been the single most dominant basketball player in NBA history.

"When Wilt came into the league, they had to change the rules," said Nate Thurmond, who played in the Warriors lineup with Chamberlain from 1963 to

1965, before Wilt was traded to the Philadelphia 76ers. "They widened the lane so he couldn't score 100 points a night. He was the strongest player in the NBA, then or now. Most people think of him as a dunker, but he had an incredible array of shots. He didn't just dunk, he had a good hook shot, a fadeaway. He even led the fast break. Wilt was a tremendous athlete."

One look at Chamberlain's statistics for the 1961-62 season is enough to

leave any basketball statistics-freak dizzy. Chamberlain went on a one-man scoring rampage that ranks among the greatest individual achievements in sports. When the season came to an end, Chamberlain had 10 NBA scoring records under his belt.

In 80 games that year, Chamberlain averaged 50.4 points, while shooting .505 from the floor, and 25.6 rebounds. For good measure, he added 2.5 assists per game. He scored 4,029 points, a figure unmatched and unchallenged since then. The second highest single-season point total of all time, Michael Jordan's 3,041 points in 1986-87, is nearly 1,000 points less than Chamberlain's record. In fact, Jordan is the only other man in NBA history to score over 3,000 points in a season. It's a safe bet no one will ever score 4,000 points in a single season again.

Chamberlain's scoring prowess peaked on March 2, 1962 when the Warriors played the New York Knicks at Hershey, Pennsylvania.

"Our coach at the time, Frank McGuire, had predicted that Wilt would score 100 points some day," former Warriors forward Tom Meschery recalled. "We all knew he could do it."

The Warriors got off to a fast start, scoring 42 points in the first quarter. Chamberlain had 23 of them. He continued to fire away and poured in 41 points by halftime. Three months earlier, Chamberlain set an NBA scoring record of 78 points in a triple-overtime game against Los Angeles. He seemed to be within striking distance of that standard.

"I remember it like it was yesterday," former Warriors guard Guy Rodgers said. "Wilt was phenomenal. He had one of those nights where he couldn't miss a thing. Whenever you go for a record like that, you need a lot of cooperation from your teammates. There was no selfish play by Wilt or anything. We were feeding him. We all wanted to see him score 100 points. It was a phenomenal feat."

In the second half, Chamberlain picked up the pace. Even the foul shots, which were the Big Dipper's career-long nemesis, were falling.

"I remember some time in the second half, the arena announcer said that Wilt had 82 points," Meschery said. "The crowd went wild and we began feeding passes to him so that he would get the 100 points."

With 46 seconds remaining Chamberlain stuffed home his 100th point of the game. The Warriors beat the Knicks convincingly, 169-147. At the time, it was the highest two-team point total in NBA history.

Chamberlain made 28 of 32 free throws and 36 of 63 field goal attempts during the game. He also grabbed 25 rebounds.

Scoring 100 points undoubtedly ranks as the highlight of the season for Chamberlain. Almost as stunning is the fact that during that 80-game season he scored 50 or more points on 44 occasions and hit the 60-point mark 15 times.

"Wilt was an incredible offensive player but one of the most amazing things about him was his stamina," said Guy Rodgers, a friend of Chamberlain's since childhood when the two became acquaintances on the playgrounds of Philadelphia. "He played almost every minute of every game even when defenses were all over him."

From 1959, his rookie season, to 1968, Chamberlain averaged over 46 minutes per game. In his record-setting 1961-62 season, he averaged 48.5 minutes per game.

"I don't remember him ever coming out of a game that season," Meschery said.

Chamberlain was more than a basket-ball star. He was a gifted all-around athlete blessed with a tremendous physical presence. At 7-foot-1, he had the agility and coordination of a gymnast.

In high school, Chamberlain ran the quarter mile in 49 seconds, and the half mile in 1:58. He could broad jump 22 feet and high jump 6 foot 6 inches. He threw the 16-pound shotput 48 feet.

Chamberlain broke into the NBA in 1959 after dominating college basketball at Kansas, then traveling with the Harlem Globetrotters for a year. In his early days with the Warriors, the only other NBA star that could challenge Chamberlain was Boston Celtics center Bill Russell.

Chamberlain entered the NBA a year after Russell, then proceeded to capture seven straight scoring titles.

The classic head-to-head matchups between the offensive-minded Chamberlain and his rival, defensive force Bill Russell, were unquestionably the NBA's highlights of the 1960s.

Between 1959 and 1969, the league's two best big men squared off seven times during postseason play. Although Wilt invariably outscored and out-rebounded Russell, the Celtics usually sent Chamberlain home early. In 1963-64, Chamberlain led the San Francisco Warriors to the NBA Finals against Russell and the Celtics. Wilt averaged 34.7 points in the playoffs while Russell averaged 13. Still, Boston won the series four games to one.

The San Francisco fans never really warmed to Chamberlain once the Warriors moved west, and the club's owners were hard pressed to pay his salary with a minimal number of fans turning out to see him play. Midway through the 1964-65 season, the Warriors traded Chamberlain to the Philadelphia 76ers for Connie Dierking, Paul Neumann, Lee Shaffer and a fat wad of cash. The trade opened the way for Nate Thurmond to move from forward to center.

"I never really felt comfortable at forward," Thurmond said. "So when Wilt was traded, I was moved back to center. I learned a lot in those early years with Wilt. Traveling with him was like traveling with Michael Jordan. He had that kind of star quality."

Ironically, Chamberlain led Philadelphia to an NBA title in 1967, beating the Warriors in six games.

When he retired in 1973, Chamberlain owned virtually every NBA career offensive record. In 14 seasons, he led the league in scoring seven times, in rebounding 11 times, in field goal percentage nine times (including a .727 percentage in 1972-73, the highest in NBA history), and in assists once. He was named MVP four times.

Although Chamberlain played just five and a half seasons with the Warriors, he is the club's all-time leading scorer with 17,783 points. Rick Barry is second with 16,447. Chris Mullin, the closest active Warriors player to Chamberlain's mark, needs another 5,000 points to catch Wilt.

"I don't think you'll ever see anyone dominate again like Wilt Chamberlain did," former teammate and ex-Warriors coach Al Attles said. "There just weren't too many people who could match up with him physically."

Paul Arizin (11) attempts to drive around Lakers forward Walt Dukes. Arizin appeared in 10 NBA All-Star Games during his Warriors career. Only Nate Thurmond played more minutes in a Warriors uniform than Arizin.

In the college draft, Philadelphia selected Maryland's Gene Shue in the first round and Niagara guard Larry Costello in the second round. Both men went on to become illustrious NBA coaches, but they offered little help to the 1954-55 Warriors. Shue averaged four points during his one season with the club, then was traded to New York. Costello averaged seven points over two seasons with the Warriors before moving on to the Syracuse Nationals.

With the retirement of George Mikan, Johnston emerged as the NBA's dominant center. Using his unstoppable hook shot, Johnston led the league in scoring for the third straight year with a 23-point average. He was also the NBA's top rebounder, pulling down 15 per game. He made the All-Star Team for the third time.

Johnston's supporting cast included Paul Arizin, who averaged 21 points, and forward Joe Graboski, who added 14 points per game and muscle underneath the hoop. Guard Jack George continued in his role as playmaker, dishing out nearly six assists per night.

Forty games into the season, coach Eddie Gottlieb decided he'd had enough and turned the coaching duties over to former Warrior guard George Senesky. Gottlieb, who was also part owner of the team, had coached the Warriors since the club's inception in 1946. During his 10 years as the head man from 1946 to 1955, Gottlieb produced a 263-318 record and took the Warriors to the playoffs six times. Gottlieb's Warriors won the World Championship in 1946-47 and were eliminated in six games in the 1947-48 NBA Finals. He had a 15-17 record in playoff competition. Only Al Attles has coached more Warrior games than Gottlieb.

Senesky led the Warriors to a 16-16 record down the stretch, but Philadelphia finished with a 33-39 record and in last place in the Eastern Division.

Forward Woody Sauldsberry (14) struggles to control a rebound against the New York Knickerbockers. Sauldsberry was an eighth round draft pick from Texas Southern in 1957. He averaged 12.8 points that season and was named Rookie of the Year.

1955–56

The Warriors made one of the most dramatic turn-arounds in NBA history, going from the cellar in 1954-55 to World Champions in one season.

Four of the Warriors' starters remained from the previous season, but the addition of first round draft pick Tom Gola proved to be instrumental in changing the team's fortunes.

Gola had been hailed as one of the best college players of all time, leading tiny LaSalle College to the N.I.T. Championship in 1952 and to the N.C.A.A. Championship in 1954. Gola took LaSalle back to the N.C.A.A. Finals in 1955, but the Explorers were bumped off by Bill Russell and the University of San Francisco.

Under the stewardship of coach George Senesky, the Warriors finally put all the pieces together. Every member of his starting five averaged over 10 points. Center Neil Johnston and forward Paul Arizin supplied the bulk of the scoring punch. Arizin averaged 24 points per game with his dead-eye jump shot, considered the best in the NBA. Johnston, the most accurate field goal shooter in the league, added 22 points and 12.5 rebounds. Both Arizin and Johnston made the All-Star Team.

The two veterans were aided by forward Joe Graboski, who supplied strong inside scoring and rebounding, and the unselfish play of guard Jack George, who averaged 6.3 assists and 14 points. George made the NBA All-Star Team for the first time.

Gola rounded out the starting lineup. At 6-foot-6, the former college forward had the speed and quickness to play the backcourt and became the first of the NBA's big guards. He averaged 11 points, six assists and nine rebounds.

Ernie Beck returned from military service to provide spark off the bench with 5.2 points per game.

TOM GOLA
1955-63

Tom Gola combined the quickness and outside shot of a guard with the strength and size of a power forward to become a basketball legend in Philadelphia before his 20th birthday.

Raised in Philadelphia, the son of a policeman, Gola distinguished himself in local playground basketball games and at LaSalle High School where he was a prep All-American. Before he knew it, he was being recruited by the nation's top basketball schools. One by one, representatives from Kentucky, North Carolina State, St. John's and a host of other colleges stopped at his door to make a pitch for his athletic services. Gola listened with interest but he was in love with his home town and didn't want to wander too far from it. So Gola did what he felt was the logical thing. He signed with LaSalle University, an extension of his high school located on the other side of the campus.

The recruiters thought he was nuts, that his basketball skills would never get showcased at tiny LaSalle. As a college freshman, the 6-foot-6, 200-pound Gola proved them wrong. He led the LaSalle Explorers to the 1952 N.I.T. Championship and was named Co-MVP of the tournament. The name Tom Gola jumped out of the headlines of every sports page in the country.

"Winning the N.I.T. my freshman year was the biggest thrill I had in basketball," Gola said. "Here I am, 18 years old and playing in Madison Square Garden, the hub of basketball. LaSalle was the last team invited to the tournament that year and we won the whole thing. To top it off, I was Co-MVP."

Gola's hardcourt heroics didn't end with the N.I.T. Championship. For the next three years, he averaged over 20 points per game and guided LaSalle to national prominence. In 1954, the Explorers won the N.C.A.A. title over Bradley and in 1955, LaSalle was in the N.C.A.A. Finals again. This time Gola ran up against Bill Russell and the U.S.F. Dons. Russell won that meeting and would become Gola's nemesis for years in the NBA.

In the 1955 college draft, Gola was labeled a "can't miss" prospect and the Philadelphia Warriors made him their first pick. He soon found himself among the world's basketball elite.

"You've got to remember there were only eight NBA teams back then," Gola said. "The Knicks generally carried 12 players but just about every other team carried 10 to cut costs. So there were only about 80 professional players in the whole country."

The Warriors were loaded with big men like Neil Johnston, Joe Graboski and Paul Arizin, so Coach George Senesky converted his new rookie to guard. At 6-foot-6, Gola became the first "big guard" in NBA history.

"I had pretty good speed and quickness for my size," Gola said. "I ran track at LaSalle so it wasn't that big of a change for me. My natural reaction has always been to rebound, even as a guard."

Gola averaged 11 points and 10 rebounds his rookie season and the Warriors won the NBA title, defeating the Fort Wayne Pistons in the finals, four games to one.

"We each got $900 for winning the championship," Gola said. "Right after that I went into the service and by the time I got out for the 1957-58 season, the Celtic dynasty with Bill Russell had started."

The Warriors found a way to combat Russell in 1959 when they drafted another Philadelphia native by the name of Wilt Chamberlain. The Big Dipper joined the Warriors after a stint with the Harlem Globetrotters and helped change the club's fortunes. In three of the next five seasons, the Warriors met Boston for the Eastern Division Championship. But Philadelphia still had trouble getting by Boston in the big game. All three seasons, the Celtics won the championship.

"When Wilt came along, he revolutionized the game," Gola said. "They had to change the rules. One thing they did was widen the lane. When George Mikan played, the lane was only five feet wide. They had to double it in size when Wilt came into the league.

"Wilt intimidated a lot of people. You could see it in the way people looked at him. He was so big and strong. As a player he could do anything he wanted to do. If he wanted to score, he'd score. If he wanted to rebound, he could rebound. One year with the Lakers he wanted to prove he could lead the league in assists and he did."

The Warriors packed their bags in 1962 and headed west to San Francisco. For Gola, it was the first time in his life he would be playing outside of his beloved Philadelphia.

"When I first heard the team was sold, I didn't want to go out to San Francisco," Gola said. "I grew up in Philadelphia and had just bought a home in 1959. Then my son was born, so I wanted to stay. (Former owner and coach) Eddie Gottlieb came and talked to us and said he really wanted us to go,

so I packed everything in the car and we drove out there.

"Once I got to San Francisco I saw that it was a beautiful town. I loved it. I still tell people that it is the most beautiful town I've ever seen and I've been all over the world.

"Initially, we stayed for three weeks at the Jack Tar Hotel on Van Ness. I couldn't find an apartment that would allow us to move in with a kid. I would have had an easier time finding a place if I had a dog or parrot, or even a monkey. You couldn't rent an apartment if you had a kid. I was all ready to go home and if I didn't have a contract, I would have. Then one of the Warriors' new owners, he owned the Mark Hopkins too, he got us an apartment on Stanford Court. It was huge. It had a maid's quarters and everything. I told the ball boy, Larry Jacobs, who came out with the club from Philadelphia, that he could stay at our apartment for free if he would babysit whenever we went out. He did."

The San Francisco Warriors didn't catch on at first. San Franciscans looked at the professional game with mild curiosity. The team didn't have a permanent home, playing at the Cow Palace, Civic Auditorium and U.S.F. Memorial Gym. Worst of all, the name Tom Gola didn't attract crowds like it had in Philadelphia.

"In San Francisco, we played all over the place," Gola recalled. "The Cow Palace was pretty big and when we played there, it looked like no one was in the stands. I think it was a matter of selling basketball to a West Coast crowd. It was more of an Eastern game. Basketball did catch on in L.A., but San Francisco was different. It had a more sophisticated crowd, a coat-and-tie crowd."

Gola played less than half a season in San Francisco, then was traded back East to the New York Knicks, where his career ended in 1966. During seven seasons with the Warriors, he averaged 13.4 points, 4.9 assists and 9.6 rebounds. More importantly, he added valuable leadership.

"I never really thought about playing pro ball until I was in college," Gola said. "I wanted to be a doctor. In high school, I did well and took all the appropriate science courses to become a doctor. Basketball just kind of came along."

Neil Johnston (6) tries to slip a shot past a New York Knickerbockers defender. Johnston was appointed head coach of the Warriors in 1958 and took the club to the Eastern Division Finals against the Boston Celtics in 1959-60.

Philadelphia rode a late season eight-game winning streak to a 45-27 record, the best in the NBA. It gave the club a chance to play Dolph Schayes and the Syracuse Nationals in the Eastern Division Finals. Syracuse advanced to the Eastern Division Finals after sneaking past the Boston Celtics. The Warriors had no trouble with Syracuse, however, and dispatched the Nationals in five games to advance to the NBA Finals against the Fort Wayne Pistons and its two big men, George Yardley and Larry Foust.

In the finals, Arizin was too much for the Pistons to handle. He averaged 29 points as the Warriors won the NBA Championship Series four games to one. Philadelphia's only loss in the series was a heartbreaking 84-83 defeat at Fort Wayne in game two.

The deciding fifth game was hotly contested until Philadelphia broke it open in the third quarter, scoring eight unanswered points to build a 72-63 lead at the end of the period. Gola sparked the Warriors with five buckets in the third quarter and 16 points overall. Philadelphia then cruised to a 99-88 win behind Graboski's team-high 29 points.

The victory capped a remarkable reversal that saw the Warriors rebound from three consecutive last place finishes to win the NBA Championship.

1956–57

The heart of the Warriors' championship team was ripped out during the off-season when guard Tom Gola, the club's best all-around player, was inducted into the armed forces. Set-shooting guard Larry Costello, the club's second round draft pick in 1954, returned to the team after completing his military duty.

He replaced Gola as the starting guard alongside Jack George.

The Warriors looked to the college draft for help in replacing Gola and selected Temple's shifty six-foot guard Hal Lear in the first round. Lear scored four points in three games for Philadelphia and was never heard from again. Among the other draft picks were Phil Rollins of Louisville and John Fannon of Notre Dame.

Without Gola, Coach Senesky increasingly looked to Paul Arizin and Neil Johnston for scoring punch. Arizin responded to the challenge by having one of his best seasons. He averaged nearly 26 points per game to capture the league scoring crown, and eight rebounds. He was named to the NBA All-Star Team.

Johnston continued to stake a claim as the league's premier center. He was selected to the All-Star Team for the fifth time after averaging 23 points and 12.5 rebounds. Joe Graboski added 14.3 points and 8.5 rebounds.

Philadelphia remained in the race for the Eastern Division title until the last month of the season, when it hit a 13-game losing streak and slumped to a 37-35 record. Despite a third place finish in the Eastern Division, Philadelphia gained a playoff spot and faced the Syracuse Nationals with stars Johnny Kerr and Dolph Schayes.

The playoffs were a disaster for Philadelphia. Arizin was unable to play because of an injury, and the Warriors were eliminated quickly as Syracuse won the first two games of the best-of-three series to send Philadelphia home for the summer.

1957–58

Lennie Rosenbluth was the first round pick of the Warriors in 1957, but the prize of the college draft turned out to be eighth round choice Woody Sauldsberry from Texas Southern. Sauldsberry, a 6-foot-7 forward who could score and rebound, immediately cracked the Warriors' starting lineup.

Tom Gola returned to the Warriors after missing a season to military duty and helped revitalize the club.

Gola and Sauldsberry teamed with Philadelphia's established stars, Paul Arizin, Neil Johnston, Joe Graboski, Ernie Beck and Jack George, to turn the club into contenders again.

As a rookie, Gola had been one of the game's most talented all-around players. He lost none of that skill during his year-long military stint. In 1957-58, he averaged 11 rebounds, six assists and 14 points. Sauldsberry contributed 13 points per game and 10 rebounds and became the first Warrior ever to be named NBA Rookie of the Year.

Arizin continued to be one of the NBA's most consistent outside shooters. He averaged 21 points, while Johnston supplied 19.5. Both Arizin and Sauldsberry were selected to the All-Star Team.

The Warriors were inconsistent throughout the year but rallied late in the season to win six straight games and finish with a 37-35 record, 12 games behind the Boston Celtics.

Philadelphia secured a playoff spot against the Syracuse Nationals, its Eastern Division rival. It marked the sixth time in nine years that the two teams met in the opening round of the playoffs. The Warriors dropped the first game, 86-82, but recovered to beat Syracuse in two consecutive contests and to advance to the Eastern Division Finals against Boston.

The Celtics were paced by an All-Star cast that included Bill Russell, Bill Sharman, Bob Cousy, Frank Ramsey and Tom Heinsohn. The Warriors never had much of a chance against Boston. Philadelphia dropped the first three games of the series before winning game four at home, 112-97, to keep alive its faint championship hopes. Gola and Arizin set the pace in the fifth game, scoring 31 points each, but Boston rallied back to clinch the Eastern Division title and move on to the NBA Finals against St. Louis.

1958–59

During the off-season, coach George Senesky was relieved of his duties after three years at the helm of the Warriors. He compiled a 119-97 record in league play and guided the Warriors to playoff appearances in all three seasons. In 1955-56, his first campaign with Phil-

GUY RODGERS
1958-66

Guy Rodgers remembers when he first picked up a basketball on the playground near his South Philadelphia home. Basketball was king in Philadelphia and Rodgers wanted to be in on the action.

"I was told I was too short to play," Rodgers said. "In fact, I heard that throughout my career. When I went to college, they said I was too short, but I did well there. Then they said I'd never make it as a pro. I always had to prove myself, but that didn't bother me."

Rodgers became one of the city's top high school talents, won All-League honors and was recruited to Philadelphia's Temple University. Although barely six feet tall, Rodgers used his compact build to his advantage. He developed quick hands, pinpoint passing skills and flashy moves to the hoop. In a town that was crazy about basketball, Rodgers was one of its top guns.

"Basketball was always so much fun," Rodgers said. "I just wanted the opportunity to play. But it turned out to give me so much more."

At Temple, he led the Owls to a 27-4 record in 1956 and a 27-3 finish in 1958. In both seasons, Temple advanced to the N.C.A.A. Semifinals before being knocked off. Rodgers then joined a college All-Star Team which traveled the country and played against the Harlem Globetrotters. The Globetrotters were impressed enough by Rodgers' skills to offer him a contract.

But Rodgers was also the first round pick of the Philadelphia Warriors in 1958. He wanted nothing more than to play in front of his home fans.

"I was looking forward to playing in Philadelphia," Rodgers said. "I grew up watching the Warriors and loved the team. We used to get into the games free because we played high school basketball. That was hot stuff, for a kid like me from the city to play for the home team."

The Warriors regularly included a number of home town lads on the roster. When Rodgers reported to the team in 1958 he was greeted by fellow Philadelphians Tom Gola, Paul Arizin and Ernie Beck.

"The fans can be hard on athletes in Philadelphia," Rodgers said. "It's a tough town. But there are a lot of knowledgeable basketball fans there. They don't go for fads. They love basketball and they like to see a good, hard game."

A year later, Wilt Chamberlain, another Philadelphia native, joined the Warriors. Chamberlain proved to be one of the league's biggest attractions.

"Wilt was from Philly and we had known each other a long time," Rodgers said. "I played against him in high school and in summer league and we had become friendly. When he came into the league, he changed everything. He was the strongest player the NBA has ever seen, then or now. Most people think all he did was dunk but he had an incredible array of shots, a hook shot, a nice fadeaway. He even led the fast break. He was a tremendous athlete."

With Rodgers in the backcourt and Chamberlain in the middle, Philadelphia went to the playoffs for three straight years from 1960-62. Inevitably, they met the Boston Celtics in their quest for a championship.

"The Celtics always had incredible depth," Rodgers said. "They could put fresh blood in, substitute guys off the bench, and it didn't slow them down. I always respected the Celtics because of their depth. They are one of the great franchises in basketball history."

In 1962, team owner Eddie Gottlieb sold the Warriors and the club was moved to San Francisco. The Philadelphia fans were irate. The city that was considered the cradle of basketball was suddenly without a team.

"Moving to San Francisco was not a big surprise to me," Rodgers said. "I was close friends with Eddie Gottlieb and (team executive) Dave Zincoff. They told me the team might be moving to San Francisco. Eddie was concerned because he wanted the players to go. He didn't want the Warriors to move to San Francisco and have just uniforms and balls. He wanted the players to go, too.

"The fans in Philadelphia were angry. That's understandable. In general the players were accepting. Personally I was looking forward to it. I had been to San Francisco before when I played with the college All-Stars against the Harlem Globetrotters and fell in love with the area.

"San Francisco is such a beautiful, cosmopolitan area. It is still at the top of my list of favorite places."

In San Francisco, Rodgers ran the backcourt with Al Attles.

"I'll never forget when Al Attles reported to the Warriors as a rookie," Rodgers said. "He was the first guy on the court and the last guy to leave. He was a hard-nosed player, just a real hard worker. The thing I remember about Al was that he had incredible speed. It was like his feet never touched the court. Here was a guy who was a fifth round pick from some little school in North Carolina (North Carolina A&T) and he beat out guys who figured they would be a cinch to make the club."

With the help of Attles, Rodgers dazzled the Warriors' new West Coast fans, averaging 14 points, a league-leading 10.4 assists, and five rebounds during 1962-63. For the first time he heard talk of something called a "triple-double."

Triple-doubles were meaningless until the 1980s when statistics-oriented public relations people began to keep tabs on such things. In an earlier era, the name Guy Rodgers would have graced the triple-double list. On eight different occasions with the Warriors, Rodgers scored in double figures in points, assists and rebounds, a Warriors career record. Rick Barry is second behind Rodgers in career triple-doubles with six.

But statistics embarrass Rodgers. He doesn't like to talk about the night in 1963 when he had 28 assists, a Warriors record, or the year he averaged 18.6 points, 10.7 assists and 5.5 rebounds, numbers that would make Magic Johnson envious. Statistics don't tell the whole story.

Indeed, a playmaking guard like Rodgers is more concerned with team accomplishments than with individual statistics. He sacrifices personal achievement and point totals in order to see that the team comes out ahead.

And that was Rodgers' way of playing basketball, to make sure that his team came out a winner. In 1963-64, the Warriors' second year in San Francisco, Rodgers guided the club to the pinnacle of basketball, a date in the NBA Finals against the Boston Celtics. But the Warriors were tired and beat up and lost to the Celtics in five games.

"We had a lot of injuries by the time we got to the finals," Rodgers recalled. "My hand was banged up, Al Attles was hurt, Gary Phillips had a bad hand. But even if we were all healthy, it would have been a feat to beat the Celtics team."

Rodgers was traded to the expansion Chicago Bulls after the 1965-66 season for Jeff Mullins, Jim King, a future draft pick and an undisclosed amount of cash. During his eight seasons with the

Warriors, he averaged 12.8 points, 8.5 assists and 5.5 rebounds.

"I still enjoy watching the game as a fan," Rodgers said. "And I still love the Warriors. I watched their games when I was a kid and that's something that sticks with you. Even now when the Warriors are on television, or I see them playing here in L.A., I find myself rooting for them. I cherish the memories of my time with the Warriors."

ABOVE: Warriors guard Ernie Beck (7) reaches for the basketball after it gets away from Fort Wayne's George Yardley (12) in the third game of the 1956 NBA Finals. George Dempsey (5) looks on. The Warriors defeated Fort Wayne four games to one to win the NBA Championship.

adelphia, he led the Warriors to the NBA Championship. Al Cervi, a former coach with the Syracuse Nationals, succeeded Senesky.

In the college draft, the Warriors used their first round pick on Guy Rodgers, a quick, playmaking guard from nearby Temple University.

Rodgers stepped right into a starting spot alongside Tom Gola in the backcourt, and was the team's leading assist man, dishing out six per game to go with 10.7 points.

The Warriors played most of the season without All-Star center Neil Johnston, who went down with a knee injury. To replace Johnston, coach Cervi moved 6-foot-8 forward Joe Graboski to center. He did a re-

spectable job in the middle, averaging 10 rebounds and 14.7 points per game, but was no match for the league's dominant big men like Bill Russell, Johnny Kerr and Bob Pettit.

Second-year man Woody Sauldsberry led the club in rebounds, hauling in 11.5 per game and scoring at a 15.4 clip. Paul Arizin continued to singe the nets with his pinpoint shooting. He was the league's second leading scorer, averaging 26.5 points. Both Sauldsberry and Arizin were selected to the All-Star squad.

The Warriors completed the disappointing season with a 32-40 record, 20 games behind the first place Boston Celtics. For the first time in three years, Philadelphia failed to make the playoffs.

1959–60

The Warriors hit the jackpot in 1959. Philadelphia possessed the draft rights to native son Wilt Chamberlain, who had quit the University of Kansas in his senior year to travel with the Harlem Globetrotters. The club convinced Chamberlain to join the Warriors after dangling a $65,000 contract in front of him. Chamberlain had an immediate impact not only on the team, but on the future of professional basketball as he drew huge crowds of curious spectators to arenas around the country.

The 7-foot-1 center put on a show everywhere he played, averaging 38 points and 27 rebounds in his rookie season, numbers which were unheard of prior to Wilt's arrival. On six different occasions, he scored over 50 points. He also brought a new aspect to the game, the slam dunk, which thrilled the legions of fans who came to see him play. In his first season in the NBA, Chamberlain was named Rookie of the Year and Most Valuable Player.

Chamberlain was surrounded by a fine supporting cast in forwards Paul Arizin and Woody Sauldsberry, and guards Tom Gola and Guy Rodgers. Arizin was among the league's top shooters again with a 22-point average, while Gola chipped in 15 points a game. Guy Rodgers developed into one of the game's premier assist men, averaging seven a game. Only Boston's Bob Cousy had more flair for finding the open man. Sauldsberry averaged 10 points and six rebounds.

Under the direction of new coach Neil Johnston, the Warriors' former All-Star center, the team flourished. Early in the season, Philadelphia put together a 10-game winning streak to take over first place in the Eastern Division. The Boston Celtics continued to plug away and eventually regained the division lead, but the Warriors finished in second place with a 49-26 mark. It was the best record in club history at the time and an improvement of 17 games over the previous season.

Philadelphia was matched with Syracuse in the Eastern Division Semifinals and easily defeated the Nationals in three games. The Warriors then advanced to the Eastern Division Finals where they met the powerful Boston Celtics, coached by Red Auerbach.

The playoff matchup between Chamberlain and Boston's Bill Russell was eagerly awaited. They were considered the league's top players, and the hype surrounding the series was equivalent to that for a heavyweight title fight.

The fans weren't disappointed. Both men averaged 26 rebounds in the series, but Chamberlain outscored Russell, averaging 33 points to Russell's 19. The Celtics had the last laugh, though, winning the bitterly fought series four games to two.

The Warriors had a chance to win the sixth game with nine seconds to play and the score tied at 117-117. Guy Rodgers, who led all scorers with 31 points in the game, went to the line but missed two free throws. On the ensuing inbounds play, Boston's Tom Heinsohn scored on a tip-in under the basket as time ran out.

OPPOSITE: Wilt Chamberlain (13) lays one in over Boston's Bill Russell (6) and Tom Heinsohn (15). The 7-foot-1 Chamberlain joined the Warriors in 1959 after a stint with the Harlem Globetrotters.

1960–1970

CHAPTER THREE
1960–1970

1960–61

The Minneapolis Lakers packed their bags after the 1959-60 season and headed into the sunset, finally settling in Los Angeles as the NBA's first West Coast team. They brought with them Elgin Baylor, a spectacular leaper who scored a record 71 points in one game, and a rookie guard from West Virginia named Jerry West.

The Philadelphia Warriors remained in "The City of Brotherly Love" but watched the Lakers' fortunes out West with interest.

In the annual college draft, the Warriors selected Maryland's Al Bunge in the first round, Bill "Pickles" Kennedy in the second round, and took a chance in the fifth round on Alvin Attles, a hard-nosed guard from North Carolina A&T.

Bunge never played in the NBA and "Pickles" Kennedy lasted just seven games for Philadelphia. Attles began a career that spanned four decades with the Warriors as a player, coach and team executive.

The nucleus of the Warriors essentially remained the same from the 1959-60 season. Tom Gola and Guy Rodgers ran the backcourt, while Paul Arizin teamed with Andy Johnson in the frontcourt. Johnson moved into a starting role after Woody Sauldsberry was traded to the St. Louis Hawks.

They blended with Wilt Chamberlain, who continued to dominate the NBA in his second season.

Chamberlain's combination of size, strength, quickness and stamina elevated him to Superman-like status. He led the league in minutes played, scoring,

OPPOSITE: Wilt Chamberlain (13) goes high over Boston Celtics center Bill Russell (6) for a lay-in. Chamberlain set new NBA scoring standards when he joined the league and averaged a league record 37.6 points in his rookie season.

rebounding and field goal percentage, and was an intimidating presence on defense. Chamberlain was simply too much for most NBA teams to handle.

In 1960-61, Chamberlain averaged 27 rebounds and 38 points, and became the first scoring leader in NBA history to shoot over .500 from the floor. He established single-game standards in both rebounding and scoring when he grabbed 55 rebounds in one game to shatter Bill Russell's single-game mark of 51. He hit 78 points in another contest. More significantly, Chamberlain was an ironman, averaging 47 minutes of playing time to top the league in that category.

Rodgers came into his own as a court magician. He set up Wilt with his pinpoint passes and averaged nearly nine assists per game, second in the league behind Oscar Robertson.

In his ninth season with the Warriors, forward Paul Arizin was again among the league's top shooters. He averaged 23 points and eight rebounds.

Johnson added 10 points per game and 4.5 rebounds, while Gola contributed 14.2 points, 10 rebounds and four assists.

The Warriors posted a 46-33 record, one of just three NBA clubs to finish over .500. They met the Syracuse Nationals, powered by Dolph Schayes, Johnny Kerr, Hal Greer and former Warrior Larry Costello, in the Eastern Division Semifinals. Syracuse swept the best of five series, three games to none.

1961–62

The American Basketball League emerged in 1961 to challenge the NBA and set up professional franchises in Los Angeles, Chicago, Hawaii, Kansas City, Pittsburgh, Washington, Cleveland and San Fran-

Wilt Chamberlain (left) receives his trophy after being named by the Philadelphia Sports Writers Association as the NBA's outstanding player in 1960. At right is Warriors Coach and General Manager Eddie Gottlieb.

cisco. A sprinkling of established players, such as Dick Barnett and Ken Sears, jumped to the new league, but for the most part it survived with NBA rejects and athletes on the verge of retirement. One of the league's most exciting stars was Pittsburgh's Connie Hawkins, who had been banned from the NBA for not reporting an attempted bribe when he was a collegiate player at Iowa.

A number of innovative ideas were enacted by the A.B.L., the most prominent being the establishment of a three-point field goal line. Hoops scored from beyond 25 feet were worth three points, an idea the NBA would adopt nearly two decades later.

John McLendon of the A.B.L.'s Cleveland Pipers became one of professional sports' first black head coaches. He led the Pipers, with Larry Siegfried,

Connie Dierking and Dick Barnett, to the A.B.L. Championship.

Philadelphia unloaded Coach Neil Johnston after two seasons and hired Frank McGuire. In his two years at the helm, Johnston compiled a 95-59 record. His .617 winning percentage is the highest of all time among Warriors coaches. Although Johnston was successful in getting the Warriors into the playoffs, they had trouble advancing. In 1959-60, they were defeated by Boston in the Eastern Division Finals, and in 1960-61 the Warriors were steamrolled by Syracuse in the first round of the playoffs.

The Warriors made excellent use of their first round pick in 1961 by selecting St. Mary's College forward Tom Meschery, a native San Franciscan who attended Lowell High School. As a rookie, he worked his way into the starting lineup alongside Tom Gola, Paul Arizin, Guy Rodgers and Wilt Chamberlain.

Coach McGuire had only one offensive strategy,

Ellis was a local product who grew up in West Oakland, then matriculated at the University of San Francisco. During his sophomore and junior years at U.S.F., Ellis helped lead the Dons to a pair of Top 20 rankings. In 1966, he was selected by the San Francisco Warriors in the second round of the college draft, the 13th player chosen overall.

"I came from a single-parent family in West Oakland, which was basically the ghetto then, and didn't have much of a chance to see pro basketball," he said. "I never thought of the possibility of playing pro ball until I was a senior at U.S.F. I was a little surprised when I got picked by the Warriors. I never thought I'd be playing here."

He reported to camp along with the club's number one pick, Clyde Lee, only to find Coach Bill Sharman was not sold on the lanky Ellis. At 6-foot-6 and 170 pounds, Sharman felt that Ellis didn't have the bulk to be a dominant player under the hoop. Ellis relied on quickness and a jump shot that could set the gym ablaze when he was hot. Sharman wasn't sure if the rookie would help his club.

"Bill Sharman didn't think I could play," Ellis said. "I gave away about 40 pounds to most other forwards and I was a streak shooter. When I was on, I could be very good. When I was off, I could be very bad."

Ellis played sparingly in his first two seasons, averaging 4.5 points. Then Sharman left the Warriors to pursue a coaching job in the American Basketball Association. George Lee was appointed head coach and Ellis' career took off.

"George Lee gave me a chance," Ellis said. "George would tell me, 'When you get in the game, you have to make things happen.' He always told me I was good enough to be a starter but that I was more of an asset to the team coming off the bench. He gave me the green light to go out and shoot."

Ellis responded by upping his average to 12 points during the 1968-69 season. The following year he had his best season, averaging 16 points and nearly eight rebounds, but the team slumped to

JOE ELLIS
1966-74

A basketball team's sixth man must be a unique individual. He must be fearless and explosive coming off the bench to give his lagging team an instantaneous jump start.

For years the Boston Celtics had the best in John Havlicek, a man who breathed life into a dying offense. The Warriors had their own resuscitator in Joe Ellis.

"I enjoyed the sixth man role," Ellis said. "It was a challenge, a mental adjustment. I just wanted to play. As long as you know you are going to play, it's not hard to get into the flow of the game. In many ways, it was an advantage for me. I would enter a game with fresh legs. I had a chance from the bench to watch the players I would be facing. When you get into the game, though, you do have to focus on making something happen right off the bat."

a 30-52 record and finished out of the playoffs.

In just two seasons, from 1967 to 1969, the club had gone from a near championship to an NBA also-ran. Much of that transformation could be attributed to the loss of star forward Rick Barry after the 1967 season, a year in which San Francisco took the Philadelphia 76ers to six games in the NBA Finals.

"Rick Barry was a guy who could flat out play basketball," Ellis said.

From a personal standpoint it wasn't a shock when Rick left. Barry's father-in-law, Bruce Hale, was the coach of the Oakland franchise in the American Basketball Association. He was instrumental in getting Barry to take his skills across the bay.

"Family ties are stronger than most other allegiances," Ellis said. "Of course he's going to go with his father-in-law in that situation. It was a shock to Franklin Mieuli, though. He was close to Rick and couldn't understand why he would leave. It was also a shock to the team because it's tough when you lose 35 points a game."

Barry's 35-point average had been instrumental in getting the Warriors to the 1967 Championship Series against the Philadelphia 76ers.

Most NBA observers felt the Warriors had no business being in the finals and that they would be speedily dispatched by the 76ers, a team that finished the season with a 68-13 record. That Philadelphia team has since been voted one of the two best teams in NBA history, along with the 1971-72 Lakers, who posted a 69-13 record. For Ellis, who was a rookie playing in his one and only championship series, the whole season was like a dream.

"I didn't understand the significance of it until much later," Ellis admitted. "Now I can look back and think we were just a couple points away from a championship.

"That 76ers team had unbelievable talent," Ellis said. "Wilt Chamberlain, Luke Jackson, Billy Cunningham, Chet Walker, Hal Greer. They won an incredible 68 games. You can throw out the names of every one of their starters and people take notice. They know who you are talking about.

"Man-for-man we didn't match up with them. We really went after them, though. Nate (Thurmond) was such a workhorse, a real player. He had that never-say-die attitude. He battled Wilt to a standstill in that series.

"Jeff Mullins was another big contributor. If you left him alone, he would kill you with his jump shot."

Ellis finished his eight-year Warriors career in 1974. He averaged nine points and five rebounds during that time and helped the Warriors secure a playoff spot during six of those seasons. But a lot of the excitement in his association with the Warriors happened off the court.

"The team's owner Franklin Mieuli was a real character," Ellis said. "I guess you could say he was kind of eccentric. He was a very nice man, much different from the other owners around the league. He thought of the Warriors as his family, and that might have been a detriment. He couldn't think of it as a business. The Warriors' market wasn't like it is today and he didn't have the money to attract star players. In this area, if you don't have a winning team there is not a lot of support.

"Radio announcer Bill King was the ultimate professional. He had notoriety around the league and was in a class with the Lakers' Chick Hearn as one of the best announcers in the game."

Without a permanent playing site in the team's early years, the Warriors played home games at San Francisco's Cow Palace, the U.S.F. gym, and Civic Auditorium. Occasionally they performed in Oakland or San Jose. The constant shuffling left some team members confused.

"You literally had to look at the schedule every night to see where you played," Ellis said. "There were times when guys went to the wrong gym. One night we played at Civic Auditorium and we were dressed and ready to go on the floor and Jeff Mullins hadn't shown up yet. Our coach, George Lee, was pacing around waiting for him. Jeff went to the Cow Palace instead.

"Basketball gave me an opportunity. Everything in my life can be attributed in some way to basketball. I got an opportunity to travel all over the world. From an economic standpoint obviously it helped me out. I wouldn't trade that experience for anything."

and that was to get the ball to Chamberlain. With Guy Rodgers feeding "The Big Dipper" underneath, he was unstoppable. Wilt responded by averaging an unprecedented 50.4 points, in addition to 25.7 rebounds. In 45 games Chamberlain scored 50 points or more and became the only man in NBA history to score over 4,000 points in a single season.

Late in the year, Chamberlain put on an offensive display that ranks as one of the most impressive records in sports annals. He scored 100 points in a game against the New York Knicks, hitting 36 field goals and 28 of 32 free throws.

"Coach Frank McGuire predicted that Wilt would score 100 points someday," former Warrior forward Tom Meschery recalled. "We all thought he could do it because he was scoring 50 and 60 points a night during that season anyway. I think it was discouraging for the Knicks, though. They couldn't do anything to stop him."

Despite Chamberlain's presence, the Eastern Division was dominated again by the Boston Celtics, who played a team-oriented style of offense. They finished with a 60-20 record, best in the NBA, and topped the Warriors by 11 games.

In the Eastern Division Semifinals, Philadelphia faced Syracuse, its annual playoff nemesis. It was the ninth time in 13 years that the two teams met in the first round of the playoffs. Syracuse, coached by Alex Hannum, opened the series at Philadelphia with a lineup that included Johnny Kerr, Dolph Schayes, Dave Gambee, Larry Costello and Lee Shaffer.

The Warriors won the first game, 110-103, then traveled to Syracuse, where they beat the Nats on their home court, 97-82, taking a 2-0 advantage in the best of five series.

The Nats struggled back, winning two consecutive games to even the series, but Philadelphia captured the deciding fifth contest, 121-104.

The Warriors moved on to the Eastern Division Finals against the defending NBA champion Boston Celtics. The unflappable Red Auerbach coached a Celtics team that boasted a slew of future Hall of Famers. In the starting lineup for Boston were Bill

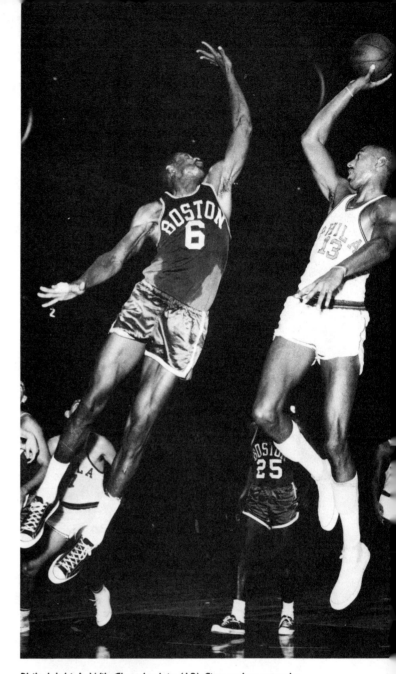

Philadelphia's Wilt Chamberlain (13) flips a shot over the outstretched hand of Boston center Bill Russell (6). Chamberlain was the NBA's leading scorer for seven straight seasons from 1959 to 1966.

Russell, Satch Sanders, Tom Heinsohn, Bob Cousy and Sam Jones. K.C. Jones and Frank Ramsey supplied bench strength.

The home team won each of the first six contests, and with the series tied at three games apiece, the two clubs returned to Boston for the decisive seventh game.

Boston took an early lead in game seven, but Philadelphia battled back and managed to tie it early in the fourth quarter. The lead changed hands a half dozen times in the final period and with time running out, the Celtics had a 109-107 advantage. Rodgers brought the ball down court for Philadelphia and tried to get it inside to Chamberlain. Boston's Bill Russell

Philadelphia's Wilt Chamberlain scores another two points against the Los Angeles Lakers in a game in 1961-62. A year later, the Warriors moved to San Francisco.

swarmed all over the Warriors' offensive sparkplug, preventing any passes to Chamberlain. With time ticking away, Philadelphia was forced to put up an outside shot that was no good, ending its title hopes. The Celtics went on to defeat Los Angeles for the NBA Championship.

1962–63

Warriors' owner Eddie Gottlieb sold the team he had nurtured since its inception to an investment group from San Francisco led by Diner's Club and Franklin Mieuli.

"Diner's Club was looking for a local investment and they talked to Gene Autry about buying the Warriors," former Warriors owner Franklin Mieuli recalled. "Autry wasn't interested but he recommended that they look me up."

Mieuli became a partner with Diner's Club in the team's ownership. A year later when the Warriors appeared to be having financial problems, Diner's Club walked away from their investment, leaving Mieuli as principal owner and president of the team.

The team's relocation necessitated a realignment of the NBA's divisions. San Francisco was placed in the Western Division while the Cincinnati Royals were moved to the East.

During their first season in San Francisco, the

Warriors played at several different sites, including the Cow Palace, Civic Auditorium and University of San Francisco's Memorial Gym. They also played home games in San Jose, Oakland and Bakersfield. Tickets ranged from $2.75 to $4.25 and could be purchased at the Warriors' ticket office in the lobby of the Bellevue Hotel at Geary and Taylor Streets in San Francisco.

The rival A.B.L. struggled along in its second campaign before giving up at midseason and sending its players home. Several of the league's stars, including Jerry Lucas and Bill Bridges, caught on with NBA clubs, but most went home to look for nine-to-five jobs.

When the Warriors moved to San Francisco, the nucleus of the club went along, too. Wilt Chamberlain, Tom Meschery, Al Attles and Guy Rodgers all found a home on the West Coast, where they were greeted by Bob Feerick, the Warriors' new head coach. But former All-Star forward Paul Arizin retired rather than move west, and shortly after the season started, guard Tom Gola was traded to New York for Ken Sears and Willie Naulls.

"When I first heard the team was sold, I didn't want to go out to San Francisco," Gola said. "I grew up in Philadelphia and had just bought a home. Then my son was born, so I wanted to stay. (Former owner and coach) Eddie Gottlieb came and talked to us and said he really wanted us to go, so I packed everything in the car and we drove out there."

Among the new faces in the Warriors' camp in 1962 were first round draft pick Wayne Hightower, forward George Lee, who was purchased from Detroit for cash, and guard Gary Phillips, who was acquired from Boston.

The San Francisco Warriors played their first home game at the Cow Palace against the Detroit Pistons before 5,600 fans. Forward Ted Luckenbill scored the first West Coast basket for the Warriors on a jump shot from the top of the key.

San Francisco took apart the Pistons, 140-113, and followed up with another victory over Detroit three nights later at U.S.F. gym before 3,600 people.

Afterward, one local scribe wrote, "The Warriors have Wilt Chamberlain, but they don't have much else. Of Guy Rodgers, Al Attles and Tom Gola, not one of them has an acceptable outside shot. And Wayne Hightower will need some time to become a suitable forward."

Meschery was anxious to prove himself in front of the hometown fans, but he was called to military duty and missed the early part of the season. He still managed to see action in 60 games, averaging 16 points and 10 rebounds.

Chamberlain put on a show for his new audience. He averaged 44.8 points and 24 rebounds to lead the league in both categories and was named to the NBA All-Star Team for the fourth time.

Guy Rodgers contributed 14 points per game and led the league in assists with a 10.6 average. Attles assisted in the backcourt, chipping in with 10 points and three assists per game while playing superb defense.

Late in the year, the Warriors were battling for a playoff spot and beat Los Angeles for the first time since moving west, 122-118, in double overtime. Chamberlain sank two free throws with 34 seconds left in the second overtime to put the Warriors in front 120-118. Guy Rodgers then stole a pass under the Los Angeles basket and hit Meschery who sank the final Warriors bucket.

The Warriors did not make the playoffs, however. They finished with a 31-49 record, 22 games behind the Lakers in the Western Division.

1963–64

Franklin Mieuli took the reins as principal owner of the Warriors and appointed Alex Hannum as head coach. Bob Feerick moved to the front office as general manager after coaching for one season.

The Warriors made one important addition to the club in 1963, selecting Nate Thurmond, a 6-foot-11 center out of Bowling Green, in the first round of the draft. He was expected to team with Wilt Chamberlain to make the Warriors unstoppable under the hoop.

Although Thurmond did not break into the starting lineup immediately, the strategy eventually paid off. Chamberlain continued to score at an unprecedented clip, averaging 37 points to lead the NBA for

Warriors guard Jeff Mullins (23) drives past Chicago Bulls guard Jim Washington (7). San Francisco center Nate Thurmond (42) watches from the free throw line.

the fifth straight year, and 22 rebounds. He was selected the league's Most Valuable Player. Thurmond made the All-Rookie Team after averaging seven points and 11 rebounds. Tom Meschery contributed 13.5 points and seven rebounds per game.

San Francisco played .500 basketball through the early portion of the schedule. At the midway point, with a 22-18 record, the Warriors began a winning streak on the road that saw them beat the Celtics in Boston, the Knicks in New York, and the 76ers in Philadelphia. They won 18 of their next 24 games and finished with a 48-32 record to capture the Western Division title by two games over the St. Louis Hawks.

For the first time since moving west, the Warriors were in the playoffs. They faced the talented Hawks, led by Cliff Hagan, Richie Guerin and Bob Pettit, in the Western Division Finals.

San Francisco needed seven games, but in the final clash of the series, the Warriors rallied from behind in the fourth period to defeat the pesky Hawks, 105-95, in front of 8,300 fans at the Cow Palace. Chamberlain scored 39 points and blocked four crucial St. Louis shots in the last three minutes of action to preserve the victory. Guard Guy Rodgers added 19 points, while Meschery pumped in 15 and Attles had 13.

"Who would have believed three months ago that we had a chance to go to the championship series?" Coach Alex Hannum asked rhetorically after winning the Western Division title. "We were able to work and grind our way back uphill while the pressure was really on us."

San Francisco advanced to the NBA Championship against the powerful Boston Celtics, who were sparked by a pair of familiar stars, former University of San Francisco greats Bill Russell and K.C. Jones.

"Against other teams, Russell plays defense on everybody," Hannum said before the series. "Against us, he is going to have to play just Wilt. That will leave our guards open, and if they drive, we should score."

Chamberlain and Thurmond proved a formidable

TOM MESCHERY
1961-67

Tom Meschery wasn't always pretty. He didn't float in the air or dribble between his legs or have a soaring fade-away jumper. He got the job done the old-fashioned way—with hustle, grit and hard-nosed defense in an era when defense was king. His teammates say he left his heart on the court 80 nights a year.

He played with broken arms and broken noses and won the affection of fans because of his never-ending

determination. But probably best of all for San Francisco Warriors fans of the 1960s, he was a local kid from Lowell High School making good in the big time.

Meschery reported to the Philadelphia Warriors in 1961 as a first round draft pick out of tiny St. Mary's College in Moraga, California. He was the seventh player selected in the draft. Choosing a player from the West Coast was a little out of character for the Warriors who traditionally drafted

players from the East Coast and primarily from the Philadelphia area. Meschery had obviously made an impression.

The 6-foot-6 forward reported to a team already brimming with stars. Center Wilt Chamberlain was about to embark on a near-mythical season, averaging 50 points and 25 rebounds. High-scoring forward Paul Arizin had a lock on one forward position while Tom Gola had his eyes on the other. Guy Rodgers and Al Attles were in the backcourt.

Excited by the rookie's ability, Coach Frank McGuire moved Gola back to guard to make room at forward for Meschery in the starting lineup. He responded by averaging 12 points and 9.5 rebounds in his first professional season.

In the off-season, the Philadelphia Warriors moved to San Francisco. For Meschery, it was a dream come true. He was going home.

"When I first heard the news," Meschery said, "I was in the army and my sergeant came over to tell me. I had no inkling the team was thinking of moving. Obviously I was ecstatic. I thought it was wonderful."

After finishing his military stint, Meschery returned to San Francisco. He was eager to strut his stuff for the home fans. Unfortunately, he found the locals didn't have much enthusiasm for professional basketball. The Warriors attracted fewer fans than an offshore yacht race. Attendance during that first season in San Francisco averaged just 3,060.

"There was a lot of skepticism about professional basketball in San Francisco," Meschery said. "We played games at U.S.F. and Civic Auditorium where you could have shot a gun off and not hit anyone. The people in the Bay Area were big college and high school basketball fans. There also were some sophisticated basketball fans who were suspicious of the pro game because they thought there was no defense. They were used to the Pete Newell teams at

Cal that played great fundamental basketball and the U.S.F. teams with Bill Russell that stressed excellent defense."

Despite having the most dominant scorer in NBA history in their own backyard, the fans were apathetic. While Wilt the Stilt was setting new scoring records on a near-nightly basis, no one was there to watch.

"The San Francisco fans didn't really take a candle to Wilt," Meschery said. "They didn't warm up to him. I don't think they realized how good he was until he was gone."

Although the fans didn't appreciate Chamberlain's ability, Meschery certainly did. He felt Chamberlain was one of the game's greatest players.

"I played with Wilt and against him," Meschery said. "Wilt could control a game like nobody else. He could do whatever he wanted to do but you could still get around him. Bill Russell was a little different. He was more of a presence on the court and may have been a little more dominant. He was a great defensive player and you couldn't ignore him."

In 1963-64, the club's second season in San Francisco, Chamberlain averaged 37 points and 22 rebounds. Meschery was the club's second leading scorer and rebounder with 13.5 points and eight rebounds. Together they led the Warriors to the NBA Finals against Bill Russell and the Boston Celtics.

"The Celtics were an unbelievable team," Meschery said. "They had won the NBA Championship several years in a row when we faced them. They had Russell at center and he was surrounded by very good players: Tommy Heinsohn, John Havlicek, Sam Jones. They also had a superior coach in Red Auerbach. Everyone had their role on that team and they played it to perfection. It was a team that executed very well."

Boston won the series in five games, although Meschery averaged 17 points. A year later Chamberlain was traded to the Philadelphia 76ers, and the Warriors were suddenly without 37 points and 25 rebounds per game. Much of the scoring

and rebounding load was heaped on Meschery. He came through with 12.7 points and nine rebounds a night in that first season without Wilt, and got plenty of help from center Nate Thurmond.

Meschery's most important chore, though, was to shut down the opposition's most effective scorer. As a defensive specialist, Meschery bumped heads with some of the NBA's most memorable players, many of whom are in the Basketball Hall of Fame.

"There will always be a long-standing argument over who was better, Jerry West or Oscar Robertson," Meschery said. "In my opinion, Oscar was bigger and stronger and could do more things but I'd go with Jerry West. He had a little more range on his shot and he was one of the best players in the clutch I ever saw."

There was one player who gave Meschery nightmares. When the Lakers came to town, it was Meschery's duty to defend Elgin Baylor. You didn't so much guard him as chase him around and wave your arms.

"Elgin Baylor was the Michael Jordan of his time," Meschery said. "He had moves that were head and shoulders above everybody else in the league. Guarding Elgin Baylor, well, that was a bad assignment. Staying with him was difficult, to say the least."

During the 1966-67 season, Meschery began to detect a different atmosphere at Warriors games. Fan interest began to intensify and there were more people in the Cow Palace seats. San Francisco averaged 7,727 fans at its home games that season, the highest in team history to date.

"Things began to change when Rick Barry came along," Meschery said. "When Rick came into his own, the Warriors began to get some recognition. The fans liked him because he was an exciting superstar. They also began to take a liking to Nate (Thurmond), and I guess there were some people that liked me because I was a local."

Most importantly, the Warriors put a

team on the floor in 1966-67 that was capable of winning a world title. They almost did it. It took a Philadelphia 76ers club led by Wilt Chamberlain to finally subdue San Francisco in the sixth game of the NBA Championship Series.

"The great irony there was that the 76ers were coached by Alex Hannum, who the Warriors had fired a year earlier, and Wilt was the team's center, who was traded by the Warriors," Meschery said. "And they beat us."

In 1968, Meschery said goodbye to his hometown when he was selected by the Seattle SuperSonics in the NBA expansion draft.

During his six seasons with the Warriors, he averaged 13 points and 8.5 rebounds and was always a fan favorite because of his hard-nosed play. In recognition of his contribution to the club, Meschery's number was retired. He is one of just four Warriors who have had their jerseys retired. Number 14 now hangs from the rafters at the Oakland Coliseum Arena.

OPPOSITE: San Francisco Warriors forward Tom Meschery (14) goes high to take a rebound from St. Louis Hawks Bill Bridges (32) and Joe Caldwell (27).

match for Boston's Bill Russell. Chamberlain averaged 35 points per game and 25 rebounds. Thurmond contributed 10 points per game and 13 rebounds. Meschery added 17 points per game.

The powerful Celtics still won the series handily, four games to one. The Warriors' lone victory came at the Cow Palace in game three, a 115-91 rout of the Celtics behind Chamberlain's 35 points and team play-off-record 38 rebounds.

Postseason accolades were bestowed on coach Alex Hannum who was saluted as NBA Coach of the Year.

1964–65

The most noteworthy of the Warriors' draft picks in 1964 was 6-foot-7 forward McCoy McLemore of Drake University. He was the Warriors' third round pick, the 25th overall selection. McLemore played two seasons with San Francisco, averaging 7.8 points and 6.2 rebounds.

The Warriors crashed to earth in 1964-65. Less than five months after playing for the NBA Championship, San Francisco got off to the worst start in team history, losing its first four games and 16 of its first 21.

Midway through the season, the Warriors were hopelessly mired in the Western Division cellar. Just after the New Year's holiday, the Warriors were entangled in a 12-game losing streak, their record a horrendous 11-35. Attendance at Warriors games was abysmal and the club was desperate for change. But Warriors fans must have thought they were suffering from a holiday hangover when they discovered that Wilt Chamberlain, the greatest scorer in the history of basketball, had been traded to the Philadelphia 76ers for Connie Dierking, Paul Neumann, Lee Shaffer and $300,000 in cash. The deal was for real.

The Warriors never saw Shaffer. He had been a holdout with the 76ers and did not sign with the Warriors. He disappeared from the NBA after the deal. Neumann enjoyed three good seasons with San Francisco and averaged 13.5 points. Dierking played one year with the Warriors, averaging eight points.

Chamberlain departed San Francisco with a 39-point average.

The development of second-year center Nate Thurmond made Chamberlain and his large contract expendable. Thurmond had rapidly turned into a force in the middle and coach Hannum felt Thurmond was ready to move from forward to center, his natural position.

Thurmond proved Hannum was right. He finished third in the NBA in rebounding, averaging 18.5 boards a game, and was the club's leading scorer with a 17 point average. He was helped by Meschery, who had 13 points and eight rebounds per game, and Guy Rodgers, who added 15 points and seven rebounds. Attles chipped in with 9.3 points and three assists per game.

San Francisco compiled a 17-63 record, worst in the league, and finished the dismal season 32 games behind first place Los Angeles.

1965–66

The future of the San Francisco Warriors dramatically changed in the 1965 college draft, when the club selected University of Miami forward Rick Barry with the second of its two first round picks.

Barry immediately became one of the NBA's most prolific scorers and supplied the Warriors with the offensive punch they lost when Wilt Chamberlain was traded. As a rookie, he averaged 25.7 points to finish fourth in the league in scoring, and hit 57 points in one game against New York. Barry was also the NBA's tenth-leading rebounder, averaging 10.6 per game, and was second in free throw percentage, using his distinctive underhand motion. He was named NBA Rookie of the Year.

With the second overall pick in the draft, the Warriors chose Davidson's 6-foot-9 forward Fred Hetzel, who supplied scoring and rebounding off the bench. Hetzel averaged seven points and five rebounds per

OPPOSITE: Rick Barry (24) drives to the hoop against the Los Angeles Lakers. He was the NBA Rookie of the Year in 1965-66. The next season, he led the league in scoring with a 35.6 average.

game and was named to the All-Rookie Team along with Barry.

Nate Thurmond emerged from the shadow of Chamberlain to develop into one of the NBA's best all-around centers. He averaged 16 points and 18 rebounds, in addition to being an intimidating defensive player. He set a San Francisco Warriors record midway through the year by pulling down a career-high 42 rebounds against Detroit.

In his last year with the Warriors, Guy Rodgers put together his best season. He averaged 18.6 points, 11 assists and 5.3 rebounds. Local favorite Tom Meschery continued his steady play by adding 13 points and nine rebounds per game.

Despite the club's improvement from the previous season, it finished the season with a 35-45 record, 10 games behind the Los Angeles Lakers in the Western Division, and missed the playoffs by one game.

1966–67

Coach Alex Hannum was fired during the off-season and replaced by Bill Sharman. In three seasons with San Francisco, Hannum compiled a 100-140 record and took the Warriors to the NBA Finals in 1963-64, where they were defeated by the Boston Celtics.

The Warriors used the third pick of the 1966 college draft to chose Vanderbilt's 6-foot-10 Clyde Lee. In the second round, the Warriors selected a local product, the University of San Francisco's 6-foot-6 forward Joe Ellis.

In another roster move that proved to be beneficial to the team over the long haul, San Francisco traded 31-year-old Guy Rodgers to Chicago for cash, a draft choice and two players to be named later. Those

TOP: San Francisco's Tom Meschery (14) steals the ball from Philadelphia's Luke Jackson (54) while Warriors forward Fred Hetzel watches from behind. Meschery, a graduate of San Francisco's Lowell High School, averaged 12.9 points per game during his six seasons with the Warriors.
BOTTOM: Rick Barry lays in two points against the Los Angeles Lakers during the 1966-67 season, when he averaged 35.6 points and was the NBA's leading scorer.

JEFF MULLINS
1966-76

The year 1966 was a benchmark in Warriors history. Over the next 10 seasons, they made the playoffs eight times, the most successful string in team annals. The only man to appear in every one of those postseason games was Jeff Mullins.

It's not just coincidence that the Warriors became a perennial contender when Mullins was added to the roster. By all accounts, he is a winner. He reported to the team in 1966 with an

Olympic gold medal from the 1964 games and an appearance with Duke in the 1964 N.C.A.A. Finals. Mullins was no stranger to championship play.

Mullins' professional career began in St. Louis where he was encouraged to change his playing style to fit in with the Hawks. As always, the frisky guard gave it his best.

"It was a frustrating year for me," Mullins said. "Richie Guerin was player/coach and he started in the backcourt

with Lenny Wilkens. Both of them were driving, penetration-type players. They wanted me to play the same style. I had a different game, though. I was more of a jump shooter who could run the floor."

At the end of the season, Mullins was selected by the Chicago Bulls in the NBA expansion draft, then traded to San Francisco along with Jim King for Guy Rodgers. He had a big pair of sneakers to fill. Rodgers had become a fan favorite in San Francisco and was quickly developing into a star.

"Bill Sharman was the head coach at San Francisco when I reported there," Mullins said. "He told me to play like I had at Duke and not to worry about the drive. The funny thing is I had become more of a penetration-type player anyway after that season in St. Louis. I was happy to go back to my old style, though."

Mullins joined a team on the upswing. Sharman was in his first season as head coach, after relieving Alex Hannum, and second-year player Rick Barry was scoring at a feverish pace.

"My first year with the Warriors was very exciting," Mullins recalled. "Rick Barry was having a terrific year. He was a Michael Jordan-type player, just phenomenal. He went on to lead the league in scoring. Nate (Thurmond) was becoming a dominant center. We had a young club and we had the feeling we could be competitive for many years."

The Warriors posted a 44-37 record and advanced to the NBA Finals. They lost in six games to a Philadelphia 76ers team that experts rank as one of the best of all time with Wilt Chamberlain, Chet Walker, Luke Jackson, Billy Cunningham, Hal Greer and Larry Costello.

A year later, the American Basketball Association started play and the Warriors were decimated when Barry jumped to the new league. Mullins also listened to the financial offers being thrown around by the A.B.A. teams.

"I have mixed emotions about the A.B.A.," Mullins said. "It helped us because basketball salaries went up. It gave us a different forum in which to compete if we weren't satisfied with our contracts. But it hurt us, because we lost Rick Barry. I always had the feeling that we would have had a tremendous team for years if we had Rick. Looking back, though, I feel the A.B.A. would have probably signed someone else from the club if they hadn't signed Rick. We had a lot of young players they could have gone after."

Even without Barry, the Warriors continued to show they were a team to be reckoned with. Mullins picked up the scoring slack, leading the club for four consecutive years with a 22-point average. Golden State made its way to the playoffs four different times without Barry, but each season it faced either the Los Angeles Lakers or Milwaukee Bucks in the first round.

"The best teams in the league during that time were the Bucks with Jabbar and Robertson, and the Lakers with West and Chamberlain," Mullins said. "We ran into one of those teams in the playoffs every year and then they would go on to the NBA Championship. If we'd had Rick during that time, we could have gone eyeball-to-eyeball with them."

During his 11-year NBA career, Mullins had some legendary battles with both Jerry West and Oscar Robertson.

"They were head and shoulders above the rest of the guards in the league," Mullins said. "West and Robertson obviously played to win at all times. They took their knocks, got up and went to the foul line. That was the thing you loved to see if they were your teammates. Nothing rattled them."

Barry returned to the team five seasons later and once again the Warriors structured the team around him. He responded by leading the 1974-75 Golden State team to its first NBA title in 19 years. By that time, Mullins was in his ninth season with the club and reduced to a part-time role.

"That was such an unbelievable year for us," Mullins said. "We weren't expected to do anything. We had a lot of guys with big hearts. There were some

outstanding role players. Butch Beard, Clifford Ray...everyone did the job they were supposed to do. It was a tremendous team effort. I think we even surprised ourselves."

It wasn't until the sixth game of the Western Division Semifinals, when the Warriors came back from a 19-point third quarter deficit to beat the Chicago Bulls, that Mullins began to see the possibilities.

"After that sixth game, I had the feeling that something special was happening," Mullins said. "It finally sunk in that we could really win the whole thing."

Golden State faced the Washington Bullets in the NBA Finals, a team that finished the regular season with a 60-22 record and demolished Buffalo and Boston to advance to the championship series.

"Washington had beaten us pretty good in the regular season," Mullins said. "But by the time we made it to the finals, we believed in ourselves.

"Everyone talked about us being a Cinderella team. A Cinderella team might win the championship if it played just one game, like in the N.C.A.A. Finals, but in a seven game series, it's a different story."

The Warriors didn't need seven games. They dispatched the Bullets in four, sending Elvin Hayes, Wes Unseld, Phil Chenier and the rest of the Washington squad back to the nation's capital empty-handed.

"That was really a special season for me," Mullins said. "It was the highlight of my career."

The Warriors meant more to Mullins than wins and losses and an annual trip to the playoffs, though. He enjoyed the unique mix of people he found in the San Francisco Bay Area and the closeness he felt with teammates and management.

"I loved every minute of playing and all the opportunities it gave me," Mullins said. "The Warriors were special. I had a real fondness for team owner Franklin Mieuli. He was a gentleman who made the team feel like a big family. During the

Rick Barry situation he showed incredible integrity. He could have traded the rights to Rick and gotten several star players but he held onto them because he felt Rick was part of the family. If Rick had stayed, Franklin might have won another championship and made more money, but he never complained about it. He was a man of high ethics. You couldn't have played for a better owner."

OPPOSITE: New York Knicks forward Dave DeBusschere (22) has his face bandaged because of a broken nose. He tries to guard San Francisco forward Jerry Lucas (47).

players turned out to be Jeff Mullins and Jim King.

Mullins reported to the Warriors with an Olympic gold medal under his belt and an appearance in the N.C.A.A. Finals. He won a starting job with the Warriors, averaging 12.9 points, 2.9 assists and five rebounds, and eventually developed into an All-Star. King averaged 11 points off the bench.

Team owner Franklin Mieuli made a bold new fashion statement in 1966 when he commissioned Walt Moreno and Dick Wilson to design new uniforms. The jerseys had a rendering of the Golden Gate Bridge and the words "The City" emblazoned on the front. On the back was the likeness of a cable car.

The Warriors dropped their first two games, played on the road at Boston and Chicago, then won 20 of their next 27. Behind the scoring of Rick Barry and Nate Thurmond's bold rebounding and defense, the Warriors surprised the Western Division.

In his second NBA season, Rick Barry developed into a superstar. He averaged 35.6 points to lead the league, becoming the first man to take the scoring title from Wilt Chamberlain. Barry was named All-NBA and played in his first All-Star Game, where he scored 38 points to take MVP honors.

Thurmond averaged 19 points and 21 rebounds, although he missed nearly 18 games with a broken hand. Forward Tom Meschery endured a broken nose to contribute 11 points and eight rebounds. Second-year man Fred Hetzel had 12 points and eight rebounds. Paul Neumann chipped in 13.9 points, 4.4 assists and 3.5 rebounds.

In the Western Division Semifinals, San Francisco manhandled the hapless Lakers, winning in three games. In the deciding third contest, the Warriors blew a 17-point second quarter lead, then came on strong midway through the fourth quarter as Jim King hit four field goals in succession to put the Warriors up 108-99. He finished with 18 points while Barry added 37, Thurmond scored 22 and Meschery chipped in with 15. San Francisco coasted to a 122-115 victory and advanced to the Western Division Finals against the St. Louis Hawks.

"We feel we are quicker than the Hawks," coach Bill Sharman said. "But they have more muscle. They are a very strong and physical team. Our team rebounding will be one of the keys."

San Francisco continued its roll toward the NBA Finals by beating the Hawks in the first two games of the series at the Cow Palace.

Things got rough when the Warriors returned to St. Louis, however. The restless fans pelted the Warriors with trash in games three and four, tossing eggs, baseballs, rocks, candy and spare coins at the San Francisco bench. Meanwhile, the Hawks won two in a row behind the scoring of Lenny Wilkens and the rugged rebounding of Bill Bridges and Zelmo Beatty, evening the series at 2-2.

The Warriors were delighted to escape St. Louis and return to the mellower atmosphere in San Francisco, where they finally took advantage of their superior speed in games five and six. Sharman employed the fast break to outrun the slower, more physical Hawks and the Warriors defeated St. Louis in six games.

The next stop for San Francisco was the NBA Finals, where it faced the Philadelphia 76ers, a team many NBA historians consider the best of all time.

Philadelphia posted a 68-13 record in regular season play with a lineup that included Wilt Chamberlain, Luke Jackson, Chet Walker, Billy Cunningham, Hal Greer and Wally Jones, and was coached by former Warriors skipper Alex Hannum. Philadelphia tuned up for the NBA Finals by thrashing Cincinnati and Boston in the playoffs.

Coach Sharman was confident of the Warriors' chances before the series started. "We won only two of seven games with them during the regular season, but we were really out of only one game," he said. "I think we've got an excellent chance."

Sharman was right. In a close and bitterly fought series, Philadelphia needed six games to put away the scrappy Warriors. The tone was set in the opening game at Philadelphia when the 76ers beat San Francisco, 141-135, in overtime. But the Warriors should have won the game in regulation. In the closing seconds, Nate Thurmond was clobbered driving to the

NATE THURMOND
1963-74

The basketball had just left Jerry West's hands on an easy six-foot baseline shot when Nate Thurmond suddenly sprang from beneath the backboard. Like a serpent rising from the deep, he rose to his full height with his arms stretched and nonchalantly flicked the ball into the stands. Then he turned and leered menacingly at the Lakers guard.

Intimidation. That was Thurmond's game.

At 6-foot-11 and 235 pounds, Thurmond was a physical presence no one could ignore. But it was the mental aspect of basketball that he cultivated and used to his advantage as one of the most feared centers in the NBA.

"I would try to demoralize my opponent right from the start," Thurmond said. "I'd try to get a blocked shot early in the game and use that on my behalf. I wanted my opponent to know that he couldn't score on me, but

that at the other end I could score on him. We never fraternized with the other team like you see now."

Thurmond put fear into the heart of anyone who traveled through the lane during his 13-year NBA career. One of the best all-around centers to ever play the game, Thurmond was named to the NBA's All-Defensive Team five times and was a six-time All-Star.

The Warriors made Thurmond their first round draft choice in 1963 after a celebrated collegiate career at Bowling Green. San Francisco signed him to a $14,000 contract, then wondered where to play their new center.

The club was already blessed with Wilt Chamberlain, the most dominant big man in basketball. Chamberlain had averaged 50 and 44 points in the two seasons prior to Thurmond's arrival, so the rookie was asked to adopt a new position at forward.

"Forward was not really my position," Thurmond said. "I didn't feel as comfortable there."

Always the team player, Thurmond made the switch with relish, averaging 10.5 rebounds and seven points. He made the All-Rookie Team and helped the Warriors advance to the NBA Finals against the Boston Celtics.

"Wilt was such a force," Thurmond said. "I learned from him every day in practice. I don't know that he consciously taught me things other than how to use my height a little better. The most important thing was I practiced against him every day and improved my defense."

Midway through Thurmond's second season, just a month after he grabbed 37 rebounds in a game against the Baltimore Bullets, Chamberlain was traded to the Philadelphia 76ers. The Warriors were making a statement, telling Thurmond they believed in his ability.

"When Wilt was traded, we had to find a whole new game," Thurmond said. "He had been doing most of our scoring. We all had to pick up the slack."

It took time. The Warriors

plummeted from contenders to cellar dwellers in 1964-65 and the Chamberlain trade looked liked the height of folly. But Thurmond flowered, once out from Chamberlain's shadow. His offensive skills gradually improved to match his defensive and rebounding prowess, and he was finally recognized as one of the league's top big men.

For years, Chamberlain and Bill Russell were considered the top centers in the league and possibly the best of all time. Lurking quietly behind them was Thurmond, a center many experts felt was a better all-around player than either Russell or Chamberlain. Thurmond may not have scored as many points as Chamberlain, nor was he the defensive intimidator Russell could be, but he put together a total game that often surpassed his rivals'.

"I always thought Nate Thurmond was the finest all-around center in the league," former Lakers star Jerry West said.

And no one played Chamberlain better than Thurmond. On November 4, 1967, long after Thurmond had taken over as the Warriors center, he did the unthinkable. Thurmond shut out Chamberlain from the floor. It was the first time in his life Chamberlain failed to score a field goal in a game.

But the toughest center Thurmond faced was neither Russell nor Chamberlain.

"I had some success against Wilt," Thurmond said. "But I think Kareem (Abdul-Jabbar) was the best center I played against. No question. He had the most devastating and dependable shot in the game. That sky hook was deadly. You couldn't block it.

"I had some battles with Willis Reed that were memorable. He played good defense and could score, plus you couldn't move him. That's what you want from the guy in the middle."

In 1967, behind the play of Thurmond and Rick Barry, the Warriors made their way to the NBA Finals.

"Rick Barry was certainly someone we needed," Thurmond said. "He could score at will. He was an incredible offensive player, a lot like Michael Jordan is today. He took the pressure off of me as far as scoring is concerned, so that I could concentrate on defense and rebounding. We complemented each other very well."

San Francisco met the Philadelphia 76ers, a team that posted a 68-13 regular season record, in the NBA Finals that year. The 76ers front line was composed of heavyweight inside players such as Chamberlain, Chet Walker, Luke Jackson and Billy Cunningham. Thurmond had his work cut out for him.

Philadelphia won in six games, but the Warriors did not go silently. Thurmond left his signature in the fifth contest, with the 76ers ahead in games, 3-1, and leading after three quarters of what appeared to be the final contest. The Warriors then went on a 33-13 scoring spree as Thurmond took control of the boards and continually started the fast break. He out-rebounded Chamberlain, 37-24, and the Warriors came back to win game five, 117-109.

Rick Barry left the Warriors for the newly formed American Basketball Association after the 1967 Finals. It was a loss that affected the Warriors' future fortunes.

"When we played Philadelphia for the championship, we were the youngest team in the playoffs," Thurmond said. "Even though we didn't win that season, we thought that was just the start of something and that we'd be a championship-caliber team for years to come. I thought we'd have other chances at a title. When Rick left, it was a disappointment."

The Warriors wouldn't reach the NBA Finals again until 1975. By then Thurmond was playing for the Chicago Bulls, having been traded at the start of the season for Clifford Ray and a first round draft choice.

"When the Warriors won the championship in 1975, I was happy for the team," Thurmond said. "I still had a number of friends that played for the Warriors. The only problem was I was playing for the Bulls and felt bad about them beating us for the Western Division Championship."

Thurmond retired in 1977 and returned to San Francisco, a city of which he has fond memories. During his 11 seasons with the Warriors, he averaged 17.4 points and 16.9 rebounds.

"The Warriors were like vagabonds in those early years," Thurmond said. "We never knew for sure where we would be playing. We had games at U.S.F., the Civic Auditorium and the Cow Palace. In later years we played in Oakland and San Jose sometimes. We didn't get the crowds like the Warriors do today, but there were some hardcore fans in those early years who we got to know personally."

In 1984, Thurmond was selected to the Basketball Hall of Fame.

"Making the Hall of Fame was the most gratifying thing to happen in my career," he said. "I didn't win a championship, so making the Hall of Fame was like them saying, 'Even though you never won a championship, it wasn't your fault. You were good anyway.'"

hoop for the winning basket. No foul was called and the game went to overtime.

Philadelphia won game two in a blowout, 126-95, and the Warriors returned home trailing in the series 2-0. San Francisco recovered to win two of the next three contests, including the fifth game at Philadelphia.

In the deciding sixth game, played before 15,612 fans at the Cow Palace, the Warriors jumped out to a 12-point third quarter lead as Barry scored 44 points and Mullins chipped in 23.

Hal Greer and Chet Walker kept the 76ers close, however, and Philadelphia was able to cut the deficit to just five points in the fourth quarter. Then Billy Cunningham scored six straight points to put Philly ahead for good.

San Francisco had one last shot to win in the final seconds. Trailing 123-122 with 15 seconds to play, Barry ate up the clock to get the final shot. With four seconds remaining, Barry put up a desperation jumper that was wide. The 76ers converted a pair of late free throws to hold off the Warriors, 125-122.

An emotionally drained Bill Sharman declared after the final game, "We're going to be heard from again if we're able to keep this team together. We have youth going for us and every man proved time and again that he can play under the toughest kind of pressure. We have a lot of potential here."

It was a statement that would come back to haunt Sharman when Barry left San Francisco the next season for greener pastures.

1967–68

The American Basketball Association began its first season of play in 1967, prompting a number of changes in the Warriors' roster. The most drastic was the loss of Rick Barry. The NBA scoring leader signed a $500,000 contract to play for the Oakland Oaks, who were coached by Barry's father-in-law, Bruce Hale.

Warriors owner Franklin Mieuli sued Barry in an effort to keep him with the club. The court ruled the star forward must sit out the 1967-68 season, but could play for the Oaks the following year. Singer Pat Boone, owner of the Oaks, put Barry to work during his hiatus,

Jeff Mullins (23) appeared in 77 playoff games as a member of the Warriors, more than any other player in team history.

as a radio commentator for Oakland's games.

The Warriors also lost three players in the NBA expansion draft. Bud Olsen and local hero Tom Meschery were selected by Seattle, while Paul Neumann, the last remnant of the Wilt Chamberlain trade, was picked up by San Diego.

In the annual college draft, San Francisco tried to replenish its dwindling roster by selecting Texas Western forward Dave "Big Daddy" Lattin in the first round. Forward Bill Turner, a third round pick from Akron, and North Carolina guard Bob Lewis also made the final cut.

The loss of veteran forwards Meschery and Barry were particularly painful to the club, so the Warriors purchased forward Rudy La Russo, a former star with the Detroit Pistons and Los Angeles Lakers, to give the club rebounding and scoring punch. He responded by averaging 22 points and 9.5 rebounds. Fred Hetzel started alongside La Russo at forward and kicked in 19 points and seven rebounds per game.

With Jeff Mullins and Jim King anchoring the backcourt, the Warriors bolted out to a 27-12 record. They made a run at first place in the Western Division, then center Nate Thurmond went down with a knee injury. Thurmond, who was off to the best start of his career, averaging 21 points and 22 rebounds, missed the final two months of the season. Without their starting center, San Francisco hit the skids, going 4-14 over the last month of the campaign. The Warriors still managed to slip into a playoff spot with a 43-39 record, which put them in third place in the West.

San Francisco faced the rough and rugged St. Louis Hawks in the Western Division Semifinals. St. Louis posted a 56-26 record and had a bruising lineup of Bill Bridges, Zelmo Beatty, Paul Silas, Lenny Wilkens, Lou Hudson and Joe Caldwell. With Thurmond sidelined for the playoffs, San Francisco didn't match up with the physically intimidating Hawks.

San Francisco pulled off a miracle in game one, beating the Hawks in St. Louis, 111-106, before 15,000 unruly fans who spent more time peppering the Warriors with trash than watching the game. The Hawks won game two, 111-103, but San Francisco came home with a new sense of confidence.

"Playing in St. Louis was always an adventure," Clyde Lee recalled. "The fans there were just vicious. They would throw trash and heckle our bench. We needed police around the bench all the time."

Back in the friendly confines of the Cow Palace, the Warriors rallied to win two straight, drubbing the Hawks, 124-109, and then squeaking by them, 108-107, in a game that broke the backs of the St. Louis squad.

San Francisco went on to win the series four games to two, completing one of the club's greatest playoff upsets. Clyde Lee took over at center for the injured Nate Thurmond and controlled the boards, collecting 14 rebounds per game in the series and 12 points. La Russo helped out inside with 10 rebounds and 20 points while Jeff Mullins caught fire and averaged 26 points per game.

The Warriors weren't as lucky in the Western Division Finals where they faced Elgin Baylor, Jerry West and the rest of the Los Angeles Lakers. San Francisco was shut down in four games.

1968–69

The NBA grew again in 1968, adding franchises in Milwaukee and Phoenix. In the expansion draft, the Warriors lost forwards Fred Hetzel and Dave "Big Daddy" Lattin, and guard Bob Warlick.

George Lee was named head coach of the Warriors after Bill Sharman left the club to take a more lucrative coaching position with the Los Angeles Stars of the A.B.A.

West Virginia guard Ron "Fritz" Williams was the Warriors' first round draft choice. He offered help off the bench, contributing eight points and 3.3 assists per game.

Center Nate Thurmond returned at full strength after injuries cut short the 1967-68 season. He averaged 21.5 points, and his 19.3 rebounds per game placed him second in the league to Wilt Chamberlain. He also was named to the NBA All-Defensive Team.

Clyde Lee added rebounding help with 14 per game in addition to 11 points. Rudy La Russo and Jeff Mullins each chipped in 20 points per game. Floor leader Al Attles averaged six assists and eight points. Forward Joe Ellis emerged as one of the league's top bench players with a 12-point average.

The Warriors finished in third place in the Western Division with a 41-41 record and won a first round playoff spot against the Los Angeles Lakers. Los Angeles, coached by Butch Van Breda Kolff, compiled a 55-27 record in regular season play and was clearly the class of the league with a starting lineup that included Wilt Chamberlain, Elgin Baylor and Jerry West.

San Francisco stunned the Lakers by winning the first two games of the series at Los Angeles. Nate Thurmond and Rudy La Russo battled Chamberlain on the boards in game one and took control under the hoop. Thurmond collected 22 rebounds, while La Russo added 12 rebounds and led all Warriors with 22 points. Thurmond's staunch defense limited Chamberlain to 12 points as San Francisco captured game one, 99-94.

OPPOSITE: Forward Rick Barry (24) uses a Nate Thurmond pick (42) as he drives against the Buffalo Braves.

Center Nate Thurmond shoots a jump hook over Milwaukee Bucks center Kareem Abdul-Jabbar (33) during a 1973 playoff game. Thurmond was also a rugged rebounder. He is the Warriors' all-time leader with 12,771 rebounds.

In game two, La Russo came through again, pumping in 29 points. Thurmond chipped in 27 points and 28 rebounds, while shutting down Chamberlain for the second straight night. Wilt scored 10 points and

had 17 rebounds. Guards Jeff Mullins and Jimmy King were on target from the outside. Mullins had 20 points and King added 18.

"I don't think we've really played our best game yet and we're two up," Coach George Lee commented after the game. "We were the underdog because the Lakers have all the superstars, but we have them on the run now."

Lee spoke too soon. With confidence and the home court advantage on their side, the Warriors returned home smelling an upset. Their joy was shortlived.

The Lakers licked their wounds then pounced all over the Warriors at the Oakland Coliseum Arena. They won four straight games to steal the series from the Warriors four games to two.

1969–70

The Warriors selected a pair of San Francisco natives in the annual college draft. They used their first round pick on 6-foot-5 forward Bob Portman, who starred at St. Ignatius High School and Creighton University, then picked San Francisco State forward Joe Callaghan in a later round.

San Francisco kept the telephone lines buzzing during the off-season as the Warriors traded Jim King and Bill Turner to Cincinnati for forward Jerry Lucas, acquired veteran forward Dave Gambee from Detroit for a first round draft choice, and sent a second round pick to Cincinnati in exchange for guard Adrian Smith.

The club was jinxed with a rash of injuries during the year. Nate Thurmond missed 39 games with a knee injury, Jerry Lucas suffered a broken hand and missed 20 games, Al Attles was lost for six weeks with a broken hand, and Joe Ellis was in and out of the lineup with a hand injury.

With the injuries and large influx of new players, San Francisco never developed any continuity and had problems early in the year. Two weeks into the season, the Warriors suffered through a six-game losing streak and never recovered. They struggled below .500, then after the All-Star break George Lee was relieved of his coaching duties. Veteran guard Al Attles took over as player/coach, but the club never recovered.

"I kind of fell into the coaching job," Attles said. "I planned on coaching until the end of the season and that would be it, I'd go back to just playing. It's difficult being a player/coach. It's hard to see what's going on on the court because you're concentrating on doing your job on the court as a player."

Attles compiled an 8-22 record during his tenure but was retained as coach and guided the Warriors over the next 13 seasons.

Clyde Lee and Jeff Mullins were the team's most consistent performers during the 1969-70 season. Mullins pumped in 22 points per game while Lee averaged 11 points and 11 rebounds. Jerry Lucas proved to be a valuable addition to the club, chipping in 15.4 points and 14.4 rebounds.

The Warriors ended the disappointing season in sixth place with a 30-52 record, 18 games behind Atlanta in the Western Division.

1970–1980

CHAPTER FOUR
1970–1980

1970–71

In an effort to improve its market, the NBA expanded, establishing new franchises in Buffalo, Cleveland and Portland. The divisions were realigned and the Warriors were placed in the new Pacific Division along with the Los Angeles Lakers, San Diego Rockets, Seattle SuperSonics and Portland Trail Blazers.

The Warriors lost a pair of players in the ensuing expansion draft when Portland chose Dale Schlueter and Bob Lewis went to the Cleveland Cavaliers.

The college draft offered little help to the Warriors, who were without their first and second round picks as a result of trades made in 1969-70. Fourth round pick Ralph Ogden, from Santa Clara, was the sole rookie to make an impact on San Francisco.

Under player/coach Al Attles, the Warriors struggled to stay above the .500 mark all year. The high point of the club's season came when it crushed Cincinnati, 133-119, to improve its record to 34-30.

The combination of Nate Thurmond and Jerry Lucas, with Clyde Lee coming off the bench, gave the Warriors one of the top rebounding trios in the league. Lucas averaged 16 rebounds and 19 points during the season, while Thurmond added 14 rebounds and 20 points. His best effort was a 43-point night against Detroit late in the year. As the club's sixth man, Lee chipped in with seven rebounds and six points. Jeff Mullins supplied accurate outside shooting and was the team's leading scorer with a 21-point average.

San Francisco ended the year with a 41-41 record, which was good enough for second place in the Pacific Division, seven games behind the Lakers. It also gave the Warriors a spot in the Western Conference Semifinals against the Milwaukee Bucks.

Milwaukee, coached by former Warriors guard Larry Costello and led by Lew Alcindor (later Kareem Abdul-Jabbar) and Oscar Robertson, dominated the first three games of the series. Despite being double-teamed, the young Alcindor was unstoppable. He averaged 31 points and controlled the boards while leading the Bucks to an easy 3-0 lead in the series.

Despite having their backs to the wall, the Warriors were loose for game four. "We had nothing to lose," Thurmond said, "so we swarmed all over them."

San Francisco took a commanding lead in the fourth quarter and led by six with just over a minute to play, when Milwaukee came back to score seven straight points. Oscar Robertson appeared to put the final nail in the Warriors' coffin by hitting a short jump shot with four seconds left to put Milwaukee ahead, 104-103.

With the Bucks on the verge of clinching the series, Attles called time out to review strategy. On the ensuing inbounds play, Joe Ellis, who had been in a shooting slump throughout the playoffs, took a pass, turned and fired a 40-foot jump shot that hit nothing but net. San Francisco came away with a 106-104 win.

Jerry Lucas led the Warriors attack with 32 points. Jeff Mullins added 20 points and a career-high 19 rebounds. It was the Warriors' last win of the season. Milwaukee rebounded in game five to blow out San Francisco, 136-86, and clinch the series.

Center Nate Thurmond was the only Warrior to receive postseason accolades. He was named to the NBA All-Defensive Team for the second straight year.

OPPOSITE: San Francisco forward Clyde Lee (43) leans into Bob Kaufman of the Chicago Bulls while putting up a hook shot. Lee was the club's first round pick in 1966.

1971–72

The San Francisco Warriors found a new home in 1971 when they moved across the bay to the Oakland Coliseum Arena for their first season as the Golden State Warriors.

The Warriors also altered their style on the hardwood floor. They tried to get away from the plodding teams of the recent past by acquiring Jim Barnett from Portland for a pair of draft choices, and by trading Jerry Lucas to New York for Cazzie Russell. Russell and Barnett bolstered the backcourt and supplied the Warriors with much needed team speed.

In keeping with tradition, the Warriors looked to local colleges for help in the draft. They selected San Jose State's Darnell Hillman in the first round and the University of California's Charles Johnson in round six.

In the supplemental draft, the Warriors made a mistake, however, when they chose Cyril Baptiste from Creighton, a pick that would come to haunt them. Baptiste ran into several off-court problems and went so far as to steal a teammate's wallet. He never made it in the NBA. To make a bad situation worse, the Warriors forfeited their first round pick in 1972 because they opted to select Baptiste in the supplemental draft.

Even with the Warriors' new backcourt duo, the club continued to revolve around center Nate Thurmond. "Nate the Great" averaged 21 points and 16 rebounds over the course of the year, while guards Russell, Barnett and Mullins supplied hot outside shooting.

Russell showed what he could do in the first week of the season when he poured in 32 points against the Lakers in a 109-105 Warriors victory. He sank a pair of free throws with seven seconds left to ice the game.

TOP: Warriors guard Jeff Mullins scores two points against New York Knicks forward Dave DeBusschere. Watching the play are New York's Jerry Lucas (32) and Clyde Lee (43) of the Warriors.
BOTTOM: Jim Barnett (25) gets under Milwaukee Bucks guard Lucius Allen (42) to score during the 1972 playoffs. Kareem Abdul-Jabbar and Oscar Robertson (1) stand by. The Bucks defeated the Warriors in five games.

JIM BARNETT
1971–74

If there was ever an athlete who truly meant it when he said he would play for free, it was Jim Barnett. For him, getting paid to play basketball was like getting paid to eat ice cream. Barnett played for fun and any money he made was just frosting on the cake.

Barnett's unending joy for the game may have been tempered by his inglorious start. He was cut from the junior varsity basketball team as a sophomore in high school. All he wanted was a chance to play.

"I had pretty humble expectations when I was a kid," Barnett said. "My goal was to eventually make the varsity basketball team by the time I was a senior. After I got cut from the J.V. team, I practiced six hours a day and I finally did make the varsity team. I just loved the game. I couldn't think of anything more fun than playing basketball."

The practice paid off and Barnett began to shine as a high school senior, even attracting the eyes of college scouts.

"I still didn't have much confidence," Barnett said. "There were a few colleges interested in me but I didn't want to go to any big schools. I didn't think I'd get any playing time. I chose Oregon because I thought I had the best chance to play in their program."

Barnett did more than just play. By the time he reached the University of Oregon campus, he had grown to 6-foot-4 and developed into a star. He set the school scoring record at Oregon and in 1966 the world champion Boston Celtics came calling. They made Barnett their first round draft pick.

"When I made it to the NBA, it was like a dream come true," Barnett said. "I had a pretty humble start. Never in my wildest dreams did I ever think I would someday be playing professional basketball. I considered it such a privilege. That's the only word for it—privilege. I played for fun first and money was just an offshoot."

Barnett received a dose of reality with the Celtics. Boston already had Sam Jones, K.C. Jones and Larry Siegfried in the backcourt with John Havlicek rotating between forward and guard. Barnett's playing time dwindled to about six minutes per game. The water cooler at the end of the bench became his closest companion.

"It's kind of funny," Barnett laughed. "My one season with the Celtics happened to be the one year they didn't win a championship."

Boston was just the first of several stops in Barnett's 11-year career. He was ready to play for anybody anytime. All he wanted was a ball and a court. After one season with Boston, he was shipped off to San Diego, then to Portland.

With the Trail Blazers in 1970-71, Barnett seemed to find his niche. He had his best season, averaging 18.5 points, four assists and five rebounds.

Numbers like that caught the Warriors' attention and at the end of the season, Golden State shipped a pair of second round draft picks to Portland for Barnett.

"I enjoyed everywhere I played," Barnett said, "But the Warriors were my favorite team. They had a great bunch of guys when I got to the team. That's what I remember most: the fun we had and the friendships."

Barnett's roommate on the road was 6-foot-10 forward Clyde Lee, a mild-mannered Southern gentleman from Vanderbilt. Lee's easy attitude made him a mark for his mischievous teammates. Barnett played more than a few practical jokes on his unsuspecting friend.

"One night we were playing in Seattle," Barnett said. "It was late and we were in bed at the hotel. During the night, Clyde got up to go to the bathroom. When he did, I snuck into his bed and made myself as skinny as possible, just pressed myself against the wall. So Clyde comes back, all 6-foot-10 of him, and gets in bed. He didn't realize I was in there. After a few minutes I said, 'Hey Clyde, it's getting kind of hot in here.' He jumped out of bed so fast. And he never swore or anything. All he said was, 'Gosh dang, what the heck are you doing in there?'"

Jeff Mullins, the Warriors' senior statesman at the time, was one of the more conservative members of the team. Together Barnett and Mullins ran the Warriors backcourt.

"Jeff Mullins was something," Barnett said. "Very few people knew that he could barely see. He wore glasses, but you never saw him on the court with glasses and he wouldn't wear contacts. We'd be running down court and he'd say, 'Hey, Barney, what's the score?' He couldn't even see the scoreboard. Don't ask me how he could shoot. But I sure saw him do it. He had that great jump shot. I saw him score 46 against Chicago one night. He couldn't miss."

During his three seasons with the Warriors, from 1971 to 1974, Barnett averaged 12 points and 3.5 assists, but it was his defense that the club valued most. Barnett generally found himself matched against the opponent's most

dangerous offensive threat.

"The Warriors really didn't need my scoring during those years, with Jeff Mullins, Cazzie Russell, Nate Thurmond and Rick Barry," Barnett said. "So I tried to make it by playing solid defense and I was a good defensive player. The guys I had problems staying with were the little guys. For me, the hardest guy to defend was Nate Archibald. He was so small and quick, like a fly you couldn't catch. He could do that little jitterbug move and be by you in a flash. He could really embarrass you if he wanted. Calvin Murphy was like that, too.

"I'd rather play against Jerry West and Oscar Robertson any time than against Archibald. I could stay with them, but of course they would still pull up and hit the jumper. They could embarrass you that way."

Owner Franklin Mieuli fostered a family atmosphere among the Warriors players and front office personnel, and as a result, many became close friends. Barnett claims there were a number of first-rate characters employed with the Warriors. Radio announcer Bill King was one of his favorites.

"Bill King was one of the team eccentrics," Barnett said. "He didn't like to wear shoes and he ate cloves of garlic, for health reasons I guess. He was a connoisseur of wine and food. He studied Russian and knew about ballet and cultural things. He was very educated and intellectual. But then he would drive the worst car he could possibly find. He always had some beat-up clunker that was falling apart. He thought it was ridiculous to waste money on a car."

In 1975, the New Orleans Jazz selected Barnett in the NBA expansion draft but it wasn't the last time the Warriors would see him. Barnett finished out his career with the Philadelphia 76ers, then returned to the Bay Area where he works as a television analyst for Warriors basketball games.

Two nights later, he hit for 43 against the Baltimore Bullets to inspire the club to another win. Russell became the only Warrior to play in the All-Star Game.

In his sixth season with the Warriors, Mullins led the club in scoring. He averaged 20.8 points, 4.5 assists and 4.4 rebounds, and had a high game of 43 against the Chicago Bulls.

Clyde Lee provided help on the boards with 14.5 rebounds per game, while "Fritz" Williams and Joe Ellis supplied scoring punch off the bench.

The Warriors stayed near the .500 mark for the first half of the campaign, then suddenly caught fire in January, winning 13 of 14 games. During the last month of the season, Golden State went 15-7 to finish with a 51-31 record. It was the first time in club history that the Warriors won 50 games in a season.

Incredibly, the Warriors still finished 18 games behind the Los Angeles Lakers. With a team that included Wilt Chamberlain, Jerry West, Gail Goodrich, Elgin Baylor, Jim McMillan and Happy Hairston, the Lakers compiled a phenomenal 69-13 mark. At one point, Los Angeles put together an NBA record 33-game winning streak. Los Angeles went on to win the NBA Championship.

The Warriors made it as far as the Western Conference Semifinals where they met the Milwaukee Bucks with Kareem Abdul-Jabbar, Bob Dandridge and an aging but still wily Oscar Robertson. The Warriors gave the Bucks a scare, beating them in game one at Milwaukee, 117-106, as Jim Barnett scored 30 points and Jeff Mullins had 29.

"After the game, we were going back to the hotel," Barnett recalled. "And Jeff Mullins said, 'Let's do it again tomorrow.' I said, 'No way. I can't do that again.' Jeff busted up. He thought that was pretty funny, that a pro didn't think he could score 30 points again."

Embarrassed and embittered, Milwaukee picked itself up and pummeled the Warriors in the next four games to win the series.

Cleveland's Walt Wesley (44) makes things difficult for Warriors guard Jeff Mullins under the hoop. Mullins is fifth on the Warriors all-time scoring list with 12,547 points during his nine seasons with the club.

1972–73

Golden State did not have a first round pick as a result of the Cyril Baptiste supplemental draft fiasco of 1971, so it did the next best thing; it selected a Chamberlain.

With their top pick, a third round draft choice, the Warriors chose forward Bill Chamberlain from North Carolina. Unfortunately, he didn't have the skills of Wilt Chamberlain and never made it with the Warriors. He ended up in the American Basketball Association.

Although the Warriors were unable to help themselves through the draft, there was an important new addition to the club. Prodigal son Rick Barry returned to the Warriors after five years of drifting around the A.B.A. It wasn't easy for the Warriors to acquire Barry's services. In fact, it took a court order. Barry had expressed a desire to stay with the New York Nets of the A.B.A. so that he could further his ambition of becoming a television personality by playing in a larger media market. He was ordered back to the Bay Area by a judge who ruled Barry had a valid contract with the Warriors.

Barry appeared to be a little rusty when he resurfaced in Oakland, but he quickly became the focal point of the Warriors' offense. He averaged 22.3 points, nine rebounds and five assists to pace the club. He was helped by Nate Thurmond and Jeff Mullins, who each contributed 17 points per game, and Cazzie Russell, who chipped in with 15.7 points.

Looking for bench strength, the Warriors signed free agent guard Mahdi Abdul-Rahman and center George Johnson early in the season. But it was Joe Ellis who continued to supply spark off the pine with 6.5 points per game.

The Warriors had an excellent year, finishing with a 47-35 record. Unfortunately, the Lakers were on fire. With Jerry West, Wilt Chamberlain and Gail Good-

OPPOSITE: Nate Thurmond (42) is guarded closely by Milwaukee center Kareem Abdul-Jabbar. Thurmond is the leading rebounder in team history, finishing his career with over 2,000 more rebounds than Wilt Chamberlain, who is second on the club's career rebounding list.

rich lighting up the Inglewood Forum, the Lakers won 60 games and finished 13 ahead of the Warriors in the Pacific Division. In his final NBA season, Chamberlain set a league record by shooting an astonishing .727 from the field while averaging 13.2 points.

For the third straight year, the Warriors were matched with the Milwaukee Bucks in the Western Conference Semifinals. The Bucks boasted a strong lineup that included Kareem Abdul-Jabbar, Oscar Robertson, Lucius Allen and Bob Dandridge.

Milwaukee took the first game of the series, 110-90, and looked like it would have no problem in game two when Rick Barry went down with an ankle injury in the first quarter and Coach Al Attles was ejected from the game after his second technical foul. Cazzie Russell picked up the slack, however, scoring 25 points to pace a 95-92 Warriors victory.

The Warriors captured two of the next three games to claim a 3-2 series lead and send the series back to Oakland. In game six, Golden State used an inspired performance by Nate Thurmond to win 100-86, and advance to the Western Conference Finals against the Los Angeles Lakers.

After posting 60 wins in the regular season, the Lakers seemed unconcerned with their Northern California rivals. But Golden State put a scare into Los Angeles in game one, taking a 53-50 halftime advantage and building a 91-82 lead with seven minutes left to play. Then the Warriors let their lead slip away. Gail Goodrich and Jerry West rallied the Lakers in the final minutes and West hit a 15-foot jumper with eight seconds remaining to win the game for Los Angeles.

The come-from-behind victory inspired the Lakers, who went on to annihilate the Warriors in five games. Golden State's lone victory came in game four, 117-109.

Rick Barry and Nate Thurmond were selected to play in the All-Star Game and Thurmond was named to the NBA All-Defensive Team. Thurmond also finished second in the league behind Chamberlain with 17.1 rebounds per game. Barry was the league's most effective foul shooter with a .902 percentage.

Warriors center Nate Thurmond reaches for the 10,000th rebound of his career against the Chicago Bulls on January 28, 1972. Bob Love (10) is behind him. Thurmond is the seventh leading rebounder of all time.

1973–74

The Warriors selected South Carolina guard Kevin Joyce in the first round of the college draft and Cincinnati's Derrick Dickey in round two. Joyce never saw a minute of action in a Warriors uniform, choosing instead to try his luck in the A.B.A. Dickey developed into a good forward who put in five seasons with Golden State.

Needing help in the backcourt, Coach Al Attles traded Mahdi Abdul-Rahman to Seattle for Butch

Beard, then teamed Beard with veteran guard Jeff Mullins. Mullins contributed 16 points per game while Beard provided 10.

Injuries hampered the club early in the year. Center Nate Thurmond sat out 20 games and backup center Clyde Lee suffered a banged-up knee that limited his playing time.

With the Warriors' two big men out of action, Rick Barry carried the scoring load, averaging 25 points per game. In a late season contest against Portland, Barry was unstoppable, hitting 30 field goals, a Golden State record, and scoring 64 points to set a personal high.

The Warriors finished 44-38, just three games behind Los Angeles in the Pacific Division, but failed to make the playoffs. A new format called for the top four teams in each conference to make the playoffs. The Warriors finished fifth in the conference.

Barry and Thurmond represented the Warriors at the All-Star Game. Barry finished fifth in the league in scoring, second in free throw percentage and fifth in steals with 2.2 per game. Thurmond was named to the All-Defensive Team for the fifth time.

1974–75

What eventually became a dream season started as a nightmare for Warriors fans when they discovered a flock of old favorites had departed. During the off-season, Golden State traded popular center Nate Thurmond to Chicago for Clifford Ray and a future draft pick. New Orleans chose guard Jim Barnett in the expansion draft. Cazzie Russell signed with Los Angeles as a free agent and Clyde Lee was traded to Atlanta.

In place of the old crowd pleasers came a stream of new blood. Golden State had one of its best drafts ever, selecting Keith "Silk" Wilkes (known later as Jamaal Wilkes) of U.C.L.A. and Phil Smith of U.S.F. with its top two picks. The pair were instrumental in reviving the franchise and leading it to a championship. In addition, the Warriors signed free agent guard Charles Dudley.

With Thurmond gone, the Warriors employed 6-foot-9 Clifford Ray at center. Keith Wilkes won a start-

RICK BARRY
1965–67 and 1972–78

The Grateful Dead aptly described Rick Barry's basketball career with the song lyric "what a long, strange trip it's been."

Barry burst onto the professional basketball scene in 1965 as a brash, jump shooting, first round pick from the University of Miami where he led the nation in scoring. The San Francisco Warriors viewed him as a savior. The fans saw him as a messiah. He won Rookie of the Year honors and turned a franchise that was considered the laughingstock of the league into an immediate contender.

"Barry could do it all," former teammate Jeff Mullins said. "He was like Michael Jordan today. He could shoot from the outside, had great moves near the basket, could rebound and pass. He made everybody around him better."

In his second year with the Warriors, Barry put all those skills together. He won the NBA scoring title, averaging 35.6 points, and became the first player in seven years to outscore Wilt Chamberlain. Barry dragged down 9.5 rebounds and added 3.5 assists a game.

He took the Warriors to the NBA Finals where they were defeated in six games by the Philadelphia 76ers, a team considered by many experts to be one of the greatest in NBA history.

In just two seasons, the Warriors had been transformed from a laughable but lovable club that finished with the NBA's worst record at 17-63, to a contender for basketball's ultimate title. The only major addition to the roster during that time was Rick Barry.

Then, just as quickly as he appeared and changed the fortunes of the Warriors, Barry vanished. He signed with the Oakland Oaks of the new American Basketball Association after the 1967 season. The Warriors wouldn't reach the pinnacle of pro basketball again until Barry returned to the team five years later.

During his self-imposed exile from the NBA, Barry became a virtual basketball vagabond. The teams moved, the owners changed and Barry found himself spending more time in the legal courts than on the hardwood courts. Each season found him playing in a different city. He went from Oakland to Washington to Virginia to New York. By 1970 he'd had enough of the A.B.A. Barry was ready to return to the Warriors. But the courts wouldn't let him out of his five-year contract. In 1972, he was finally able to wear a Warriors uniform again.

"I expected some animosity from the fans when I came back from the A.B.A.," Barry said. "But I figured if I played well, that would go away. I did play well and we won the NBA Championship."

The 1974-75 season was a dream come true for Barry. After drifting around the A.B.A., he finally got what he wanted; another chance to play for an NBA title.

"That was my best season in the NBA," Barry said. "I was named team captain that year, which meant a lot to me. The championship series with Washington was one of the great playoffs in NBA history. It was unbelievable, but it didn't get the recognition it deserved. We didn't even make the cover of *Sports Illustrated*."

With a lineup that included Wes Unseld, Elvin Hayes, Nick Weatherspoon, Phil Chenier and Kevin Porter, the Washington Bullets were heavily favored to whip the Warriors, who squeaked by Chicago to get to the finals.

"I remember it like it was yesterday," Barry said. "It took a fantastic team effort to beat Washington. That's what it was—a team effort. We had two excellent rookies, Phil Smith and Jamaal Wilkes. Clifford Ray did a great job at center. Charles Dudley, Butch Beard, Jeff Mullins, George Johnson...I could go down the line. There were so many contributors and many of them went unrecognized.

"The fans were great. They went wild. I remember coming back to San Francisco and we had to land in Oakland because there were so many fans in the airport. People were jumping on the cabs. Someone got on the roof of my cab and crushed it."

Reaching the top of the basketball world took perseverance. Although Barry had the confidence and the athletic skill to make it look easy at times, there were a number of people that helped him along the way.

"When I first got to the Warriors Tom Meschery helped me out quite a bit," Barry said. "He was a tough old pro, a very physical player, and he showed me some of the things I needed to do to survive in the NBA. I knew that if I could play against Tom in practice, I could do okay against the rest of the league.

"Alex Hannum was the coach my rookie year. He was quite a character. He ran a brutally tough camp. I came to camp in great shape and was still sore after his workouts. Fred Hetzel was the other first round pick that year and he was tough, but he ended up in bed with IVs running into his arm because he was so dehydrated."

Despite Barry's undeniable skill he couldn't win basketball games single-handedly. There was one teammate who was special.

"Playing with Nate Thurmond made a big difference," he said. "It was the only time I played with a great center. We ran the pick-and-roll together as well as anyone."

And in his early years, Barry was observant as well. He watched the NBA's great players to see how they got things done.

"Elgin Baylor was always a role model for me," Barry said. "In college I emulated his moves, his body control. When I got to the NBA and was actually playing against guys like Jerry West and Elgin Baylor, I had to pinch myself. I still have a *Sport* magazine when I made the NBA All-Star Team and I was on the cover with Elgin, Wilt and the rest of the All-Star Team. I couldn't believe it was actually me on the cover with them."

On most lists of professional basketball's greatest forwards, Rick Barry is near the top. The numbers speak for themselves. Over 14 professional seasons, 10 in the NBA and four in the A.B.A., Barry averaged 25 points, five assists and seven rebounds. He's the best free throw shooter in pro basketball history with an .893 percentage. He's number two in career steals by a forward with 2,380, trailing only Julius Erving. He's third on the all-time list of assists by a forward with 4,952. Some of his former teammates feel statistics don't do justice to Barry.

"I played with the best forward in the league," Jeff Mullins said. "The record book probably doesn't reflect Rick Barry's greatness. He was an exceptionally skilled athlete. Unfortunately, he had his career interrupted by playing in the A.B.A., and by the time he returned to the Warriors he'd had knee surgery and he was a little bit older. He'd been bandied about a little, but then he came back and still had a fantastic year in 1974-75. It was the best season I've ever seen a player have."

As for individual accomplishments, he was the NBA Rookie of the Year in 1966, the NBA scoring leader in 1967, the All-Star Game MVP in 1967, and

MVP of the 1975 NBA Finals. Five times Barry was an NBA All-Star and four times he made the A.B.A. All-Star Team. But the individual awards pale when compared to his feelings for the people he met in his years with the Warriors.

"The Warriors were always special to me," Barry said. "I never wanted to leave the team but it came down to $10,000, which was a matter of principle. I really loved the Bay Area and still do. Franklin Mieuli was always great to me. He didn't typify the NBA owner. He was a unique person, one of the characters that made the Warriors such a different organization.

"There were so many great people associated with the team. Maybe it was because San Francisco was such a cosmopolitan city that the Warriors attracted these unique characters. One of the things that made the Warriors special was the team's closeness."

OPPOSITE: Golden State's Cazzie Russell (32) prepares to fire a pass over New York's Earl Monroe (15). The Warriors obtained Russell from the Knicks in 1971 in a trade for Jerry Lucas. Russell averaged 19.2 points during his three seasons with Golden State.

ing job alongside Rick Barry at forward, while Charles Johnson and Butch Beard took over at the guard spots.

Golden State got off to one of its best starts in years, going 10-3 through the first month of the season. The Warriors proved they were for real during that stretch by beating Boston and Los Angeles on the road.

By the All-Star break, Golden State was 14 games over .500 and looking at a playoff spot.

Just a week after the All-Star Game, Rick Barry put on a show for the Oakland Coliseum Arena fans by scoring 55 points against Philadelphia, his season high. Barry went on to have one of his best years ever, averaging 30.6 points, second only to Bob MacAdoo's 34-point average.

As the season began to wind down, Golden State found itself fighting with Seattle for the division crown. To bolster their lineup for the upcoming playoffs, the Warriors signed veteran bruiser Bill Bridges. Golden State then won seven of its last nine games, finishing with a 48-34 record to clinch first place in the Pacific Division. Seattle finished four games behind in second place and was matched with Golden State in the Western Conference Semifinals.

Seattle was coached by the legendary Bill Russell and had an offense that revolved around forward Spencer Haywood, 7-foot-3 center Tom Burleson and hot-shooting guard Fred Brown. The Warriors needed six games to handle the frisky SuperSonics.

Golden State won the first game handily, 123-96, but the Sonics came back to take two of the next three as Burleson proved unstoppable for the smaller Warrior team. Golden State returned home for game five with the series deadlocked at two games apiece, wondering how to contain Seattle's 7-foot-3 center.

With 6-foot-9 Clifford Ray and 6-foot-11 George Johnson alternating at center, the Warriors were able to subdue Burleson in games five and six while Rick

TOP: Jeff Mullins (23) goes for two against the Chicago Bulls in the 1974-75 playoffs. Former Warriors teammate Nate Thurmond (42) is in the background.
BOTTOM: The Warriors won the 1974-75 NBA Championship under the guidance of Al Attles. He accumulated a .518 winning percentage during his 13 seasons as head coach.

Barry and Keith Wilkes took over the scoring chores for Golden State. They paced the Warriors in back-to-back wins to send Seattle home for the summer.

In the Western Conference Finals, Golden State faced the Chicago Bulls. The Bulls were a rough-and-tumble team that featured 7-foot center Tom Boerwinkle, high-scoring forwards Chet Walker and Bob Love, Jerry Sloan, a 6-foot-6 guard, and the outside shooting of Norm Van Lier. Sharing time with Boerwinkle at center was former Warriors great Nate Thurmond.

The Warriors had their hands full with Chicago. Golden State won the first game at home, 107-89, then lost a pair of heartbreakers at Chicago, 90-89, and 108-101. Down two games to one, the Warriors returned home to capture game four, 111-106, and even the series. Chicago won game five and could have clinched the series in game six, but Golden State rebounded from a 19-point third quarter deficit to win the sixth game and set up a deciding seventh game at the Oakland Coliseum Arena.

"After we came back to win game six, I knew something special was happening," Jeff Mullins said. "It looked like we were going to be eliminated but this was a team that just wouldn't give up."

Game seven turned out to be a defensive battle. Warriors forward Bill Bridges shut down Chicago's Bob Love, while Barry and Mullins supplied just enough offense, as the Warriors came from behind in the fourth quarter to win, 83-79.

The Warriors advanced to the NBA Championship Series for the first time since 1967, when a young Rick Barry took them to the finals against the Philadelphia 76ers.

Golden State did not match up with the Eastern Division Champion Washington Bullets and their intimidating front line of Wes Unseld, Elvin Hayes and Nick Weatherspoon. Guard Phil Chenier was one of the league's top scorers and Kevin Porter led the league

Rick Barry (24) pops a jumper against the Houston Rockets. Barry was an eight-time All-Star in the NBA and played in four A.B.A. All-Star Games.

Golden State's Jamaal Wilkes brings down a rebound against the Portland Trail Blazers in a game in 1975. Portland's Sidney Wicks (21) sends a foot flying.

from a small television in the locker room.

The Warriors regrouped under assistant coach Joe Roberts, but fell behind by 14 points. As the game began to wind down, Washington still had a commanding eight-point lead with just over four minutes to play. Then the ball began to bounce the Warriors' way. The Bullets hit a cold spell, while Barry and Keith Wilkes hit a pair of field goals to cut the lead.

With 1:45 left on the clock, Butch Beard scored on a driving layup to put the Warriors ahead, 94-93. A series of tension-building turnovers ensued, then Beard was fouled and sank a pair of free throws to make the score 96-93. Washington sank one last basket before time ran out, but the Warriors were champions for the first time since moving to the West Coast. They did it by playing excellent defense against a bigger, more talented team.

"We never panicked. We just did what we had to do," said Barry, who averaged 28 points in the series. "Even when we fell behind by eight late in the fourth quarter, we knew we were going to win. We could see they were tired."

Barry was named MVP of the Championship Series, but several other team members received postseason awards including Keith Wilkes, who was named NBA Rookie of the Year, and Warriors general manager Dick Vertlieb, who was selected Executive of the Year.

1975–76

The Warriors picked LaSalle forward Joe Bryant with its first round draft pick in 1975 then sold his rights to Philadelphia. U.S.C. guard Gus Williams was selected in the second round and became an immediate starter at guard. The third round pick was Robert "Bubbles" Hawkins who contributed off the bench with a four-point average.

With the emergence of Gus Williams and the improved play of Phil Smith, guard Butch Beard became expendable. Beard, one of the heroes of the 1975 playoffs, was traded to Cleveland for Dwight Davis, a 6-foot-8 forward, who was expected to give the club rebounding help.

in assists. It seemed as if Bullets coach K.C. Jones had assembled a team with few weaknesses.

The Warriors stole the first game from the heavily-favored Bullets, 101-95, at Washington's Capital Centre. Then, back home at Oakland, the Warriors snuck by the Bullets in game two, 92-91. In game three, Rick Barry exploded for 38 points as the Warriors defeated the Bullets, 109-101, to take an unlikely 3-0 edge in the series.

Game four in Washington got off to a wild start. Less than four minutes into it, Bullets guard Mike Riordan, who had the unenviable task of defending Rick Barry, committed his third foul by mugging Barry on a layup attempt. The overly aggressive contact sparked a fierce pushing and shoving match. Coach Al Attles leaped off the bench in an attempt to protect his players and went after Riordan, then Wes Unseld, the biggest man on the court. Attles was ejected from the game and was forced to watch the rest of the action

Forward Jamaal Wilkes drives past Chicago's Mickey Johnson. Wilkes averaged 16.5 points per game during his three years with the Warriors. In 1977 he played out his option and signed with the Los Angeles Lakers.

The NBA Champion Warriors continued their winning ways in the 1975-76 season, blazing through the first half of their schedule with a 32-10 record, best in the league.

Phil Smith blossomed into the club's backcourt leader and most consistent scorer. He had the best day of his career against Phoenix midway through the season when he exploded for 51 points. Smith averaged 20 points, 4.5 rebounds and 4.4 assists.

On the last day of the regular season, Golden State had already clinched the Pacific Division Championship but had an opportunity to set a franchise record as the only Warriors team ever to win 60 games in a season. Seattle defeated Golden State, 119-103, but the Warriors posted a 59-23 record, best in team history.

Golden State faced the Detroit Pistons with Bob Lanier and Curtis Rowe in the Western Conference

Semifinals. The series opened at the Oakland Coliseum Arena where the Warriors outclassed the Pistons in game one, 127-103. The two clubs traded victories as Detroit came back to soundly beat the Warriors in game two, 123-111. Golden State won game three easily, 113-90, and the Pistons won the fourth game, 106-103, to deadlock the series at two games apiece. Golden State captured game five, 128-109, to take a one-game edge in the series.

Game six was one of the most dramatic of the season as Phil Smith and Gus Williams put on a show in a 118-116 Warriors overtime win. Smith poured in 37 points and had seven assists and Williams had 14 points in the critical third quarter to put Golden State ahead.

"We won four games but it was a battle all the way," said forward Rick Barry after the deciding game. "They made us work for this one."

The Phoenix Suns, fresh off a semifinal playoff victory over the Seattle SuperSonics and led by Paul Westphal and Alvan Adams, were happily waiting for the Warriors in the Western Conference Finals.

Golden State made it look easy in game one with a nonchalant 128-103 win at the Oakland Coliseum Arena as Barry, Smith and Jamaal Wilkes all scored in double figures. The Warriors effortless victory may have caused them to relax in game two, because the Suns jumped off the deck and spanked Golden State at the Coliseum Arena, 108-101.

After capturing game three, 99-91, the Warriors lost one of the most exhausting games in memory, a double-overtime thriller at Phoenix, 133-129.

"It seemed like it was going to go on forever," said Golden State guard Phil Smith, who led all scorers with 30 points. "We had an opportunity to put it away and blew it."

Golden State was on top in the fourth game, 112-110, with eight seconds to play in regulation when Keith Erickson took a pass and hit a 25-foot jumper to trigger the first overtime. In the first extra period, Ricky Sobers rescued the Suns with two clutch free throws to send the game into a second overtime.

The discouraging loss started the Warriors on their demise. Although they won game five, 111-95, to take a 3-2 edge in the best of seven series, the Warriors appeared to run out of gas. They lost another heartbreaker at Phoenix in game six, 105-104, when Erickson hit Suns rookie center Alvan Adams on a backdoor pass under the hoop with nine seconds remaining. Adams canned the winning layup.

The series returned to Oakland for game seven and the Suns' superior size took over. "The reason they beat us is offensive rebounding," Coach Al Attles said. "When a team gets 49 rebounds and 20 of them are offensive rebounds you're going to get beat."

Phoenix took game seven, 94-86, to end the Warriors' dream of back-to-back NBA championships.

Rick Barry, Phil Smith and Jamaal Wilkes were selected to the All-Star Team. Smith and Wilkes were also named to the All-Defensive Team. Barry averaged 21 points to lead the Warriors in scoring and contributed six assists per game. Gus Williams made the All-Rookie Team.

1976–77

The American Basketball Association ceased operation in 1976 after nine exciting and innovative years, but four teams were assimilated into the NBA after paying a $3 million entry fee. The A.B.A. teams entering the promised land were the New York Nets, Denver Nuggets, San Antonio Spurs and Indiana Pacers. They brought with them a covey of A.B.A. stars including Julius "Dr. J" Erving, Moses Malone, Bobby Jones, Artis Gilmore, George Gervin, Dan Issel and David Thompson.

The Warriors had an outstanding draft, picking up Centenary center Robert Parish in the first round and Texas A&M forward Sonny Parker in round two. Both men would figure prominently in the Warriors' future.

Coach Al Attles' starting five remained basically unchanged from the 1975-76 season, with Clifford Ray at center, Jamaal Wilkes and Rick Barry at forward, and Phil Smith and Gus Williams at guard.

The 37-year-old Barry continued to be the focal point of the offense with a 21.8 average. Some of the scoring load was taken off Barry, however, by the rapidly improving Smith, who averaged 19 points, and Wilkes, who contributed 17.7 per game. Williams added 9.3 points and 3.6 assists, and Ray was good for eight points and eight rebounds.

The Warriors got bench help from Parish, who contributed nine points and seven rebounds per game. Reserve guard Charles Dudley averaged seven points and 4.5 assists.

The club got off to a rocky start and just one month into the season was already struggling with a 7-10 record. Then, Barry went on a hot streak, averaging over 30 points during a 10-game stretch as the Warriors won eight times. By midway through the season, Golden State had improved its record to 22-19. As the year progressed, the Warriors continued to refine their offense and improved their record to 46-36, which was good enough for third place in the Pacific Division.

In the first round of the playoffs, Golden State met the Detroit Pistons, who finished the season with a

CLYDE LEE
1966-74

Clyde Lee was venturing into the unknown when he reported to the San Francisco Warriors in the fall of 1966.

Lee had been a standout at Nashville, Tennessee's Vanderbilt University but the professional game was a big step forward. Despite being the Warriors' first round draft pick, the third player selected overall, Lee was unsure of himself. He didn't know if he would succeed in the NBA or where he might fit in with the Warriors.

San Francisco already had one of the game's best big men in Nate Thurmond who was coming off another All-Star season. The 6-foot-10 Lee would not be needed at center, and the forward positions were held down by Rick Barry, Tom Meschery and Fred Hetzel. For the first time in his life, Lee began to doubt his ability as a basketball player.

"When I first got to San Francisco, Rick Barry was the star forward and the team's biggest scorer," Lee said. "Nate

Thurmond was a defensive center and rebounder but he could also score. I didn't know where I would play. The coaches took me aside and told me if I wanted playing time, I would need to be a defensive player and rebounder. That way Rick (Barry) could get a rest on defense. I had been a scorer in college so this was a little different role. But I did it. I usually got the scoring forward to guard. I was content playing defense."

Lee developed into the consummate team player. He adapted to the team's changing style and personnel. He was always ready when needed. And when Thurmond suffered through a variety of injuries during Lee's first two years with the club, it was Lee who was put to work as a center in place of Thurmond.

"I felt more comfortable as a forward," Lee said. "But Nate was injured during my early years and I ended up playing a lot of center. I never felt comfortable there. I didn't think I was big enough. But I did the best I could."

Lee averaged seven points and seven rebounds as a rookie and learned valuable lessons about life in the NBA. Much of his education was done on the job at the hands of Bill Russell, Wilt Chamberlain, Zelmo Beatty, Willis Reed, Bill Bridges and the league's other fierce inside players.

Thurmond missed nearly 20 games in Lee's rookie season and the first-year man filled his shoes admirably. With Rick Barry scoring at a clip of 35 points per game, the Warriors captured a spot in the playoffs. They shocked the basketball world by advancing to the NBA Finals against the Philadelphia 76ers.

"In my rookie year we made it to the finals against Philadelphia," Lee said. "They had a heck of a team. Chet Walker was the guy I usually matched up with. I was pleased just to get there to the finals. We played well but I thought we'd be back to the finals more often. We had a young team so I thought that was just the start for us. I guess I should have appreciated it more when it happened."

It turned out to be Lee's only shot at a championship. The following season Rick Barry drifted off to the American Basketball Association, Nate Thurmond missed nearly 30 games due to injuries, and the team limped into the playoffs where it was defeated by the Los Angeles Lakers in the Western Division Finals, four games to one.

But Lee's sophomore season turned out to be one of his best. Picking up the slack for the missing Barry, and often filling in at center for the ailing Thurmond, he averaged 12 points and 14 rebounds and made the All-Star Team. One of the year's highlights occurred in the postseason, when the Warriors faced the fearsome St. Louis Hawks in the first round of the playoffs.

St. Louis ripped through the Western Division in 1967-68 compiling a 56-26 record, 13 games better than San Francisco. With Bill Bridges, Paul Silas and Zelmo "the Elbow" Beatty dominating the inside, the Hawks were one of the league's most physically intimidating teams.

"We developed a big rivalry with the Hawks," Lee said. "They played a rough game and you really hated to play there in St. Louis. Those fans were vicious. When we had Rick Barry, they would really get on him. He had a Snickers candy bar commercial so whenever Rick went to the line they would throw Snickers bars at him. When they ran out of those, they threw cigarette lighters, coins, whatever they could find."

San Francisco knocked off the Hawks in six games to advance to the Western Division Finals before losing to Los Angeles. But the playoff victory over St. Louis was satisfying. It was during the playoffs that Lee began to get the respect he deserved. He believes his teammate Nate Thurmond should get recognition for the role he played.

"Nate was always a big help," Lee said. "When he was in the lineup, he made things a lot easier on the rest of the team. I remember games where he would block out people so I could get

the rebound. Whenever we played the Bucks, Nate would concentrate on blocking out Jabbar and then he'd yell to me, 'Go get it, Clyde.'"

In 1969, Lew Alcindor came into the league and transformed the Milwaukee Bucks from a cellar-dwelling expansion team into an instant title contender. The Bucks also became one of the Warriors' annual playoff rivals. Every season between 1971 and 1973, the Warriors met the Bucks in the Western Conference Semifinals.

"The most satisfying moment of my career came in the '73 playoffs," Lee said. "None of the reporters thought we had a chance against the Bucks and Jabbar. Some of the national reporters didn't even cover the series because they thought the Bucks would beat us so easily."

Lee averaged 11 points and 16 rebounds and the Warriors beat Milwaukee in six games.

"When we returned home, the fans gave me a standing ovation," Lee said. "I'll always remember that. It meant a lot to me.

"There were always good fans in San Francisco. I enjoyed every minute that I was out there. I lived in the Marina district and always felt like I grew up in San Francisco because it was the first time I was really away from home. It was a different time. The hippies were around and there were the protests over the war. It was an interesting area. My daughter was born there."

Lee was traded to the Atlanta Hawks in 1974 after eight years of service with the Warriors. He was the proverbial "player to be named later," handed to Atlanta to fulfill a trade that occurred four years earlier when San Francisco acquired the rights to Zelmo Beatty. Ironically, Beatty never signed with the Warriors. During his eight seasons with the club, Lee averaged 8.5 points and 11 rebounds. Most importantly, he played defense the way the Warriors wanted.

"I took pride in my defense," Lee said. "I usually played against the other team's best-scoring forward. The one guy who

usually gave me problems was Connie Hawkins. He was quick and had such good moves. He could go to the basket or just pop an outside shot. And he was a good outside shooter."

Playing professional basketball and being paid to do what he loved best is something that still excites Lee.

"I never had a goal to be a pro basketball player," Lee said. "I just loved playing. Even now, when I walk through a gym, if I see a ball, I feel like picking it up and shooting. I never dreamed I could make a living at it."

44-38 record behind the play of M.L. Carr, Bob Lanier and Howard Porter.

Lanier dominated the first game of the best-of-three playoff series as the Pistons defeated the Warriors at the Oakland Coliseum Arena, 95-90. Golden State rebounded by blowing out Detroit in game two, 138-108.

The decisive third game at the Oakland Coliseum Arena turned into a slugfest with six minutes left in the third quarter and the Pistons clinging to a 67-64 lead. The skirmish started when Golden State's Charles Dudley and Detroit's Eric Money squared off. As the punching got serious, Al Attles and Clifford Ray sprang from the Warriors' bench to break it up. The fighting spilled over a press table and into the stands where a fan decked Detroit's M.L. Carr. The fan then had his nose crushed by Detroit's 6-foot-10 center Bob Lanier. To add insult to injury, Carr later filed a battery complaint against the fan.

The battle seemed to revitalize the Warriors. When play resumed, Rick Barry ran off six straight buckets to give Golden State a lead it never relinquished. Barry ended up with 35 points, shooting 14 of 29 from the field.

"I think it got us going," Jamaal Wilkes said of the fight. "It changed the tempo. We seemed to take control."

"I did feel a little adrenaline flowing," Phil Smith said. "But basketball is an emotional thing. You get fired up."

Robert Parish chipped in with 17 points and 18 rebounds while neutralizing Lanier, as the Warriors advanced to the Western Conference Semifinals against the Los Angeles Lakers.

Despite having a lineup that included such stars as Kareem Abdul-Jabbar, Cazzie Russell and Lucius Allen, the heavily-favored Lakers needed seven games to dispose of the Warriors. The Lakers won the first two games handily, but after returning to Oakland the

During his six seasons with the Warriors, Phil Smith (20) averaged 17.1 points. In 1976 and 1977 he was selected to play in the NBA All-Star Game.

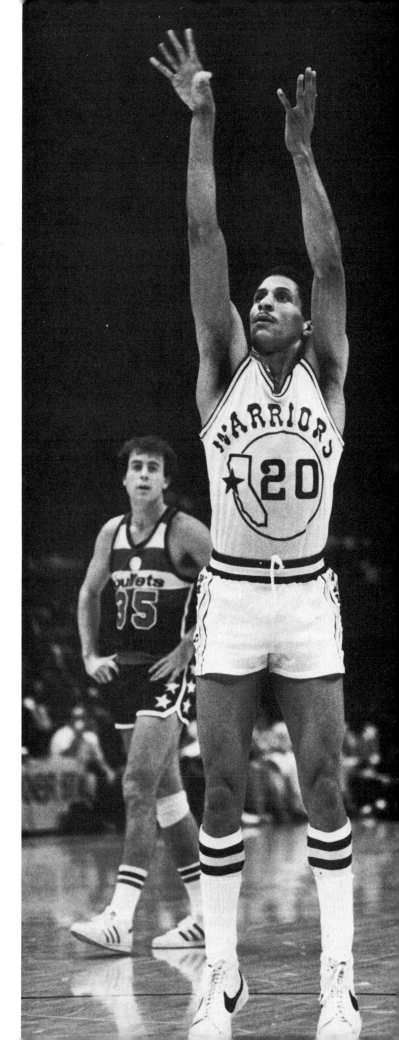

Warriors struck back, taking two in a row to even the series.

Jabbar took control in game five as Los Angeles escaped with a 112-105 win, but once again the Warriors showed their resiliency. They bounced back to capture game six, 115-106, and to force a seventh game at Los Angeles.

The concluding seventh game was played before 17,500 fans at the Inglewood Forum. They watched passively as Golden State jumped out to a 14-point second quarter lead. But the Lakers were patient and gradually chipped away at the lead until they tied the game with eight minutes to play. At that point, the ball stopped dropping through the hoop for Golden State. The Warriors made just three field goals in the final eight minutes and converted only 6 of 22 from the floor in the fourth quarter. Meanwhile, Jabbar put on a sensational performance for the Lakers, finishing the night with 36 points and 25 rebounds as Los Angeles pulled out a 97-84 win.

Wilkes had 16 points in the first half and finished with 24, but Barry and Smith had sub-par games. Barry, who averaged 30 points in the series, scored just 15. Smith made just 3 of 13 field goal attempts for nine points, well below his 19-point average.

During the regular season, Barry set an NBA record by connecting on 60 consecutive free throws and reached the 20,000-point mark for his career.

1977–78

The Warriors lost two of their starters to free agency when guard Gus Williams signed with the Seattle SuperSonics and star forward Jamaal Wilkes went south to the Los Angeles Lakers. NBA commissioner Larry O'Brien stepped in, however, and ruled that Golden State was entitled to a first round draft pick from the Lakers as compensation for Wilkes.

Golden State used its picks wisely, selecting a trio of talented collegiate stars in the annual draft. Among the rookies that found a place on the Warriors' roster were first round choices Rickey Green of Michigan and Wesley Cox of Louisville. They also picked up Manhattan's Rickey Marsh in the eighth round and signed veteran forward E.C. Coleman from New Orleans.

Rick Barry and Phil Smith continued to provide the club with offensive spark. Barry averaged 23 points over the course of the season, while Smith chipped in 19.7 points. Clifford Ray held down the center spot, but Robert Parish began to show he was a force off the bench, contributing 8.3 rebounds and 12.5 points. Sonny Parker also added scoring punch with his 11.5 average. Coleman turned into the Warriors' best defensive player and made the NBA's All-Defensive Team.

Despite an impressive starting lineup, the Warriors had the bad fortune of playing in the talent-rich Pacific Division. The defending NBA Champion Portland Trail Blazers were the class of the league with Bill Walton, but hot on their heels were the Phoenix Suns with Walter Davis and Paul Westphal, the Seattle Sonics with Jack Sikma and Marvin Webster, and the Los Angeles Lakers featuring Kareem Abdul-Jabbar, Adrian Dantley and ex-Warrior Jamaal Wilkes.

Golden State won 14 of its last 19 games to post a 43-39 record but finished dead last in the Pacific Division. On the final day of the season, the Warriors flew to Seattle needing a victory to clinch the last playoff spot.

Under coach Lenny Wilkens, the Sonics had a 27-3 record at Seattle's old Coliseum Center, known by the Warriors as the "House of Horrors" because of their rotten luck in Seattle over the years. The bad fortune continued. Rick Barry went the entire first half without hitting a field goal and finished the night four of 18 from the field as Seattle beat the Warriors, 111-105, and ended the Warriors playoff hopes.

OPPOSITE: Warriors guard Phil Smith (20) finds a lane as Philadelphia 76ers forward Doug Collins watches.

In his last season with the Warriors, Barry set a team record by shooting .924 from the free throw line.

1978–79

Free agency put a damper on the Warriors' off-season for the second year in a row as Rick Barry decided to jump ship and head off to the Houston Rockets. NBA commissioner Larry O'Brien demanded the Warriors receive fair compensation, however, and the Rockets sent guard John Lucas west in exchange for Barry.

The Warriors uncovered a couple of nuggets in the college draft, selecting Jackson State forward Purvis Short and U.C.L.A. guard Ray Townsend in the first round, and Wayne Cooper from the University of New Orleans in the second round.

Robert Parish worked his way into the starting lineup, replacing Clifford Ray, and began to develop into one of the league's top centers. He averaged 17 points and 12 rebounds during the season and set a team record with 217 blocked shots. Parish also joined the exclusive 30-30 club in a game against New York when he grabbed 32 rebounds and scored 30 points. He became the first Warrior to accomplish that feat since Nate Thurmond in 1969.

Parish was helped offensively by a quick, young crew that averaged 24 years of age but just 2.3 years of NBA experience. The starting five included rookie forward Purvis Short, third-year man Sonny Parker, who averaged 15 points, playmaking guard John Lucas, who averaged 16 points and nine assists, and Phil Smith, the veteran of the group. Golden State's fast-breaking style seemed to work early in the season as it bolted out to a 9-5 record.

Midway through the year, Smith, who was averaging 20 points and 4.5 assists, went down with a leg

TOP: *Guard John Lucas drives past Los Angeles Lakers center Kareem Abdul-Jabbar for two points. Lucas once had 12 assists in a single quarter against the Chicago Bulls in 1978, a club record.*
BOTTOM: *Warriors center Robert Parish (00) drives past Milwaukee's Kent Benson (54). Parish averaged 13.8 points and 9.5 points during his four seasons with the club.*

PHIL SMITH
1974-80

The Warriors were looking for a completely new starting lineup.

Smith and first round draft choice Keith "Silk" Wilkes (later Jamaal Wilkes) were the youngest members of the Warriors' new regime. Wilkes won a starting job at forward alongside Rick Barry, averaged 14 points and eight rebounds, and was named NBA Rookie of the Year. Smith became the Warriors' fourth guard behind Butch Beard, Jeff Mullins and Charles Johnson. He averaged eight points and two assists off the bench as the Warriors went on to win the NBA Championship.

"The thing that made us so successful in 1975 was that everyone made a contribution," Smith said. "There was a lot of individual sacrifice which went to the betterment of the team. It took an all-out team effort and our goal was winning a championship."

Rick Barry was the club leader with a 30.6 scoring average, 6.2 assists and 5.7 rebounds; Beard averaged 12.8 points, and Johnson added 11, but everyone had a hand in the team's success. The Warriors had the league's highest scoring offense and much of the spark was coming from the bench.

"Different people would stand out at different times," Smith said. "One night it might be Clifford Ray, another night it might be Butch Beard, then another night it might be Jamaal Wilkes."

With a year in the NBA under his belt and a championship ring on his finger, Smith's career took off. He went to work on the aspects of his game that needed improvement and the results were remarkable. In 1975-76, Smith won a starting job and was second in the club in minutes played. He averaged 20 points and made the NBA All-Star Team.

"Shooting was the one thing I needed to work on the most if I was going to make the jump from the college game to the pros," Smith said. "I worked on that and developed into a better shooter over time.

"After my rookie season, I saw that I could succeed in the pros. I realized that

After six years with the Golden State Warriors, Phil Smith began to wonder if he would ever get out of San Francisco. He'd played basketball his whole life in the Bay Area, starring at San Francisco's George Washington High School, then matriculating at the University of San Francisco before joining the Warriors in 1974 as their second round draft pick.

The Warriors club he joined was a team in the midst of transition. Prior to the start of the 1974-75 season, the Warriors dealt a number of old favorites including Nate Thurmond, Cazzie Russell and Clyde Lee. Guard Jim Barnett was lost in the expansion draft.

hard work would pay off. I also understood that I was blessed with physical gifts. I had God-given talent. I had quickness, fast hands to bat the ball away. I could jump pretty good. The thing that made me a success was the ability to focus on my job and concentrate on what I had to do.

"I always felt I could pass. That was one of the better parts of my game. I learned a lot from watching the people around me. I watched Rick (Barry) and saw how he could pass. I picked up a lot of techniques from watching opponents too, defensive techniques and things like that."

In 1975-76, Golden State won 59 games, the most in team history, with a starting lineup that included second-year players Smith, Wilkes and Clifford Ray, rookie guard Gus Williams and high-scoring veteran Rick Barry. With a bounty of young bucks eager to play basketball, coach Al Attles looked like he had a dynasty on his hands.

"After winning a championship and getting a little more playing time, my confidence was much higher," Smith said. "That 1975-76 season was the most memorable for me. I went from a bench role to a starting job. We won 59 games and it looked like we had all the ingredients to win the championship again. Gus Williams was becoming a star and we had a young backcourt. We went through the league and just whipped on people. The whole team was confident. We knew we could win."

Golden State beat Detroit in the first round of the playoffs but fizzled in the Western Conference Finals. After leading the series three games to two over the Phoenix Suns, the Warriors dropped two straight and the dynasty began to unravel.

Wilkes played one more season with the Warriors before heading south to Los Angeles where he teamed with Kareem Abdul-Jabbar, and later Magic Johnson, to bring a dynasty to Los Angeles. Williams went north where he signed with Seattle. Barry sought refuge with the Houston Rockets. And Jeff

Mullins retired and went home to North Carolina.

Smith remained behind to play for the team he watched as a kid and became the Warriors' focal point. He averaged 19 to 20 points per game over the next three seasons and emerged as the club's most steady and reliable player.

But even Smith's days were numbered in his home town. He finally was traded to the San Diego Clippers in 1980 for World B. Free. Around that time, Smith realized there was something about Bay Area basketball that was attractive to him.

"I loved playing in pickup games around the Bay Area," Smith said. "I went around to all the local gyms, the junior colleges, outdoor courts, anywhere you could get a game. A lot of the time the people didn't know me and I didn't know them. At different courts you had to read what was going on. Every group had its own dynamics. I learned a lot about the game that way."

It was in those playground games that Smith gained confidence in his ability. While a collegiate star at U.S.F. he had the opportunity to play pickup basketball against professionals like Joe Ellis, Jim Barnett and Rick Barry who were known to frequent local gyms. Smith had an inkling that the NBA might be in his future.

"I became friendly with a couple of the Warriors when I was at U.S.F.," Smith said. "I played against them one-on-one and did okay, so I had the impression I could make it as a professional if I worked hard."

Barnett remembers Smith as more than a gym rat. He was a dynamic young player who had a definite NBA future.

"We used to put on these clinics for the kids in the community," Barnett said. "I remember Phil would come by to play and a few times he lit me up pretty good."

Smith ended his nine-year NBA career with the Seattle SuperSonics in 1983. He averaged 15 points, four assists and three rebounds during that time. Some of his fondest memories are of

playing in front of his hometown fans.

"I really enjoyed playing in the Bay Area," Smith said. "I had a good support system—lots of friends and family. They could get in the way a little bit at times. If I was to do it again I would probably go about things in a more businesslike manner to try to limit the distractions. But I think the people in the Bay Area appreciated what I did a little more because I was from there and they knew me."

OPPOSITE: Golden State center Clifford Ray (44) grabs a rebound against Atlanta's Ollie Johnson (27). Ray was an important part of the 1974-75 Warriors team which won the NBA championship.

John Lucas averaged 16.1 points and 9.3 assists during the 1978-79 season, his best year with the Warriors.

injury. In desperate need of a seasoned veteran to replace Smith and stabilize the young starters, the Warriors obtained 32-year-old guard Jo Jo White from the Boston Celtics in exchange for a first round pick in 1979.

White added 12 points and 4.5 assists per game but Golden State never recovered from the loss of Smith. The Warriors ended the year with a 38-44 record, 14 games behind first place Seattle and out of the playoff picture. The Sonics went on to win the NBA title.

The future looked bright for the Warriors, however, as Purvis Short and Wayne Cooper were both selected to the All-Rookie Team.

1979–80

The Warriors did not have a first round pick, having sent it to Boston in exchange for Jo Jo White midway through the 1978-79 season, so the roster remained relatively intact from the previous year. The only draft choice to make the club, Lynbert "Cheese" Johnson, was better known for his mouth-watering nickname than his playing ability. Johnson was a third round pick from Wichita, who played sparingly and contributed three points per game.

Injuries hampered the Warriors throughout the year. Phil Smith missed the first 31 games of the season due to a torn Achilles tendon. Purvis Short sat out a dozen games with a shoulder problem. Ted Abernathy was forced to the sidelines for several weeks after suffering an ankle injury. Even coach Al Attles had problems. He tore an Achilles tendon while practicing with the team and missed the final month of the campaign. Assistant coach John Bach guided the club in Attles' absence but by that time the season was lost. Under Bach, the Warriors went 6-15 and ended the year with a 24-58 record, the second worst in the NBA.

Guard John Lucas was one of the bright spots on the young squad. He began to come into his own as the league's top playmaker, averaging 7.5 assists and 13 points per game. Center Robert Parish was among the top centers in the league, averaging 11 rebounds and 17 points. Second-year man Purvis Short also had a 17-point average.

1980–1990

CHAPTER FIVE
1980–1990

1980–81

The Warriors' front office made more deals than Monte Hall during the off-season. They started by trading center Robert Parish and their first round pick (number three) to Boston for the Celtics' two first-round choices (numbers one and 13).

With the first pick in the draft, the Warriors chose seven-foot center Joe Barry Carroll from Purdue. Golden State used its other first round selection to take Mississippi's 6-foot-10 forward/center Rickey Brown.

Golden State made good use of its later draft picks. Strong forward Larry Smith from Alcorn State was selected in the second round, Washington guard Lorenzo Romar was a seventh round pick, and U.S.F.'s Billy Reid was a ninth round choice. Carroll and Smith became rookie starters while Reid, Romar and Brown provided time as backups.

The Warriors weren't finished dealing, though. They traded guard Phil Smith and a first round choice in 1984 to San Diego for World B. Free. Then Wayne Cooper and a second round pick in 1981 were sent to Utah for forward Bernard King. Veteran guard Jo Jo White was sold to Kansas City.

Coach Al Attles opened the season with a completely new lineup. John Lucas was the only starter remaining from the 1979-80 team. He began the year at guard alongside Free, while Carroll took over at center, and King and Smith moved into the forward spots.

The new club showed dramatic improvement and played exciting basketball. A month into the season, the Warriors proved to be the surprise of the NBA as

they sat perched atop the Pacific Division with a 12-6 record. Free thrilled the Oakland Coliseum Arena crowds with his fall-away jumpers, while Lucas and King were breathtaking on the fast break.

Lucas ran the floor, dishing off seven assists per game to go with 8.4 points. Free led the club in scoring with 24 points per game. King added 22 points, 6.8 rebounds and 3.5 assists, and established a club record by shooting .588 from the field. He was named NBA Comeback Player of the Year, after returning to the league following an alcohol problem.

First-year players Larry Smith and J.B. Carroll also provided quality time and were selected to the All-Rookie Team. From the opening tip of the season, Smith showed he had a nose for the ball, dragging down 12 rebounds per game and averaging 10 points. Carroll averaged 19 points and nine rebounds.

Golden State cooled off after its early hot spell, but finished the season with a 39-43 record, an improvement of 15 games from 1979-80.

With the season winding down, Golden State needed to win one of its last two games to make the playoffs. Instead, it dropped a pair of heartbreakers, losing at home to Denver, 142-139, and on the road at Seattle, 96-92.

Although the Warriors failed to make the playoffs for the fourth straight year, the future looked bright. The club had a solid nucleus of young talent and the average age of the starters was just 24. There was trouble in the ranks, however. John Lucas had missed a series of practices and games and was suspended for the final month of the season. It was later disclosed that he was having drug and alcohol problems.

OPPOSITE: World B. Free (21) was one of the Warriors' most exciting performers from 1980-82. He averaged 23.4 points but was traded to Cleveland for Ron Brewer midway through the 1982-83 season.

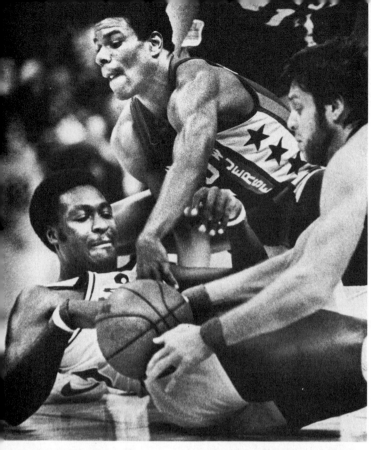

1981–82

Point guard John Lucas was shipped to the Washington Bullets for a pair of second round picks during the off-season, but the rest of the Warriors starting lineup from 1980-81 remained intact.

In the college draft, Golden State looked for rebounding help and used its top choice on Arizona State forward Sam Williams. The 6-foot-8 rookie averaged five rebounds and six points until suffering a leg injury that hampered him late in the year. Drake forward Lewis Lloyd was chosen in the fourth round and Memphis State forward Hank McDowell was a fifth round pick. Both played sparingly.

To strengthen the backcourt, Golden State acquired veteran guard Mike Gale from Portland in exchange for a pair of future second round draft picks.

During the first month of the season, Golden State posted a 13-7 record and began to look like a team on the rise. The early season highlight was a dramatic double-overtime win over the powerful Phoenix Suns that showed the rest of the league that the Warriors were for real.

Forward Bernard King continued to inspire teammates and fans with his remarkable recovery from substance abuse problems. He developed into the club's unmistakable court leader, giving 110 percent every time he took the floor. King averaged 23 points and helped the Warriors get off to a strong start. He became the first Warrior to appear in the All-Star Game since Rick Barry in 1978.

World B. Free provided the fireworks, launching bombs from anywhere on the court. He posted a 23-point average and was among the flashiest and most entertaining players in the NBA. Free and King finished among the league's Top Ten scorers, becoming

TOP: Warriors forward Purvis Short scrambles for a loose ball while New Jersey's Mike Newline (right) tries to take it away. Short was the Warriors' leading scorer four times between 1980-1986.

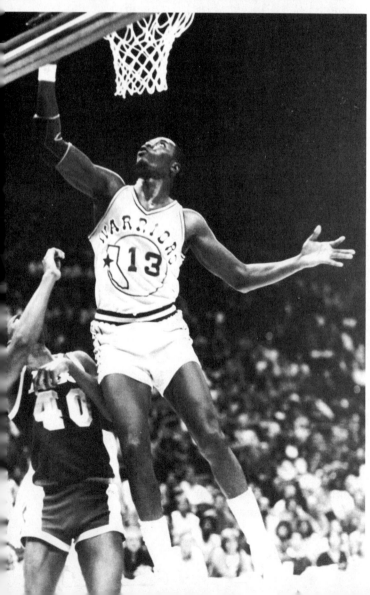

BOTTOM: The Warriors selected Alcorn State's Larry Smith (13) in the second round of the 1980 college draft. He turned into one of the NBA's dominant rebounders, averaging 10.5 per game during his Warriors career.

AL ATTLES
1960-

Through four decades in three cities, Al Attles has worn a variety of hats for the Philadelphia, San Francisco and Golden State Warriors.

From player to coach to general manager to team vice-president, Attles has overseen virtually every phase of the Warriors' operation since joining the team in 1960 as a lowly fifth round draft pick out of North Carolina A&T. Attles showed up at the Philadelphia Warriors camp with enough clothes to last a

week. He wasn't making any long-range plans for staying with the club.

"When I was drafted I never expected to make the team, let alone stick around for over 30 years," Attles said. "I figured I'd last a couple days and then go on to a teaching job I had lined up. I wanted to be a school teacher and play basketball in the Eastern League on weekends. But I'm a firm believer in the idea that timing plays a big role in everything. I just happened to be the right guy in the right

place at the right time. The Warriors needed a guard that played my style of game so I made the team."

During his 11-year playing career, from 1960-1971, Attles averaged nine points and 3.5 assists, not overwhelming numbers. But he was a hardworking team player whose infectious enthusiasm rubbed off on his teammates. He also played tenacious defense, earning the nickname "The Destroyer" in an era marked by rugged defensive play. It was his aggressive style that helped him win a job with the Philadelphia Warriors.

"When I reported to the Warriors, they already had Wilt Chamberlain, who was averaging 50 points, and Paul Arizin, who averaged 20," Attles said. "They didn't need another scorer. If I was a shooting guard I probably wouldn't have made the team. They needed a guy who played my style of basketball."

Attles played two years with the Philadelphia Warriors before the team unexpectedly moved west in 1962. Although attendance at Philadelphia Warriors games had tapered off in the 1960s, East Coast fans were generally more enthusiastic about basketball. It took time before the Warriors caught on in San Francisco.

"Philadelphia was a good basketball town but the only times we had large crowds was when we played the Celtics or Lakers," Attles said. "When we moved out here, the Bay Area was more interested in college basketball. Cal had recently played in the N.C.A.A. Finals and U.S.F. was a big draw, so we didn't get many people at the games, maybe 3,000 a night. Wilt was scoring big numbers then, but he never got much recognition in San Francisco. It was funny because we'd get huge crowds on the road and then come home and there was no one in the stands."

Because of his defensive skill, Attles was often matched against the league's best players. With just eight teams in the league, Attles saw the NBA's biggest stars at least 10 times a season.

"Oscar Robertson was probably the

toughest player to defend against," Attles said. "He was a big guard at 6-foot-5. Most other guards of that time were about six feet. He played forward in college, so he kind of redefined the guard position. He could shoot, pass, rebound and was just a great all-around player.

"Jerry West took longer to develop. He was a rookie in 1960, too. But he was a heck of a player, a great shooter and very competitive."

During his second season, Attles witnessed one of the most memorable events in NBA history as Wilt Chamberlain scored 100 points against the New York Knicks.

"It was just another game for us," Attles said. "Wilt was averaging 50 points that season and a lot of us had been predicting he could score 100. When you look back now, it really was a remarkable feat. I don't think you'll ever see anybody break that record. With the three-point basket, someone could get really hot and do it, but for the most part, defense is so much tougher now. Someone like Michael Jordan would be exhausted trying to beat today's tough defenses to score 100."

With 30 games left in the 1969-70 season, Attles was asked to replace George Lee as coach of the Warriors. Once again, Attles was in the right place at the right time. He expected to take over as player/coach until the end of the season, then go back to being strictly a player.

"I kind of fell into coaching," Attles said. "I turned it down initially, then thought I'd do it for the final 30 games of the season and go back to playing. I didn't have aspirations to be a head coach. It's especially difficult to be a player/coach. It's too hard to take off one hat and put on another. The only successful player/coach in the NBA was Bill Russell and that's because he was such a great player.

"The transition from player to coach was difficult because I had always been able to take care of myself, but now I had to take care of 11 other guys too."

Once Attles settled into the coaching role, he found he had a number of knowledgeable stars ready to help with advice.

"I enjoyed coaching but I was never 100 percent comfortable," he said. "I learned on the job. I got input from a lot of great players like Nate Thurmond, Rick Barry, Jeff Mullins. It would have been ignorant for me to not listen to them."

Attles went on to coach 1,071 regular season games for the Warriors over 13 seasons, posting a 555-516 record. The most memorable year was 1974-75 when the Warriors won their only West Coast NBA Championship. That team was considered young and inexperienced because the Warriors had lost a host of veterans after the 1973-74 season to trades and free agency. Clyde Lee, Nate Thurmond and Cazzie Russell were replaced by a crop of hungry young players led by veteran Rick Barry.

"Clifford Ray was not considered a great center but he was instrumental in getting us that championship," Attles said. "He was a team player. Butch Beard was another one. He played everywhere and did everything we asked. Jamaal Wilkes was just blossoming into the great player that he became. Everything clicked for us."

The Warriors beat Seattle in six games and Chicago in seven to advance to the NBA Finals against the Washington Bullets, a team widely favored to destroy the Warriors.

"No one expected us to win," Attles said. "But we never believed the negative things people said. It was considered such an upset because this was a West Coast team that got very little publicity or exposure before the playoffs. We all played toward a common goal. If you get enough people pulling in one direction you can reach your goal.

"People always ask me if the best team really won that championship series. I have to say that in a one-game situation maybe the best team will not

always win, but when you sweep a series in four games, then the best team has won."

Ironically, Attles was not on the floor for the deciding fourth game of the finals. He was in the locker room watching it on television. He'd been tossed out of the game in the first quarter after a fight erupted between Washington's Mike Riordan, who was whistled for three fouls in the first three minutes, and Rick Barry.

"I had to protect my star player," Attles said. "They were trying to get Rick into a fight so he'd get kicked out of the game. It's a lot harder to win a game when your star is kicked out than when the coach is.

"I'll always cherish that memory and I'm sure the players will too."

OPPOSITE: Bernard King (30) rebounded from a substance abuse problem to become one of the NBA's most exciting players. During his two seasons with the club, he averaged 22.5 points.

the first pair of Warriors to achieve that feat since Wilt Chamberlain and Paul Arizin in 1960-61.

Center Joe Barry Carroll continued to plug along with 17 points and eight rebounds per game. Forward Larry Smith, known as "Mr. Mean" around the league because of his intimidating presence around the hoop, did the club's dirty work. He averaged 11 rebounds and seven points while providing the Warriors with an enforcer in the paint. They were aided by Purvis Short, who doubled as a forward and as a guard, contributing 14.5 points per game.

In early January, Al Attles won his 500th game as a head coach, a plateau reached by only five other coaches in NBA history, and the Warriors looked like they were on the way to the playoffs.

On the last day of the season, Golden State had a 45-36 record but faced a familiar predicament. It needed a victory in its final game against the Seattle SuperSonics to gain a playoff berth. Seattle knocked the Warriors out of contention, beating them in a heartbreaker, 95-94. Golden State missed the playoffs by one game.

1982–83

The Warriors lost the soul of their club during the off-season when free agent Bernard King signed an offer sheet from the New York Knicks. Golden State matched the offer, but traded King to the Knicks for guard Micheal Ray Richardson and a future draft pick. Richardson then refused to report to the Warriors until November, missing nearly a month of the season.

The club's top draft choice was Oregon State guard Lester Connor. Second round pick Derek Smith of Louisville and third round selection Chris Engler, a seven-foot center from Wyoming, also made the final roster.

Golden State started the season well, winning its first three games before hitting the skids. The Warriors lost 12 of the next 14 games and tumbled hopelessly into the Pacific Division cellar. By December, the club was in desperate need of change, so fan favorite World B. Free was traded to Cleveland for guard Ron Brewer. In 53 games with the Warriors in 1982-83, Brewer av-

eraged 11 points, less than half of Free's average nightly output.

Before long the Warriors' locker room began to look like a hospital emergency ward. Mike Gale, Derek Smith, Joe Hassett and Purvis Short all went down with injuries as Golden State suited up 19 different players during the season. In the course of the year, the team members missed an incredible 238 games due to injury or illness, the most recorded in the history of the NBA.

Joe Barry Carroll averaged 24 points, seventh best in the NBA, and 8.7 rebounds to pace the club. Purvis Short chipped in 21.4 points per game, and Larry Smith contributed 8.4 points and 10 rebounds. They got little help.

As the playoffs drew near, it became obvious that Michael Ray Richardson was not the player the Warriors wanted. They traded him to New Jersey for forward Mickey Johnson and guard Eric "Sleepy" Floyd. In his 30 games with Golden State, Richardson averaged 12.5 points and 7.4 assists. He eventually was kicked out of the league after failing numerous drug tests.

Golden State ended its year of bad luck with a 30-52 record, 28 games behind the Los Angeles Lakers. The rocky season took a toll on coach Al Attles. He turned the coaching duties over to John Bach and moved to the front office as general manager of the Warriors. Between 1970 and 1983, Attles coached in 1,071 Warriors games, posting a 555-516 record. He was 31-30 in playoff competition and guided Golden State to the NBA Championship in 1974-75.

1983–84

With the sixth pick in the college draft, the Warriors hoped to select an impact player who could erase the bitter memories of the disastrous 1982-83 season. Unfortunately, they made things worse by choosing 6-foot-10 Purdue center Russell Cross. The former Boilermaker's NBA career lasted just 45 games. He averaged 3.5 points and 1.7 rebounds for Golden State before hanging up his Converses.

In the second round of the draft, the Warriors se-

WORLD B. FREE
1980-83

John Bach, the Warriors' no-nonsense assistant coach during the 1980-81 season, Free's first with the club, was one of the skeptics.

"He wanted me to call him World," Bach said. "Can you imagine? All-World? A 27-year old guy in the NBA called All-World?"

Free never quite lived up to his All-World billing while playing with the Philadelphia 76ers, and later the San Diego Clippers, in the early years of his career. He averaged 13 points during three years with Philadelphia and 29 points during his two seasons with the Clippers.

Then in the fall of 1980, Free joined the Warriors in a trade with San Diego. To obtain Free, Golden State gave up a first round pick in the 1984 draft and guard Phil Smith, a popular local player who starred at University of San Francisco before being drafted by the Warriors. Many felt the price was too high for a 6-foot-2 gunning guard of Free's dubious character and defensive ability.

The Warriors front office was initially hesitant to make the deal until former Philadelphia 76ers coach Jack McMahon recommended Free. "He told me Free was a great player," former coach and general manager Al Attles said. Attles saw that the trade was made, then went a step further by naming Free the Warriors' team captain.

With his new role as team leader, Free needed to prove himself to his coaches and teammates in a hurry.

"I needed to show what I could do because I always was talking about it," Free said.

His bombs-away style immediately excited the Oakland Coliseum Arena fans and he became one of the most celebrated players on a lackluster Warriors team. He averaged 24.1 points per game during his first season with Golden State to lead the club in scoring. More importantly, he helped engineer a team turnaround that saw Golden State improve by 15 games, going from last place in the Western Conference in

Lloyd Free never lacked for confidence. He earned his stripes on the playgrounds of New York City and became one of the legends of schoolyard basketball. He earned a reputation as the man with the sky-scraping jumper, the flashy moves and the fast-paced lifestyle.

He took his flamboyance into the NBA and it carried over to his game, where he irritated opponents, and at times his own teammates, with a running commentary on his playing ability. At the same time, he won fans in arenas throughout the league who enjoyed his entertaining playing style.

When he insisted on being called World Free, as in All-World, many people thought he had gone too far.

"There have always been nonbelievers," Free said. "Eventually they come around to my point of view."

1979-80, to within one game of a playoff spot in 1980-81.

Even Coach Bach began to change his stance toward the cocky 27-year-old with the rainbow jumper.

Despite his confidence, it took time for Free to catch on in the NBA. He joined the Philadelphia 76ers in 1976 after a spectacular college career at Guilford College. Many scouts thought he was overrated, a schoolyard player who would never make the transition to the big time.

As a rookie with the 76ers, he learned some hard lessons. Philadelphia was led by a group of old school veterans that included Doug Collins, Billy Cunningham and George McGinnis. They didn't take kindly to a ball-hogging rookie.

Free recalls a practice where he came down court and used one of his schoolyard moves in an effort to impress his colleagues—a between-the-legs dribble combined with a fancy spin before putting up a high-arching jumper. The ball clanged off the rim and Billy Cunningham stopped the practice to scold Free. "This ain't the park," he said. "Make the shot or pass the ball."

"I learned from that," Free said.

But Free continued to talk incessantly, and the acrimonious Philadelphia press picked up and printed every word, whether he was serious or not. When he rattled on about being the greatest player of all time, usually with tongue in cheek, the papers reported it. Before long, the tough Philadelphia fans were all over Free. It was just a matter of time before his act wore thin in "The City of Brotherly Love." When it did, Free relished a change of scenery.

At San Diego, Free was the acknowledged team leader, a one-man show averaging nearly 30 points per game in his two seasons with the club. He finished second in the NBA in scoring both years, behind San Antonio's George Gervin. But an image of selfishness had grown around him. He was a man who always wanted the ball, and once it was in his hands, he never gave it up.

The selfish image was perpetuated when Free demanded a new contract from the Clippers after the 1979-80 season. San Diego said he was locked into a $160,000-a-year contract. Free pushed for a trade and when a deal was finally consummated, the Warriors agreed that Free was indeed worth more. They tore up his contract and gave him a salary fit for an up-and-coming NBA star.

With the revised contract, and a novel role as team captain, Free felt pressure when he joined his new team.

"I admit I was self-conscious about it," Free said. "The Warriors already had scorers Sonny Parker and Purvis Short coming back, and John Lucas was the honcho on the floor. I was reluctant to take over the show."

Free was uncharacteristically timid at first. At the start of the 1980-81 season, he limited his shots so that his team-mates could see he wasn't a selfish player, that he could dish off the ball as well as backcourt mate John Lucas. During the first few weeks of the season, Free averaged just 20 points on 12 to 13 shots. Coach Al Attles noticed his new guard was holding back. He told Free it was okay to go out and light up the sky.

That was all the encouragement the "Brownsville Bomber" needed. Within a month, Free increased his scoring average from 20 to nearly 28 points per game.

The following season, Free teamed with Bernard King to give the Warriors one of the most exciting scoring duos in basketball. Free averaged 23 points to finish ninth in the league in scoring, while King pumped in 23.2 points per game, and finished as the NBA's eighth-leading scorer. It was the first time the Warriors had two players among the league's top 10 in scoring in the same year since Wilt Chamberlain and Paul Arizin did it in 1960-61 with the Philadelphia Warriors.

But that was to be Free's last year with Golden State. Midway through the 1982-83 season, the club was slumping badly and in need of change. In an effort

to revamp the team, Free was traded to Cleveland for Ron Brewer. By all accounts it was a rotten deal. Free departed with a 24-point average but his legacy still remains.

"World was always exciting," former coach Al Attles said. "He gave the fans their money's worth."

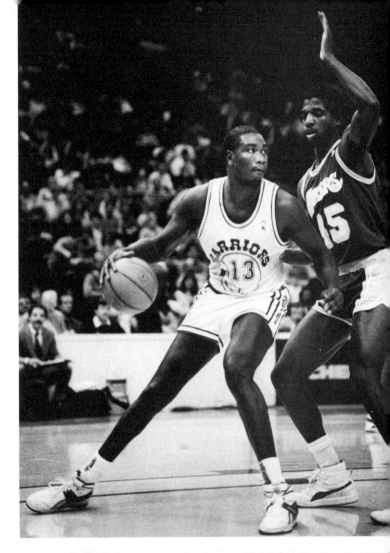

lected 6-foot-7 Utah forward Pace Mannion. He had limited success, too, playing just 57 games for Golden State, averaging two points and one rebound.

Unable to find adequate help through the draft, the Warriors signed free agent guard Mike Bratz and acquired forward Darren Tillis from Cleveland for a future draft choice.

Under coach John Bach, the Warriors showed marked improvement early in the year. Playing in the rugged Pacific Division, Golden State stayed near the .500 mark until late January. Then the club lost nine out of 11 games during a tough Eastern road swing and began to sink like lead.

Down the stretch, the Warriors still had an outside shot at making the playoffs. They won five of their last seven contests to finish in fifth place with a 37-45 record, 17 games behind Los Angeles. One more win would have earned Golden State a trip to the playoffs.

Purvis Short developed into the Warriors' top shooter with a 23-point average and displayed the ability to dominate a game with his high, arching jumper. He was the league's tenth-leading scorer and had an NBA season high of 57 points in a game against San Antonio.

Center Joe Barry Carroll added 20 points and eight rebounds per game. Lester Connor moved into a starting guard position alongside "Sleepy" Floyd. Connor averaged 11 points and five assists while Floyd contributed 17 points and three assists per night.

Veteran forward Mickey Johnson provided leadership and spark off the bench with 14 points and seven rebounds per game.

1984–85

Center Joe Barry Carroll said *arrivederci* to the Warriors and headed off to Italy where he earned plenty of lira playing for the Simac team in Milan and enjoyed the world's best panettone.

TOP: *Forward Larry Smith (13) prepares to go to the hoop against the Los Angeles Lakers.*

BOTTOM: *Coach Al Attles congratulates John Lucas (4) as the Warriors' point guard comes off the court during a game in 1980.*

Warriors center Joe Barry Carroll (2) gets set to put up a hook shot against the Lakers' Kareem Abdul-Jabbar. Carroll averaged 20.4 points during his seven years with the club.

The Warriors did not have a first round pick, having surrendered it to the San Diego Clippers back in 1980 in a trade for World B. Free. As a result, the draft produced several forgettable players, although guard Steve Burtt and forward Gary Plummer made the final roster.

The Warriors searched high and low for a big man to take the place of Carroll before settling on Jerome Whitehead, a reserve center with the Clippers. Whitehead, who averaged eight rebounds and 13 points for the Warriors in 1984-85, was obtained for second round pick Jay Murphy.

Golden State gave up on Russell Cross and Pace Mannion, the club's first and second round picks in 1983, and placed them on waivers. Free agent forward Peter Thibeaux, a collegiate star at nearby St. Mary's College, was signed to give the Warriors bench strength.

The 1984-85 season was hopeless from the start. Golden State dropped 10 of its first 13 games and suf-fered through one of the worst years in franchise history. The club went the entire month of January without a victory, dropping 16 contests in a row, and a total of 22 out of 23.

Purvis Short was the one bright light in an otherwise dismal season. He averaged 28 points, fourth best in the league, and scored 59 points in a losing effort against New Jersey early in the campaign. It was the highest single-game point total by a Warrior in 10 years.

Forward Larry Smith quietly pulled in 10 rebounds per game, and Sleepy Floyd began to emerge as a top-notch guard, averaging 19.5 points and five assists. Lester Connor contributed eight points and 4.7 assists.

Veteran forward Mickey Johnson tried to keep the team together, chipping in 13.3 points and six rebounds per game.

When the season mercifully came to an end, Golden State had won just five games on the road and had given up the most points in the NBA.

The club's horrid luck extended into the postseason when the NBA held its first draft lottery. Despite tying Indiana at 22-60 for the worst record in basketball, the Warriors ended up with the seventh lottery pick and missed out on the year's prize collegiate star, Georgetown center Patrick Ewing.

1985–86

The Warriors made a conscious effort to bolster the roster with established NBA players in the off-season, signing free agents Terry Teagle, Guy Williams, Geoff Huston and Peter Verhooven. They also traded a pair of second round draft picks for Washington forward Greg Ballard. Most importantly, they made good use of their first round pick, selecting college basketball's Player of the Year, Chris Mullin of St. John's.

Center J.B. (Giuseppe) Carroll returned to the Warriors after a year of hanging out at the Piazza del

OPPOSITE: Eric "Sleepy" Floyd (21) set an NBA playoff record in 1987 when he scored 29 points in a single quarter against the Los Angeles Lakers.

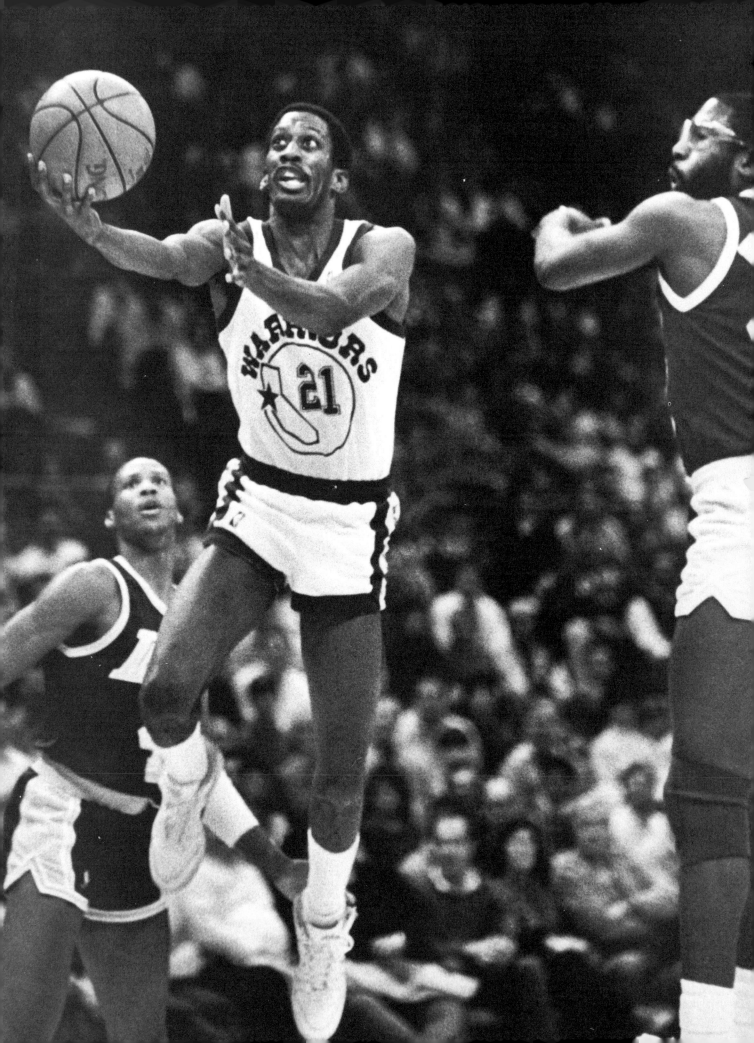

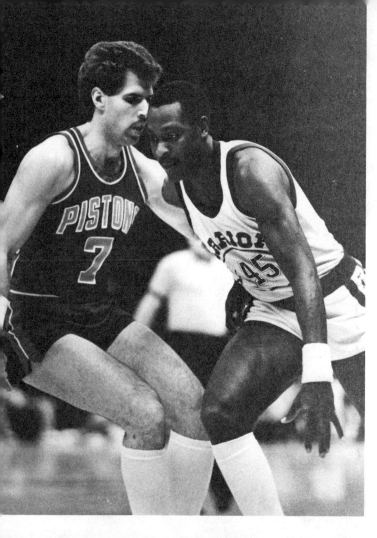

Duomo and shooting hoops for the Simac team in Milan, Italy. Carroll picked up right where he left off, averaging 21 points and 8.5 rebounds as Golden State showed marked improvement early in the season.

After a month of play, the Warriors had a 7-7 record. Then the defeats began to pile up. First there was a four-game losing streak, then a five-game losing streak, and later a six-game streak. The defeats were like poison and coach John Bach had no antidote. In January, Golden State outdid itself by dropping eight games in a row. With a 14-36 record, the Warriors were hopelessly out of the playoff race.

Despite the mounting losses, Purvis Short maintained his shooting touch and lit up the scoreboard with his rainbow jumper. He averaged 25.5 points, fifth best in the NBA. Guard Sleepy Floyd chipped in with 17.2 points and nine assists.

Rookie Chris Mullin reported to the team late because of contract negotiations and played in only 55 games. He averaged 14 points, two rebounds and two assists, but disappointed many observers who expected the former college All-American to be a dominant NBA player. His .896 free throw percentage was second in the league.

Forward Larry Smith continued to sweep the glass night after night, averaging 11 rebounds, sixth best in the league. Smith also averaged 10 points and established a team record by pulling down 16 offensive rebounds in a late-season game against Denver. Forward Terry Teagle added 14 points and three rebounds per game.

Greg Ballard, the club's old pro at 30, proved to be a valuable asset off the bench. He averaged 5.6 rebounds and nine points.

Golden State ended the year with a 30-52 record, 32 games behind the Los Angeles Lakers.

TOP: Purvis Short (45) drives around Detroit's Kelly Tripucka (7). Short averaged 28 points in 1984-85 and finished fourth in the NBA scoring race.

BOTTOM: Chris Mullin (17) manages to get off a pass during a game in 1986 despite being sandwiched by Brad Daugherty (43) and an unidentified Cleveland Cavaliers player.

CHRIS MULLIN
1985-

Chris Mullin stood alone under the backboard after a two-hour workout with the Golden State Warriors and tossed the ball into the hoop every way imaginable. Right hand. Left hand. Spin off the glass. Tip off the rim. Lean in. Fall away. Finger roll.

Mullin started slowly at first, then picked up the pace. The ball began to move at a dizzying speed. He never moved out of the paint and the ball rarely touched the hardwood floor.

Ninety percent of the time his shot found the hole.

This was Mullin at work, refining the aspect of his game that has made him a five-time All-Star. Hand control. Ball control. Caressing the leather then flicking it into the basket from every possible close-range angle.

At 6-foot-7, Mullin has the size to be an NBA player, but many scouts felt he lacked the other physical necessities: speed, moves and jumping ability. Mullin

will never be mistaken for Michael Jordan.

While Mullin may not get the hang time of Jordan, he turns heads and blows minds with his fancy spin shots and no-look lay-ins. He flips those shots into the hoop like a grounded Dr. J. That's what he practices at the end of a two-hour workout. Soft, quick hands and unmistakable court savvy are Mullin's equalizers in the high-flying NBA.

Mullin came to the Warriors as a first round pick, the seventh player chosen in 1985. In a way, he was a disappointment right off the bat and it wasn't even his fault.

Golden State finished the 1984-85 season with a 22-60 mark, tied with Indiana for the worst record in the NBA. In any previous year, Golden State and Indiana would have flipped a coin to determine who had the first pick and the opportunity to sign college basketball's prize player, Georgetown center Patrick Ewing.

But 1985 just happened to be the first year of the draft lottery. Luck didn't seem to be on the Warriors' side in the 1980s and the Warriors ended up with the seventh selection. Mullin was available when the Warriors' turn came around.

Mullin was no slouch. After all, he won the John Wooden Award in 1985 as college basketball's top player, and was a two-time All-American. And it was Mullin's magnificent play that got the St. John's Redmen to the N.C.A.A. Final Four in 1985.

The trouble was, Mullin wasn't sure he wanted to play in Oakland, a city as foreign to a Brooklyn native as Bangladesh. In New York, he was a celebrity; people took care of him. While a student at St. John's, Coach Lou Carnesecca personally watched over his star forward.

And Mullin was the king of the schoolyards in Brooklyn, the Bronx and parts of greater Manhattan. Former St. John's teammate Billy Goodwin said of Mullin, "He's the only white boy I've ever seen who understood street ball."

Outside of New York, Mullin was just another player.

Now the Golden State Warriors were calling from 3,000 miles away with the opportunity he always dreamed about, the chance to play professional basketball. But he wasn't sure if he was ready to leave his neighborhood and the support it gave him.

Mullin found the courage to move West and report to the Warriors. He missed training camp and the first six games of the season while his agent negotiated a four-year, multimillion-dollar contract. He reported to Golden State out of shape and found a team in disarray, one still trying to regroup after posting basketball's worst record in 1985.

Mullin was met by a core group of players more worried about being shown-up in practice than winning games. One veteran went so far as to stop Mullin during one of his post-practice shooting routines to tell him he was making the rest of the players look bad.

Mullin didn't know what to think. Basketball wasn't fun anymore. He sat out the final 20 games of his rookie season with a heel injury, not sure if professional basketball was in his future. He'd never had such feelings before, never really faced adversity. Mullin was always the brightest star on one of the best teams in the biggest city in North America. Now he was in the cellar with a team that didn't seem to care. He didn't feel like he belonged. To forget about his problems, he began hitting the bottle. He grew fat and out-of-shape and eventually his skills began to erode. Worse yet, he skipped practices and the Warriors' Don Nelson saw fit to suspend him from the team.

"There were days when I didn't care if I ever played again," he said.

In 1987, Golden State hired Nelson as executive vice-president. A year later he would take over as head coach. He gradually weeded out the club's malcontents. He also confronted Mullin

and told him to get help for his drinking problem.

"Here I was in the NBA, something I dreamed about as a kid," Mullin said. "I was living my dream and I wasn't happy. Something had to change."

Mullin took the first step. He checked into a 30-day rehabilitation program in Southern California and joined Alcoholics Anonymous. Then he devoted himself to his craft like never before. He was like a hurricane, an untapped bundle of energy hitting the Stairmaster, the stationary bike, the weight room, the pool and the gym. And when he was finished, he did it over again.

In a matter of months, he trimmed down from a puffy 245 pounds to a svelte 210 with six-percent body fat. His on-court performances soared. Best of all, the fans understood and sympathized with Mullin. When he returned from rehab, he was greeted with a standing ovation at the Oakland Coliseum Arena.

"That made me feel good," Mullin said.

Back on the court, his numbers jumped dramatically. In his first two seasons with the Warriors, he averaged 14.7 points. After returning from rehab, he averaged 20.5 for the remainder of the season, then topped it the following year with a 26.5 average and a spot in the All-Star Game.

The new Mullin caused Magic Johnson to remark, "When God made basketball he just carved Chris Mullin out and said, 'This is a player.'"

Now, more than four years after he checked into the rehab center, Mullin is one of the NBA's brightest stars, and the cornerstone of a revamped Warriors squad.

He's played in four All-Star Games and was a member of The Dream Team that stormed the Olympic Games in Barcelona. Mullin was the gold medal-winning Dream Team's second leading scorer, averaging 14.3 points.

But Mullin has his heart set on an NBA title now. In preparation, the

conditioning never stops. It paid off in 1991 and '92 when he led the league in minutes played for two straight seasons while being one of the game's most accurate shooters.

But the best is yet to come for Chris Mullin. The sky's the limit.

1986–87

The Warriors came under new ownership in 1986 when Jim Fitzgerald and Dan Finnane purchased the Warriors from Franklin Mieuli. Fitzgerald and Finnane had served in executive positions with the Milwaukee Bucks for several years before taking control of the Warriors. Mieuli had single-handedly guided the team after it moved from Philadelphia to San Francisco in 1962.

The new ownership group relieved coach John Bach of his duties and replaced him with former Cleveland Cavaliers coach George Karl. Between 1983-86, the Warriors compiled a 97-174 record under Bach.

As one of the seven worst teams in professional basketball in 1985-86, the Warriors earned a place in the NBA draft lottery for the second year in a row. This time they received the third overall pick. But the club continued its Draft Day mishaps by selecting North Carolina State's Chris Washburn. The 6-foot-11 center caused coaches, teammates, fans and local police heartburn from the day he stepped off a 747 at San Francisco International Airport. Washburn had a hard time making it to practice and often looked befuddled on the court. He played in just 35 games as a rookie, averaging 2.9 rebounds and 3.8 points. Midway through the year, he entered a drug rehabilitation program. In his second season, he played in just eight games before the Warriors decided to cut their loses and gave him to Atlanta.

Washburn was the only draft pick to stick with the team, so Golden State added bench strength by signing free agent forwards Ben McDonald and Rod Higgins.

Under coach Karl, the team showed noticeable improvement, beating Pacific Division rivals Los Angeles and Portland early in the year. By midseason, Golden State was six games over .500 and began to eye

TOP: Larry Smith (13) contributes two of the 5,225 points he scored for the Warriors over nine seasons. He averaged 8.5 points per game during his career.

BOTTOM: Terry Teagle (20) spent six seasons with the Warriors, but one of his best nights came against the Utah Jazz in the 1987 playoffs, when he scored 30 points to lead the Warriors to victory.

the playoffs for the first time since the glory days of the mid-1970s.

Purvis Short averaged 18.3 points but no longer shouldered the offense. The scoring load was spread around by point guard Sleepy Floyd, who averaged 19 points and a team-record 10.3 assists, second in the league. He also set a team record with 73 three-point field goals during the year.

Joe Barry Carroll had a 21-point average, but his anemic rebounding numbers, seven a game, began to grate on the team's fans. Forward Larry Smith continued to be the Warriors' main man on the boards. He finished sixth in the league in rebounding with 11.5 per game and 8.8 points.

Second-year guard Chris Mullin averaged 15 points, 2.2 rebounds and 3.3 assists. Sixth man Terry Teagle provided additional scoring punch with 11 points per game.

With 22 games left in the season, the Warriors had a 28-32 record and were still eyeing a playoff spot. Inspired by the prospect of being the first Warrior team in 10 years to appear in postseason competition, Golden State went 14-8 during that stretch to nose out the Houston Rockets for the final playoff spot.

Golden State met the Utah Jazz in the first round of the playoffs. Utah featured Karl Malone, John Stockton, Thurl Bailey, Darrell Griffith and 7-foot-4 center Mark Eaton, and posted a 44-38 record during the regular season.

Utah dismantled the Warriors in the first two games of the best of five series and looked like it would dispose of the Warriors easily. History was on Utah's side. Not a single NBA team in 30 years had rebounded from a 2-0 deficit to win a five-game playoff series.

At the Oakland Coliseum Arena for game three, the Warriors rallied behind the hot shooting of Purvis Short and Terry Teagle for a 110-95 win, then took game four, 98-94, to tie the series.

The Jazz returned to the friendly confines of Salt Lake City's Salt Palace for game five but the pressure was on Karl Malone and company.

Once the game got started, forward Larry Smith

made it hotter for the Jazz. Smith controlled the boards and dominated the inside as the Warriors completed their dramatic comeback by defeating the Jazz, 118-113.

Magic Johnson, James Worthy, Kareem Abdul-Jabbar and the rest of the Los Angeles Lakers were waiting for the Warriors in the Western Conference Semifinals. Oddsmakers figured it would take a minor miracle for Golden State to win one game. They were right.

Los Angeles took the first three games without a problem, but in game four the Warriors' Sleepy Floyd staged a spectacular show. In the second half of a tight game, he scored 39 points, including 29 in the fourth quarter, to set an NBA playoff record. He finished the game with 51 points.

"Sleepy was unconscious out there," Magic Johnson said after the game. "I've never seen anybody get in a zone like that where everything goes in. I don't like to lose but that was a pleasure to watch."

Golden State won game four, 129-121, but it was the club's only victory. Los Angeles clinched the series in five games.

1987–88

In a year of widespread changes, Golden State started by bringing in former Milwaukee Bucks coach Don Nelson as executive vice-president.

High-scoring forward Purvis Short was the first player to be traded. After nine years with the Warriors, he was sent to the Houston Rockets for 7-foot center Dave Feitl, guard Dirk Minniefield and a first round draft pick.

Golden State used its first round pick, the 14th overall, to select Western Kentucky's Tellis Frank, a 6-foot-10 board banger. Frank was the only draft choice to make the club. He averaged eight points and four rebounds coming off the bench during the 1987-88 season.

The Warriors started poorly and got continually

OPPOSITE: Coach Don Nelson checks strategy with his club during a time-out.

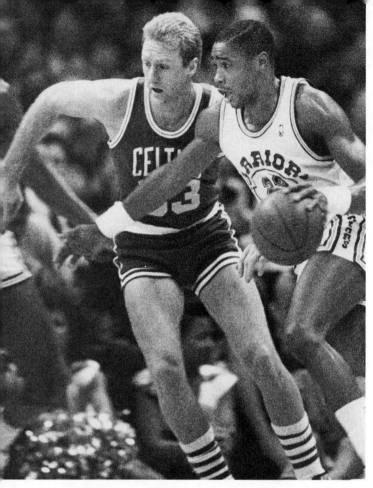

Rod Higgins and Larry Bird go head to head. Higgins, a 6-foot-7 forward, averaged 10.9 points during six seasons with the Warriors.

worse. Golden State had a 1-10 record before squeaking by Philadelphia for its second victory of the year, then promptly lost 10 of its next 12 games.

Rebounding forward Larry Smith went on the injured list with leg problems and missed nearly 60 games. Before long, the Warriors were 4-20 and in danger of setting NBA records for ineptitude. In obvious need of a major overhaul, the Warriors made a series of blockbuster moves over a ten-day period in December. They began by trading center Joe Barry Carroll, a veteran of eight campaigns with the Warriors, and guard Sleepy Floyd to the Houston Rockets for 7-foot-4 center Ralph Sampson and guard Steve Harris. Free agent guard Winston Garland was signed, and Otis Smith was acquired from Denver for cash.

In addition, the Warriors finally gave up on former first round pick Chris Washburn, handing him over to Atlanta. In exchange, the Warriors received the draft rights to Ken Barlow, who never played in the NBA.

The club made one other personnel change that would have a significant impact on the team's future. Chris Mullin was placed on the injured list when he voluntarily entered a Los Angeles hospital to be treated for an alcohol abuse problem.

The roster moves did little to change the team's performance. Golden State continued to lose games at a breathtaking pace. Surprisingly, the Warriors' fans found excitement in the newly revamped team and attendance surged to 11,350 per game, the highest in nearly 10 years.

The 27-year-old Sampson was no longer the intimidating center he had been at the University of Virginia, although he showed flashes of brilliance. He hobbled along on bad legs and managed to see action in 29 games for Golden State after the trade, averaging 10 rebounds and 15.5 points.

Sampson got help from Rod Higgins, who scored 15 points per game, and Otis Smith, who averaged 13 points.

Chris Mullin returned to the club in March and was greeted warmly by the fans with a standing ovation. He appeared in 60 games and averaged 20 points, 4.8 assists and 3.4 rebounds, his best numbers since joining the team.

As the disappointing season began to wind down, coach Karl tendered his resignation and assistant coach Ed Gregory filled in for the remaining few weeks. When the season mercifully came to an end, the Warriors were 42 games out of first place with a 20-62 record.

1988–89

Don Nelson moved out of the front office in 1988 and began his tenure as head coach and general manager of the Golden State Warriors.

In one of his initial personnel moves, Nelson used the club's first round pick, the fifth overall, to select Kansas State guard Mitch Richmond.

Richmond turned out to be one of the Warriors' best picks in years. He became an immediate starter, averaging 22 points and 5.9 rebounds, and was named NBA Rookie of the Year.

The center position proved to be the team's area of weakness. It was clear that Ralph Sampson's fragile knees could not carry him through an entire NBA season. Midway through the campaign, he went on the

PURVIS SHORT
1978–87

season of 1975-76. Rick Barry had just departed for Houston and the club's leadership role went to quiet Phil Smith.

But the team was about to go into serious decline. It began to drift without an anchor. The Warriors wouldn't make the playoffs again until 1987. By that time, Short was in his ninth and final season with Golden State.

The 6-foot-7, 215-pound Short found himself in a new role when he joined the Warriors in 1978. He was made a spot starter and sixth man, the club's sparkplug off the bench, an unfamiliar role for a player accustomed to being the offense's focus. He averaged 10.6 points per game and 4.8 rebounds while rotating between guard and forward. At the conclusion of his first season, he was selected to the NBA All-Rookie Team along with teammate Wayne Cooper.

Although Short drew personal accolades, the franchise fell into disrepair. The Warriors posted a 38-44 record, their first losing season in ten years. It was just the beginning of a decade-long slide.

Short didn't allow the chaos around him to affect his play. He became a full-time starter in the 1979-80 season, although a shoulder injury forced him to miss 20 games. Short responded to his starting role by averaging 17 points and five rebounds.

Over his first four seasons, Short was a model of consistency. World B. Free and Bernard King supplied most of the offense in the early 1980s. Short chipped in just enough to keep his employers happy, averaging 15 points. His one shining moment came against Kansas City in 1981 when he schooled the Kings' Eddie Johnson, scoring 32 points and ringing up his first and only triple-double as a member of the Warriors.

Then suddenly in the 1982-83 season, Short began to take his game to a new level. King was dealt to New York prior to the start of the campaign and Free was traded to Cleveland. The scoring load was heaped on the shoulders of Short and center Joe Barry Carroll.

Short accepted the responsibility and

It's no coincidence that when Purvis Short left the Warriors in 1987, Northern California went into a five-year drought. Short's sky-piercing rainbow jumper was the one thing that could be counted on to bring rain.

It was admired by fans, envied by teammates, and despised by defending players. Like the Mona Lisa's smile, Short's jumper attracted everyone's opinion, be it good or bad.

Some said Short's jump shot was too high, it was too light, it had the wrong rotation, or too much arch. Coaches, friends and fellow players all gave advice. But there was no question that Short's shot was a work of art, a thing of beauty. It always pleased the fans.

Short joined the Warriors in 1978 off the Jackson State campus as a first round draft selection, the fifth player picked overall. He joined a team that was still basking in the afterglow of the 1974-75 NBA Championship and the 59-win showed the Warriors what they had been waiting to see. He shredded the nets, scoring 21.4 points per game and adding 5.3 rebounds, although he suffered a shoulder injury late in the season that hampered his game.

Short also found an advocate on the offensive end when the Warriors acquired Sleepy Floyd midway through the 1982-83 season. Floyd quickly developed into the club's floor leader and leading assist man. Most of those assists went to Short who benefited from Floyd's crisp passing.

Suddenly, Short was one of the most dangerous jump shooters in the NBA. From 1983 to 1986, over three consecutive seasons, he led the Warriors in scoring.

During the 1983-84 campaign, Short broke into the NBA's top ten in scoring for the first time with a 22.8 average. Against San Antonio midway through the year, he posted an NBA season high by scoring 57 points, and was named the league's Player of the Week. He also became the first Warrior other than Rick Barry, Wilt Chamberlain and Joe Fulks to score over 50 points in a game.

The following season, center J.B. Carroll defected, choosing to play in Italy for a year. With Carroll gone, Short was the Warriors' only serious scoring threat. He took that responsibility earnestly. Early in the year, he lit up the Oakland Coliseum, scoring 59 points, more than half the team's total, against the New Jersey Nets in a losing effort.

Short ended the 1984-85 season as the league's fourth-leading scorer, averaging a career-high 28 points. He finished just behind Bernard King, Larry Bird and Michael Jordan among the scoring leaders. But it was a bittersweet accomplishment for Short. The Warriors finished in the NBA cellar tied with Indiana. The club's 22-60 record was its worst in 20 years.

"During those lean years (in the 1980s), Purvis Short was one of the players who really gave the fans their money's worth," said former Warriors coach Al Attles. "He had an excellent jump shot and was a real impact player from an offensive standpoint."

Carroll returned to the club for the 1985-86 season and Chris Mullin joined the Warriors as a first round draft choice, but the Warriors still looked to Short for scoring. He responded again, giving the club 25.5 points per game, fifth-best in the NBA. It turned out to be Short's last great year for Golden State.

The following season, Short suffered various injuries and played in just 34 games. Ironically, it was the only year he appeared in the playoffs for the Warriors. When he finally saw postseason action, Short wasn't at his best.

The Warriors upset the Utah Jazz in five games in the 1986-87 playoffs, then got bounced around by the Los Angeles Lakers. Short averaged just 14.6 points in the 10 playoff games, well below his Warriors career average of 19.4 points. Fans accused him of pulling a disappearing act when the real pressure was on.

Golden State changed directions in 1987 when Don Nelson joined the club as executive vice-president. Early in the season, Short was dealt to Houston for Dave Feitl, Dirk Minniefield and a first round draft choice.

When he was traded, Short was in the career Top Ten in virtually every Warriors offensive category. He ranks sixth on the club's all-time scoring list with 11,894 points, sixth in field goals with 4,830, third in steals with 710, fifth in rebounds with 2,976 and seventh in games played with 614.

Short was never selected to play in an All-Star Game. But for most of the 1980s, he was an All-Star caliber attraction.

ABOVE: Tim Hardaway (10) launches a three-pointer. He is second among the Warriors career leaders (behind Chris Mullin) in three-point field goals.

RIGHT, TOP & CENTER: Tyrone Hill (32), a 51-percent shooter from the field, fires up a jumper from 18 feet. Hill was the second power forward selected in the 1990 NBA draft behind Derrick Coleman. He averaged 5.3 points and 5.2 rebounds as a rookie.

RIGHT, BOTTOM: Jeff Grayer (44) defends against Chicago's Michael Jordan. Grayer spent four seasons with the Milwaukee Bucks before joining the Warriors in 1991-92.

ABOVE: Jud Buechler and Chris Mullin embrace after pulling out a close win during the 1992-93 season.

LEFT: Guard Sarunas Marciulionis was the leading scorer on the gold-medal winning Soviet team at the 1988 Olympics. In the 1992 Olympics he carried the Lithuanian team to the bronze medal.

LEFT: Head coach Don Nelson signals instruction to his players on the court. Nelson has participated in more N.B.A. games as either a player, head coach or general manager than anyone else in league history.

NEXT PAGE: Latrell Sprewell goes past Utah Jazz All Stars John Stockton to get two points.

ABOVE: Trainer Tom Abdenour, Tim Hardaway, Chris Mullin and Alton Lister (left to right) relax on the bench with a Warriors victory just seconds away.

NEXT PAGE: Tim Hardaway drives past Philadelphia 76ers center Manute Bol for a layup.

BELOW LEFT: Tim Hardaway receives last minute instructions from Coach Don Nelson. Hardaway is fourth on the Warriors all-time steals list.

BELOW RIGHT: Billy Owens (30) stretches to knock a ball away from the hoop.

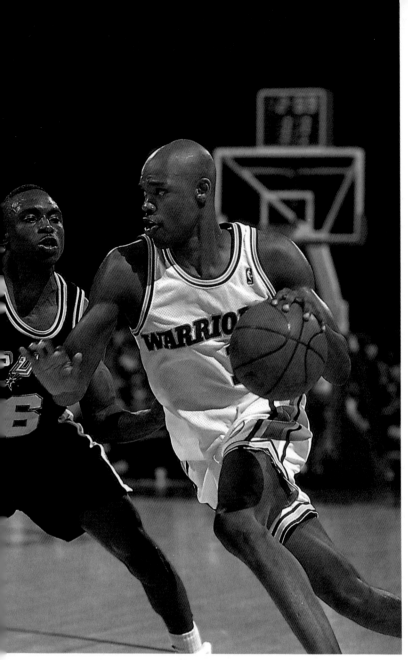

2

1

THESE PAGES, CLOCKWISE FROM LEFT: 1—Billy Owens, a career .675 shooter from the free-throw line, sizes up and then sinks a shot from the charity stripe. 2—Latrell Sprewell (15) was the Warriors first round draft pick in 1992 after a stellar collegiate career at Alabama. 3—Victor Alexander (left) and Byron Houston (middle) battle with Boston center Robert Parish for a rebound. 4—Byron Houston (21) slams home two points. Originally a first round choice of the Chicago Bulls in 1992, the Warriors acquired Houston for a future first round pick. 5—Victor Alexander goes high above a trio of Detroit Pistons defenders. Alexander is a career .525 shooter from the field.

FOLLOWING PAGE: The Chicago Bull's Horace Grant is rejected by Chris Gatling (25). Gatling has averaged 40 blocks per season since joining the club in 1991.

3

5

4

injured list to have arthroscopic knee surgery. Sampson still appeared in 61 games but averaged just 18 minutes, contributing 6.4 points and five rebounds.

In their unending search for a big man to relieve Sampson, the Warriors acquired 7-foot-7 Manute Bol from Washington in exchange for Dave Feitl and a future draft choice. Bol saw considerable time in the middle despite his offensive limitations. He averaged 3.9 points and five rebounds but was disruptive on defense. He led the league with 345 blocked shots, an average of 4.3 per game.

The Warriors compensated for their lack of a scoring center by using an unorthodox, "small" lineup that consisted of four guards and a forward. When Golden State went to its small game, Rod Higgins or Terry Teagle would generally team with Chris Mullin, Mitch Richmond, Winston Garland and Larry Smith in a motion-style offense.

Under Coach Nelson, Chris Mullin blossomed into an NBA superstar. He had his best season ever, averaging 26.5 points per game, fifth in the league, six rebounds and five assists. He was named to the All-Star Team.

The versatile Higgins was used at forward, guard and center and contributed 10.6 points and 4.2 rebounds. Garland supplied the Warriors with 14.5 points, 6.4 assists and 4.3 rebounds, while Teagle provided 15.2 points and 4.1 rebounds per game.

Nelson's methods proved effective as the Warriors made a dramatic improvement. With six games left in the season, they were 10 games over .500 with a 43-33 record, then they inexplicably lost their final six games. The team still made the playoffs and faced the Utah Jazz in the opening round.

Utah posted a 51-31 record under coach Jerry Sloan and finished first in the Midwest Division. Led by Karl Malone, Thurl Bailey and John Stockton, the Jazz were the clear favorite in the best of five series.

Nelson went to his small lineup for most of the series using Mullin, Higgins, Richmond, Garland and Teagle. Golden State surprised the Jazz by sweeping the series in three games, winning the first two games at Utah, then coming home to win game three at the Oakland Coliseum Arena.

Chris Mullin (17) keeps his eyes glued to the basket as he drives the lane against the Indiana Pacers. Mullin is sixth on the Warriors' all-time points list.

Mullin averaged 29 points to lead the Warriors in scoring during the series.

Phoenix was the next stop on the Warriors' itinerary. The Suns, coached by Cotton Fitzsimmons, posted a 55-27 regular season record, then knocked off the Denver Nuggets to advance to the Western Conference Semifinals. Tom Chambers, Kevin Johnson, Dan Majerle and Eddie Johnson were the team's catalysts.

Phoenix flattened the Warriors in five games. Golden State won game two on the road, 127-122, but the Warriors were no match for the blistering Suns.

1989–90

Golden State found the floor leader it needed when it selected Texas-El Paso point guard Tim Hardaway with the 14th pick in the college draft. With the emergence of Hardaway, Winston Garland became expendable and was dealt to the Los Angeles Clippers for a pair of second round picks. Hardaway was just one part of the puzzle, however. The Warriors still were fishing for a reliable center.

Terry Teagle (20) tries to slap away a shot from Seattle's Alton Lister. Teagle was traded to the Lakers for a first round pick in 1991. Lister later joined the Warriors as a center.

Golden State made a number of off-season deals in search of the elusive big man it needed to round out its roster. By the end of the 1989-90 campaign, the Oakland Coliseum Arena looked like the home for wayward centers as the Warriors tried eight different men in the middle. After two disappointing seasons, Ralph Sampson was sent to Sacramento for 6-foot-10 center Jim Petersen. The Warriors acquired Seattle's seven-foot center Alton Lister in exchange for a first round draft pick, and signed 7-foot-1 free agent Uwe Blab. Shortly after his arrival, Lister ruptured an Achilles tendon and was lost for the season. Seven-foot centers Chris Welp, John Shasky and Mike Smrek also spent time in a Warriors uniform before the season was over.

None of the big men acquired by the Warriors worked out to the club's satisfaction, so coach Nelson continued to confound the league with the small

lineup that had proven successful in 1988-89. Six-foot-seven Rod Higgins worked at center, with Chris Mullin and Terry Teagle at forward, and Mitch Richmond and Tim Hardaway at the guard spots.

Opposing teams had caught on to the Warriors' strategy and without inside enforcer Larry Smith, who went south to the Houston Rockets as a free agent, or an effective big man, rebounding became a problem. It was reflected in the standings. During the first month of the season, Golden State posted a 4-14 record.

Hardaway ran the NBA's highest scoring offense smoothly and confidently, averaging 8.7 assists and 14.7 points. Mullin continued to fire away, supplying 25 points per game and leading the club in rebounding with 5.9 per game. Second-year man Mitch Richmond added 22 points, 2.9 assists and 4.6 rebounds per game. Teagle averaged 16 points and 4.5 rebounds.

Sarunas Marciulionis, a member of the Soviet Union's 1988 Olympic gold-medal winning team, became the first Soviet player to sign with an NBA team. Marciulionis became an immediate fan favorite with his exciting, physical style of play and added 12 points per game as the team's sixth man.

The Warriors took a 35-39 record into the season's final three weeks and had a good shot at securing a playoff berth. But they lost six of their last eight games to end their postseason hopes.

Despite the disappointing finish, the Warriors proved to be an exciting young team with Hardaway, Mullin and Richmond leading the way. Hardaway was selected to the NBA All-Rookie Team and Chris Mullin made the All-Star Team.

The fans seemed to agree. Golden State set a team attendance record, selling out all 41 home games for the first time in franchise history.

1990–2000

CHAPTER SIX
1990–2000

1990–91

As the 1990s began, the Warriors were still searching for that elusive big man that would make them a contender.

In an effort to fill that gap, Golden State selected Tyrone Hill, a 6-foot-9 forward from Xavier with its first round pick and went after Iowa's seven-foot center, Les Jepsen, in the second round. Kansas guard Kevin Pritchard was a later second round pick.

With an eye to the future, Golden State sent forward Terry Teagle to the Los Angeles Lakers for a first round pick in 1991.

Although the center position remained the club's Achilles' heel, the Warriors put an entertaining and competitive team on the floor. Once again they relied on the league's top-scoring trio of Chris Mullin, Tim Hardaway and Mitch Richmond (nicknamed "Run TMC.") Mullin continued as the club's scoring leader, pouring in 25.7 points per night while Tim Hardaway came into his own as an all-around player, averaging 23 points and 9.7 assists. Mitch Richmond added 24 points and could be counted on for rebounding help. He pulled down nearly six rebounds per game. Rod Higgins started alongside Mullin at forward.

Despite injury problems, center Alton Lister averaged 20 minutes per game and supplied the team with tough defense and rebounding strength.

The Warriors also had a deep bench that included Sarunas Marciulionis, Tom Tolbert, Jim Petersen and Mario Elie, who was signed as a free agent. Rookie Tyrone Hill developed slowly but added five rebounds and five points per game.

Injuries caused problems for Golden State throughout the year. Mitch Richmond suffered a fractured thumb in November and lost playing time while he recuperated. Marciulionis sprained his knee and needed two different stints on the injured list. Tolbert and Jepsen also missed playing time because of leg problems.

Mullin took up the slack for his injured teammates. He developed into one of the NBA's ironmen, leading the league in minutes played, with an average of 40 a night.

With one of the highest scoring offenses in the league, Golden State posted a 44-38 record, its best regular season finish in nine years. The first playoff stop for the Warriors was San Antonio to take on David Robinson and the rest of the Spurs.

In the opening game of the playoffs, Robinson demonstrated why he is considered one of the league's premier centers as he led the Spurs to a 130-121 victory. The win just served to infuriate the Warriors, however. Golden State came back to win the next three games, despite Robinson's 26 points and 13.5 rebounds per game, and sent San Antonio home for the summer.

Golden State advanced to the Western Conference Semifinals against the Los Angeles Lakers, a team that had always been the Warriors nemesis in the playoffs. Once again the Lakers proved to be Golden State's undoing, beating the Warriors three games to one. The Warriors squeaked by Los Angeles in game two, 125-124, for its only victory in the best of five series.

OPPOSITE: Tyrone Hill (32), a 6-foot-9 forward, averaged 7.3 points during his three seasons with the Warriors.

NEXT PAGE: Billy Owens (30) was a unanimous selection to the 1991-92 NBA All-Rookie Team after averaging 14.3 points and eight rebounds.

TIM HARDAWAY
1989–

Tim Hardaway's crossover move is basketball's equivalent to a caged and hungry panther. When it's let loose, it'll eat you alive.

It didn't take long for NBA players to start comparing notes on ways to stop Hardaway's renowned crossover. It is already rated with Kareem's skyhook, Wilt's thundering dunk, and Magic's no-look pass as one of basketball's unstoppable forces.

In theory, it seems deceptively simple. The crossover starts with a right-handed dribble between the legs to the left hand. Then crossover from the left back to the right and go to the hoop. But that's before Hardaway begins to improvise like Charlie Parker at Birdland.

"As long as Tim has that crossover move, he's the king," ex-Laker star Magic Johnson said. "It can't be stopped. It's bang bang, you're dead."

"Next to Michael Jordan, Hardaway might be the toughest player in the league to stop," agreed Phoenix guard Danny Ainge.

Hardaway developed the crossover after his freshman year at the University of Texas-El Paso, when he saw New Jersey's Pearl Washington make a similar move during a televised game. After studying Washington's fancy footwork on several later plays, Hardaway decided it was a move he had to add to his repertoire.

"I played around with it a little bit," Hardaway said. "But I couldn't get it right. That summer, me and my brother (Donald) went to the playground and I said to him, 'Try to stop me.' The first time, he sort of did. But not the second, or third, or any time since then."

Hardaway's brother is not alone. It is a move that leaves opponents bumbling like the Three Stooges, even when they see it coming. Hardaway took the crossover back to UTEP and used it to boost his average to 22 points and 5.4 assists by his senior year, when he was named Western Athletic Conference Player of the Year. That season, he surpassed Tiny Archibald to become UTEP's all-time leading scorer.

But UTEP never had the media exposure of teams like Duke, U.C.L.A. and Indiana, and Hardaway began to wonder where he stood on the NBA scouts' draft charts. The 1989 college draft featured a number of quality players at point guard, and Hardaway felt he could play with any of them.

As it turned out, Hardaway didn't need to worry. Warriors chief scout Ed Gregory recommended Hardaway to Coach Don Nelson, stating in his report, "Explosive! He could be a star."

But everyone knew Nelson wanted a big man on draft day. When it was the Warriors' turn to pick with the 14th selection, Hardaway's name was still listed on the board. The Warriors surprised everyone and chose the six-foot, 195-pound Hardaway instead of a center or power forward. He was the third point guard chosen behind Jerome "Pooh" Richardson, taken with the 10th pick by Minnesota, and Oklahoma's Mookie Blaylock, who was chosen by the New Jersey Nets.

If Nelson and Gregory were happy, the fans clearly were not. They howled in displeasure.

"We consider ourselves very lucky to pick Tim Hardaway," Warriors Coach Don Nelson said at the time. "We evaluated him positively in every category. We thought he has a chance to be special, to be a star. You'll be calling me a genius six months from now."

Nelson was right. Hardaway has lived up to and surpassed Nelson's expectations. In his rookie season, Hardaway averaged 14.7 points and 8.7 assists and was named to the All-Rookie Team. In his second season, he improved to 22.9 points, 9.7 assists, four rebounds and 2.6 steals per game and made the All-Star Team.

By the time Hardaway was in his third NBA season, he was in a class by himself. He was the leading vote-getter among point guards for the All-Star Team and averaged 20.4 points and 9.5 assists. Furthermore, he was approaching the company of legends. The only player in NBA history with more points and assists after three seasons was Hall of Famer Oscar Robertson.

"He has turned out to be a tremendous player," Minnesota Timberwolves Coach Jimmy Rodgers said. "I think a lot of it has to do with his tenacity. He's a very tough-minded, strong-bodied point guard. He really has the best of two worlds. He's developed an outside shot, and he also has the ability to get into the heart of the defense. You're talking about a guy who's really stepped up to be one of the best point guards in the league."

Scott Layden, director of player personnel for the Utah Jazz, agrees with that assessment. "He punishes teams from the point guard position. He's such a tough guy. Usually when you think of point guards, you don't think of damage, but he has the power to destroy teams. There's no way to stop him. He's turned

Golden State from a mediocre team to a great team."

Tim Hardaway didn't become a tough guy who destroys opponents by hanging around millionaire athletes at the country club. He learned the game on the mean streets of Chicago's South Side and earned respect playing in the schoolyards. As a teenager, he trailed behind his father, 6-foot-3 playground legend Donald Hardaway, and begged for a chance to show his stuff.

"I used to go down to the playgrounds with him, mostly at South Shore Park," Hardaway said. "I'd stand on the sidelines just begging to play. My dad kept saying no, that it was too tough, too physical. I guess I bugged him so much, he finally let me play just to shut me up and show me. I was playing against guys 30 years old and they'd say, 'Go away little man.' They pushed me to the ground and fouled me hard."

But Hardaway didn't quit and that's what made him tough. He picked himself up and went right back to the game.

"Even if you broke your wrist or your arm, you'd still be out there playing," said Hardaway, "because you didn't want to give anyone the satisfaction of knocking you out."

Hardaway molded his game further at Chicago's Carver High School, an institution which produced NBA standouts Cazzie Russell and Terry Cummings. Hardaway followed in their footsteps by leading Carver to the Chicago City Championships in 1985, although it lost to rival San Simeon.

Hordes of scouts attended the game to drool over the college prospects they saw on the floor. UTEP's Rex Bradburd was attracted to Hardaway. But it wasn't until he caught a glimpse of Hardaway playing in a schoolyard game that he was persuaded to recruit him.

"Tim was doing things you can't teach," Bradburd said. "He had this uncanny knack. When he hit a guy with a pass, he always hit him at just the right time."

Coach Nelson believes that Hardaway could be just the person to

lead the Warriors to an NBA title.

"There is no doubt in my mind that Timmy has developed into one of the premier point guards in the league," Nelson said. "I think we are all about ready as a team to take that next step."

And Warriors fans in the Bay Area will be just a step behind.

Chris Mullin and Tim Hardaway share some thoughts as they walk to the Warriors bench during a time-out.

1991–92

With three first round picks in the 1991 draft, the Warriors continued to go after big men. They selected Old Dominion's 6-foot-10 forward Chris Gatling, Iowa State's 6-foot-9 center/forward Victor Alexander, and 6-foot-10 forward Shaun Vandiver of Colorado. While Gatling and Alexander found a place on the final roster, Vandiver decided to try his luck in Italy and signed a contract with Bologna.

Just as the regular season was about to start, Golden State traded popular guard Mitch Richmond and center Les Jepsen to Sacramento for guard/forward Billy Owens, who was the Kings' first round pick in 1991.

Owens made an immediate impact with Golden State and quickly won a starting job in the Warriors' front line alongside Chris Mullin. He averaged 14.3 points and eight rebounds a game.

Tim Hardaway and Chris Mullin were the undisputed team leaders but in the absence of Richmond, Sarunas Marciulionis stepped in to pick up the scoring. He chipped in 19 points a game and played an inspired brand of offense with his slashing drives to the hoop.

The new mix seemed to work. The Warriors had their best season in 16 years with a 55-27 record and finished two games behind the Portland Trail Blazers in the Pacific Division.

For the second time in three years, the Warriors led the league in scoring, averaging 118.7 points. Mullin's 25.6 points per game ranked him third in the league and Hardaway's 23.4 placed him sixth in the NBA.

The Warriors' regular season success didn't translate into postseason rewards. In the playoffs, Golden State was matched with the Seattle SuperSonics, coached by former Warriors head man George Karl.

The Sonics were led by Ricky Pierce and Shawn Kemp, but appeared to be no match for the Warriors. Kemp came into his own in the playoffs. He dominated the boards and the Warriors lost the series, three games to one.

Despite the playoff disappointment, several Warriors were honored with postseason awards. Mullin was named to the All-NBA First Team and Hardaway made the All-NBA Second Team. Owens was chosen to the NBA All-Rookie Team. Coach Don Nelson was named Coach of the Year. And Sarunas Marciulionis finished second in voting for the Sixth Man Award. Mullin was also named to the U.S. Olympic "Dream Team."

1992–93

In a season marked by injuries, the Warriors fell from the top of the heap to the bottom of the pile. After posting 55 wins in 1991-92, the Warriors collapsed amid a rash of cuts, bruises and broken bones.

One of the best days of the year came during the NBA draft when the Warriors selected guard Latrell Sprewell with their first round pick. Sprewell gave the club another three-point threat while proving he could run the club in the absence of Tim Hardaway and play tough defense. In April, he had a monster night, scoring 36 points against the Lakers with nine rebounds and nine assists. He finished the year with a 15.4 scoring average.

The Warriors also acquired Byron Houston from Chicago in a three-team deal prior to the start of the campaign, after sending a first round draft pick to the Dallas Mavericks. The 6-foot-5, 250-pound forward gave the Warriors an enforcer underneath. He averaged four rebounds and 5.3 points while giving the league's power forwards headaches.

The injuries came early and often for the Warriors.

TOP: In the 1991-92 season, guard Tim Hardaway (10) became the first Warrior guard since Phil Smith in 1975-76 to win All-NBA honors.

BOTTOM: Chris Gatling (25) was the Sun Belt Conference Player of the Year at Old Dominion before becoming the Warriors' first round draft choice in 1991.

SARUNAS MARCIULIONIS
1989–

the feathery left-handed jumper. In the 1987 NBA draft, the Warriors selected Marciulionis in the sixth round. League officials later disallowed the pick, claiming Marciulionis was eight days too old to have been eligible for the draft.

But the Warriors were committed to the Lithuanian and Marciulionis seemed just as eager to play for Golden State. Like a pair of war-torn lovers, they waited and hoped.

After the 1988 Olympics, when the Soviet Union seemed destined to crack apart, Marciulionis made his move. He signed a Warriors contract at a reported $1.3 million per year on June 23, 1989, the first Soviet athlete to sign with an NBA team.

His transition to the big time was not without problems. It took time for Marciulionis to adapt. At first he was awestruck by NBA stars like Michael Jordan, Patrick Ewing and Karl Malone. Furthermore, he spoke almost no English.

Warriors coach Don Nelson realized he had an athlete of enormous potential. He just wasn't sure how to harness his runaway colt. He'd never coached a guard who seemed to prefer plowing through defenders than driving around them. But patience paid off.

By the 1991-92 season, Marciulionis had risen to become one of the league's top players. He was the highest scoring non-starter in the NBA in 1991-92, with 18.9 points per game, and was runner-up to Detlef Schrempf for the Sixth Man Award. Among guards, he had the league's highest shooting percentage. And only Michael Jordan, Clyde Drexler and Karl Malone produced more points per minute.

"He's so explosive," Don Nelson said. "He can come off the bench and get points quickly. Without any warm-up he can step on the court and be dominant."

But Marciulionis' explosive style has its costs. He missed nearly 100 games between 1990 and 1993 due to injury. The most drastic occurred in September 1992. Ironically, it happened off the court as he was preparing to

Sarunas Marciulionis drives the lane and bodies are cast like rickety bowling pins. He's a 6-foot-5, 215-pound guard with a fullback mentality and kamikaze playing style.

Marciulionis was scattering Soviet players long before he drove the lane in the National Basketball Association. At the age of 19, in 1983, he was selected to the Soviet Junior Team. Soon after, Warriors assistant coach Donnie Nelson took notice.

Marciulionis first met Nelson, son of Warriors head coach Don Nelson, in the summer of 1985. Nelson was playing for Athletes in Action, a touring team that made a goodwill stop in Kaunas, Lithuania, Marciulionis' hometown of 400,000 people. Although neither man could speak the other's language, they exchanged pleasantries and became friendly.

Nelson brought home scouting reports on the explosive Lithuanian with return to the United States from Lithuania.

While jogging in the woods near his home, Marciulionis fell, fracturing a fibula and dislocating his right ankle. He was flown back to California for surgery but the first two months of the 1992-93 season were shot. Although Marciulionis worked feverishly with Warriors conditioning coach Mark Grabow, his comeback wasn't complete until mid-December. He missed the first 24 games of the season.

When he returned to action against the Dallas Mavericks, it was as if he had never left. He knocked in five field goals during his first two and a half minutes back on the court. Marciulionis ended his first night back in uniform with 12 points in 19 minutes, then helped the Warriors win seven of the next eight games in which he appeared.

But as February came to an end, Marciulionis went down again. This time he suffered tendonitis in his right ankle and missed the final 27 games of the season.

Despite playing in just 30 games in 1992-93, Marciulionis averaged 17.4 points while shooting .543 percent, and contributed 3.2 rebounds and 3.5 assists per game. He had his best night against Philadelphia in early January, scoring 34 points in 42 minutes.

Although the 1992-93 Warriors season ended miserably for Marciulionis with a stint on the injured list, it began with newfound optimism after he made history at the 1992 Olympics. But then the Olympic Games have become something of a showcase for Marciulionis' talents.

Several American basketball players can boast of owning a pair of Olympic medals, including Golden State's Chris Mullin, Chicago's Michael Jordan and New York's Patrick Ewing, who all captured gold medals as part of the U.S. basketball teams in both 1984 and 1992. Very few athletes can say they won Olympic medals for two different countries. Marciulionis is one of those who can.

In 1988, Marciulionis was the leading scorer on the Soviet team that won the gold medal in Seoul, Korea. After the break-up of the Soviet Union in March 1990, Marciulionis played for his Lithuanian homeland in the 1992 Olympics at Barcelona, Spain. He finished third among Olympic scorers with a 23.4 point average, and first in assists with 8.3, as Lithuania captured a bronze medal.

More importantly, however, Marciulionis almost single-handedly organized and found sponsors to support a team for a country that was just getting on its feet after declaring its independence. With help from the Grateful Dead, which donated money and provided the Lithuanian players with tie-dyed uniforms, Marciulionis put together a team in a matter of months that included 7-foot-3 center Arvidas Sabonis.

The highlight of the Olympic Games for Marciulionis was Lithuania's 82-78 victory over the former Soviet Union team, which was playing as the Commonwealth of Independent States. The win gave Lithuania the bronze medal and Marciulionis an unsurpassed feeling of satisfaction. He scored 29 points in a game he considers one of the most important of his career.

The bronze medal is ancient history now, and Marciulionis' attention returns to Oakland and the Coliseum Arena. The tendonitis has waned and the ankle seems completely healed, although zipper-like scars run up the sides. The man who is driven to excel, to change things, to be the very best, is ready to return to his rightful place as one of the league's top performers.

Sarunas Marciulionis, one of the league's premier sixth men, was lost before the season got under way when he broke his leg and dislocated his ankle while jogging in Lithuania. Midway through the season, Billy Owens needed knee surgery and sat out 45 games. Most devastating of all was the loss of Chris Mullin who suffered ligament damage to his thumb and missed 36 contests. He still finished the year as the club's top scorer with a 25.9 average and was the NBA's second best three-point shooter with a .451 average.

By the time Tim Hardaway injured his knee in March, the Warriors had dropped out of the playoff race. Hardaway still appeared in 66 games and averaged 21.5 points and 10.6 assists, second in the league.

With the club's nucleus sidelined, coach Don Nelson looked to his bench and found considerable help. Tyrone Hill and Victor Alexander were two players who took advantage of the club's injuries to showcase their talents.

Hill finished the season with a 10.2 rebounding average and proved to be the club's most consistent rebounder since Larry Smith averaged 11.5 in 1986-87. In December, he pulled down 20 rebounds against Minnesota, the most by a Warrior in six years. He was named the Warriors' Most Improved Player.

Alexander developed into a formidable scorer during the later part of the season. He averaged 19 points and 10 rebounds during the final 11 games of the year.

Golden State finished the season with a 34-48 record, 28 games behind the Pacific Division Champion Phoenix Suns. By finishing with the seventh-worst record in the league, Coach Nelson's Warriors clinched a place in the NBA Draft Lottery.

TOP: Victor Alexander (52), a 6-foot-9 center/forward, clogs the middle and prepares to block a shot.

BOTTOM: Chris Mullin (17) hooks a shot over the outstretched arms of New York Knicks center Patrick Ewing.

NEXT PAGE: Phoenix guard Kevin Johnson looks for a way out after he is surrounded by Warriors while trying to finish a layup.

DON NELSON
1987–

the 19th choice overall. Soon after, the Zephyrs sold the 6-foot-6 Nelson to the Los Angeles Lakers.

At Los Angeles, Nelson found himself playing behind All-Star forwards Elgin Baylor and Rudy La Russo. As the first man off the bench, Nelson contributed six points and five rebounds per game.

Two seasons later, Nelson signed with the Boston Celtics as a free agent. Boston already had collected seven straight NBA titles when Nelson came aboard. Under Coach Red Auerbach, the club continued to flourish with a lineup that included Bill Russell, John Havlicek, Satch Sanders, Sam Jones and K.C. Jones. As a spot starter and sixth man, Nelson played a pivotal role in the continuation of the Celtics dynasty.

During his 11 seasons with the Celtics, the club's nucleus changed. Russell, then Tom Heinsohn, took over as coach. But the results were inevitably the same. Nelson won five NBA Championships while wearing Celtic green.

One of the great games in Celtics history featured Nelson in a starring role. In the 1969 NBA Finals against a crack Los Angeles Lakers team that included Jerry West, Elgin Baylor and Wilt Chamberlain, Nelson nailed an off-balance jumper in the final seconds of game seven to clinch the championship, 108-106.

Nelson finally retired in 1976. He averaged 10.3 points and five rebounds in 14 NBA seasons. But he wasn't done with basketball. The game was in his blood. He felt he still had a future as a teacher and coach. Midway through the 1976-77 season, less than a year after packing his sneakers in mothballs, Nelson took over the coaching reins of the Milwaukee Bucks. He guided them to the playoffs in his first full season at the helm and went on to become the winningest coach in Bucks history. In 11 seasons with Milwaukee, he posted a 540-344 record. The Bucks won 50 or more games in seven straight seasons as well as seven consecutive division titles.

The Warriors brought Nelson aboard in 1987 to serve as vice president under

It's tough to outfox Don Nelson on the basketball court. He's as wily as a Cajun on an alligator hunt.

Nelson's craftiness can be attributed to one thing—experience. No one has seen more National Basketball Association action. Nelson has participated in more regular and postseason games, as either a player or a coach, than anybody in league history.

More importantly, Nelson gained his knowledge and skill from the masters,

the class of the league. He has always been affiliated with the NBA's top-of-the-line clubs. Nelson spent most of his playing career with the Los Angeles Lakers and Boston Celtics, two of the most successful franchises in sports history.

Nelson's four decades of professional basketball schooling began in 1962. That year, the NBA's Chicago Zephyrs selected Nelson out of the University of Iowa with their third round draft pick, new owners Jim Fitzgerald and Dan Finnane. But near the tail end of the 1987-88 season, Warriors coach George Karl tendered his resignation. Nelson threw his hat back into the ring. He took over as head coach for the 1988-89 season. There was a catch, however. Before Nelson could become involved in coaching again, Golden State was required to give Milwaukee a second round draft pick. Sensing a bargain, Fitzgerald and Finnane readily agreed to give up the draft choice.

Nelson started reshaping the Warriors long before he took over as coach. Almost immediately upon joining the club, he began searching for an effective NBA center. He unloaded dead weight, dumping Chris Washburn, the club's first round pick in 1986. And in a blockbuster trade, he sent center Joe Barry Carroll and All-Star guard Sleepy Floyd to Houston for 7-foot-4 center Ralph Sampson and guard Steve Harris.

But Sampson proved to be ineffective. He was playing on bad wheels when he joined the Warriors and never regained the form he showed as a collegiate standout. When it became apparent that Sampson was not the answer to the center position problem, Nelson tried again in 1988. He traded Dave Feitl to Washington for 7-foot-7 Manute Bol. Bol was consistently among the league leaders in blocked shots, but the rest of his game fell below NBA standards.

Nelson's obsession with centers continued in 1990. He sent a first round pick to Seattle for Alton Lister, but the bad luck persisted. Lister, an NBA ironman prior to joining the Warriors, tore his Achilles tendon in his third game with the club and never played up to his potential.

On Draft Day 1993, everything finally jelled for Nelson. He put together a stunning deal to obtain the big man he had been searching for. The Warriors acquired from Orlando the number one collegiate pick, Michigan center/forward Chris Webber. In exchange, the Warriors gave up the number three pick, Anfernee Hardaway, and three

future first round picks. The deal instantly transformed Golden State into a championship-caliber team.

"I feel we have a dominant inside player who will be with the Warriors for many years to come," Nelson said. "He possesses a lot of skills, he's 20 years old, and his growth is going to be excellent throughout his career."

The 6-foot-9 Webber is just the final piece of a puzzle Nelson has patiently put together. Although his early efforts to obtain a premier center were thwarted, he made several other excellent personnel moves to shape the present Warriors team. One of Nelson's best decisions came in 1989 when he signed Lithuania's Sarunas Marciulionis on the recommendation of his son Donnie Nelson. Marciulionis since has developed into one of the NBA's best sixth men.

Nelson already has left his imprint on Warriors basketball. He is the third winningest coach in team history behind Al Attles and Eddie Gottlieb, and only seven men have won more games in league history.

Nelson's signature year with Golden State came in 1991-92. He took a team that finished 37-45 just two years earlier and transformed it into the class of the Western Division. Golden State won 55 games, its best regular season showing in 16 years, and led the league in scoring with 118.7 points per game. At the conclusion of the season, Nelson was named NBA Coach of the Year for an unprecedented third time in his career.

The 1992-93 season may have been one of the most frustrating of Nelson's career. Expectations for the team were high after winning 55 games just a year earlier. Some prognosticators foresaw the Warriors as Western Conference Champions. But Golden State suffered more injuries than the Redcoats at Bunker Hill. By midseason, three of the club's original starting five were sidelined. Leading scorer Chris Mullin was lost with a torn thumb ligament, Sarunas Marciulionis suffered a broken leg and then tendonitis, Billy Owens tore

cartilage in his knee and Tim Hardaway suffered a bruised knee.

But the injuries have healed and the club is ready to go to war.

"We feel comfortable that our time is now," said Nelson. "I think we're ready to challenge as contenders. I think we're going to have a strong team from beginning to end."

CHRIS WEBBER
1993–

In Coach Don Nelson's dream, a power forward would have the size of Karl Malone, the strength of Charles Barkley and the hands of Larry Bird.

On Draft Day 1993, Nelson's dream came true.

In one of the most stunning draft moves the NBA has seen in years, Nelson swung a deal with the Orlando Magic acquiring Chris Webber, the first player picked in the draft, for Anfernee Hardaway and three future picks. The acquisition made the Golden State Warriors immediate title contenders.

The 6-foot-9, 265-pound Webber, a center and power forward, can score, rebound and dominate the inside with his size and bulk. He gives the Warriors the inside enforcer they need to move into the league's top echelon.

"I'll never be intimidated by anybody," Webber said. "I'm not afraid of anyone on the court. I've taken my bumps and bruises, but I've given them out, too."

Before joining the Warriors, Webber, a consensus All-American at the University of Michigan, averaged 19.2 points and 2.5 assists while shooting an astounding 61.9 percent from the field. He led the Wolverines to the N.C.A.A. Finals in both 1992 and 1993 and is the only college player in history to make the N.C.A.A. All-Tournament Team as both a freshman and sophomore. Webber elected to leave Michigan after his sophomore year to enter the NBA draft.

An imposing rebounder and shot-blocker, Webber gives the Warriors the big man they have lacked for nearly a decade. He led Michigan in rebounds with 10.1 per game and blocked shots with 2.5. But Nelson feels he needs some improvement to match up in the NBA.

"He needs some work on the low blocks, no question about it," Nelson said. "He has lots of natural instincts that he relies on right now. We feel with a lot of hard work, he'll be an excellent offensive player and a dominating rebounder.

"Since I've been here, we've had to deal with a small team because of injuries to our big players and then just not having players of size. But now we have a fellow who is going to play some forward and center for us. He feels he is a power forward, but we'll find combinations to use his strength, size and quickness."

Webber is a tough customer who can play with pain. He showed his resiliency at Michigan when he blocked seven shots in a game against Minnesota, just a day after undergoing surgery for a broken nose.

That type of aggressiveness hasn't been lost on his Warriors teammates. They are thrilled by his presence and know full well that the addition of Webber could mean the difference between a fat playoff check and a long off-season.

"We got a guy we want to go to war with," Chris Mullin said of Webber.

"For the first time since I've been with

this club, I feel we have a dominant inside player who will be with the Warriors for years to come," Nelson said.

"The man can play," says point guard Tim Hardaway. "It will take him a while to learn, but he runs the floor, he has great hands, and he's got the desire to do well. I think we're going to work well together."

And Webber is just as happy to be with the Warriors. Nelson expects him to match up with the league's enforcers like Charles Barkley, Karl Malone, Shawn Kemp, and Shaquille O'Neal. But he's quick to point out that Webber is not going to be an NBA goon. He sees Webber as a gentle giant with a soft touch.

"He's probably got the best hands I've ever seen," Nelson said. "When he practiced with the Dream Team, they all were talking about one thing, his hands. His hands are on par with Chris Mullin's."

And his soft hands will help him fit into the Warriors' offensive scheme.

"The Warriors play my style of basketball," Webber said. "I've seen them in situations where Tim Hardaway is posted up and Billy Owens is at the point. It reminds me a lot of some things we did at Michigan. There is a lot of versatility."

Coaches, teammates and spectators have been marveling at Webber's ability since he laced up his first pair of sneakers. According to Mitch Albom, who is writing a book on the "Fab Five," Webber dominated the high school ranks so completely, his team was moved from Class D to Class C to Class B after destroying all the competition in its path. The team won two different classes of state championships. In one of the championship games, Webber played with a sprained ankle.

"His high school coach always talks about the game in which an alley-oop pass came in way too high for him," Albom said. "It went over his head and off the backboard, but he somehow stayed in the air, caught it one-handed when it ricocheted off the backboard and slammed it."

Webber joined the Warriors as one of the most acclaimed players to come out of the collegiate ranks in recent years, after leading Michigan's "Fab Five" to the Final Four in two different seasons. But his last memories of college basketball are of frustration.

In the waning seconds of the 1993 N.C.A.A. title game against North Carolina, Webber called a frantic time-out as Michigan fell behind. Unfortunately, his team didn't have any time-outs remaining. The ensuing technical foul clinched the game for the Tar Heels and hung the "goat" label on Webber. But Webber is not one to sulk. He quickly rebounded from the incident, handled the press with aplomb and announced he was ready to turn pro.

"I think the deal will make the Warriors a title contender," Webber said. "They were a contender before this. I'm glad to be coming to an organization that is already established."

1993–94

The basketball gods smiled on the Warriors for a change on NBA Lottery Day. Golden State wound up with the third pick in the draft.

Armed with the third overall choice, coach Don Nelson did some shrewd wheeling and dealing. On Draft Day, he selected Anfernee Hardaway, then immediately traded Hardaway and a trio of future first round picks to the Orlando Magic for Chris Webber, who was selected by Orlando with the first pick in the draft.

Suddenly the future looked bright for Golden State. The 6-foot-9 Webber, a forward/center from Michigan, gave the Warriors the one ingredient they lacked: a legitimate inside threat.

"We're excited about this," Coach Don Nelson said. "Chris gives us the kind of player we've been after for a long time."

The fans are hoping he will help give Golden State the championship they have dreamed about for a long time.

RECORDS & STATISTICS

ALL-TIME RECORDS

ALL-TIME YEARLY RESULTS

SEASON	HOME	AWAY	NEUTRAL	OVERALL
1946-47	23-7	12-18	—	35-25
1947-48	14-10	13-11	—	27-21
1948-49	19-10	9-21	0-1	28-32
1949-50	15-15	8-23	3-4	26-42
1950-51	29-3	10-22	1-1	40-26
1951-52	24-7	6-25	3-1	33-33
1952-53	4-13	1-28	7-16	12-57
1953-54	10-9	6-16	13-18	29-43
1954-55	16-5	4-19	13-15	33-39
1955-56	21-7	11-17	13-3	45-27
1956-57	26-5	5-26	6-4	37-35
1957-58	16-12	12-19	9-4	37-35
1958-59	17-9	7-24	8-7	32-40
1959-60	22-6	12-19	15-1	49-26
1960-61	23-6	12-21	11-6	46-33
1961-62	18-11	18-19	13-1	49-31
1962-63	13-20	11-25	7-4	31-49
1963-64	25-14	21-15	2-3	48-32
1964-65	10-26	5-31	2-6	17-63
1965-66	12-14	8-19	15-12	35-45
1966-67	18-10	11-19	15-8	44-37
1967-68	27-14	16-23	0-2	43-39
1968-69	22-19	18-21	1-1	41-41
1969-70	16-20	14-26	0-6	30-52
1970-71	20-18	19-21	2-2	41-41
1971-72	27-8	21-20	3-3	51-31
1972-73	27-14	18-20	2-1	47-35
1973-74	23-18	20-20	1-0	44-38
1974-75	31-10	17-24	—	48-34
1975-76	36-5	23-18	—	59-23
1976-77	29-12	17-24	—	46-36
1977-78	30-11	13-28	—	43-39
1978-79	23-18	15-26	—	38-44
1979-80	15-26	9-32	—	24-58
1980-81	26-15	13-28	—	39-43
1981-82	28-13	17-24	—	45-37
1982-83	21-20	9-32	—	30-52
1983-84	27-14	10-31	—	37-45
1984-85	17-24	5-36	—	22-60
1985-86	24-17	6-35	—	30-52
1986-87	25-16	17-24	—	42-40
1987-88	16-25	4-37	—	20-62
1988-89	29-12	14-27	—	43-39
1989-90	27-14	10-31	—	37-45
1990-91	30-11	14-27	—	44-38
1991-92	31-10	24-17	—	55-27
1992-93	19-22	15-26	—	34-48

Philadelphia Totals:	H: 297-135	A: 146-328	N: 115-82	O: 558-545
Bay Area Totals:	H: 724-490	A: 434-787	N: 50-48	O: 1208-1325
All-Time Totals:	H: 1021-625	A: 580-1115	N: 165-130	O: 1766-1870

ALL-TIME COACHES RECORDS

COACH	YEARS	GAMES	RECORD	PCT	PLAYOFFS	PCT
Edward Gottlieb	1946-55	581	263-318	.453	15-17	.469
George Senesky	1955-58	216	119-97	.551	10-10	.500
Al Cervi	1958-59	72	32-40	.444	—	—
Neil Johnston	1959-61	154	95-59	.617	4-8	.333
Frank McGuire	1961-62	80	49-31	.613	6-6	.500
Bob Feerick	1962-63	80	31-49	.388	—	—
Alex Hannum	1963-66	240	100-140	.417	5-4	.556
Bill Sharman	1966-68	163	87-76	.534	13-12	.520
George Lee	1968-70	134	63-71	.470	2-4	.333
Alvin Attles	1970-83	1071	555-516	.518	31-30	.508
John Bach	1983-86	271	97-174	.358	—	—
George Karl	1986-88	146	58-88	.330	4-6	.400
Ed Gregory	1988	18	4-14	.222	—	—
Don Nelson	1988-93	410	213-197	.520	9-12	.429
Totals		3636	1766-1870	.486	99-112	.469

Editor's Note: John Bach's record includes duty as interim Head Coach in 1980 for the last 21 games (6-15) and again in 1982 for the last 4 games (2-2).

WARRIORS ALL-TIME SEASON HIGH PERFORMANCES

TEAM

Points	10,035	1961-62	(Avg. 125.4)
Field Goals Made	3,917	1961-62	(Avg. 49.0)
Field Goals Attempted	8,929	1961-62	(Avg. 111.6)
Field Goal Percentage	.507	1991-92	
Three-Point Field Goals Made	298	1992-93	(Avg. 3.6)
Three-Point Field Goals Attempted	852	1992-93	(Avg. 10.4)
Three-Point Field Goal Percentage	.350	1992-93	
Free Throws Made	2,334	1967-68	(Avg. 28.5)
Free Throws Attempted	3,207	1961-62	(Avg. 40.1)
Free Throw Percentage	.809	1989-90	
Offensive Rebounds	1,416	1974-75	(Avg. 17.3)
Defensive Rebounds	3,035	1973-74	(Avg. 37.0)
Total Rebounds	6,029	1967-68	(Avg. 73.5)
Assists	2,120	1976-77	(Avg. 25.9)
Steals	972	1974-75	(Avg. 11.9)
Blocked Shots	643	1988-89	(Avg. 7.8)
Turnovers	1,716	1974-75	(Avg. 20.9)
Personal Fouls	2,265	1967-68	(Avg. 27.6)
Disqualifications	71	1961-62	

INDIVIDUAL

Total Points	4,029	Wilt Chamberlain, 1961-62*
Scoring Average	50.4	Wilt Chamberlain, 1961-62*
Field Goals Made	1,597	Wilt Chamberlain, 1961-62*
Field Goals Attempted	3,159	Wilt Chamberlain, 1961-62
Field Goal Percentage	.588	Bernard King, 1980-81
Three-Point Field Goals Made	127	Tim Hardaway, 1991-92
Three-Point Field Goals Att.	376	Tim Hardaway, 1991-92
Three-Point Field Goal Pct.	.451	Chris Mullin, 1992-93
Free Throws Made	753	Rick Barry, 1966-67
Free Throws Attempted	1,363	Wilt Chamberlain, 1961-62*

NBA All-Time Record

ALL-TIME RECORDS

WARRIORS ALL-TIME SEASON HIGH PERFORMANCES

INDIVIDUAL

Free Throw Percentage	.924	Rick Barry, 1977-78
Offensive Rebounds	433	Larry Smith, 1980-81
Defensive Rebounds	651	Robert Parish, 1978-79
Total Rebounds	2,149	Wilt Chamberlain, 1960-61*
Average Rebounds	27.2	Wilt Chamberlain, 1960-61*
Assists	848	Eric Floyd, 1986-87
Average Assists	10.7	Guy Rodgers, 1965-66
Steals	228	Rick Barry, 1974-75
Average Steals	2.85	Rick Barry, 1974-75
Blocked Shots	345	Manute Bol, 1988-89
Average Blocked Shots	4.31	Manute Bol, 1988-89
Turnovers	296	Chris Mullin, 1988-89
Personal Fouls	337	Rudy LaRusso, 1967-68
Disqualifications	20	Joe Fulks, 1952-53
Minutes Played	3,882	Wilt Chamberlain, 1961-62*
Average Minutes Played	48.5	Wilt Chamberlain, 1961-62*

*NBA All-Time Record

WARRIORS ALL-TIME TOP SCORING PERFORMANCES

PTS.	PLAYER	OPPONENT	DATE
100	Wilt Chamberlain	vs. New York at Hershey, PA	3/2/62
78	Wilt Chamberlain	vs. Los Angeles (3OT)	12/8/61
73	Wilt Chamberlain	vs. Chicago	1/13/62
	Wilt Chamberlain	at New York	12/16/62
72	Wilt Chamberlain	at Los Angeles	11/3/62
70	Wilt Chamberlain	at Syracuse	3/10/63
67	Wilt Chamberlain	vs. New York	3/9/61
	Wilt Chamberlain	at St. Louis	2/17/62
	Wilt Chamberlain	vs. New York	2/26/62
	Wilt Chamberlain	vs. Los Angeles	1/17/63
65	Wilt Chamberlain	at Cincinnati	2/13/62
	Wilt Chamberlain	at St. Louis	2/27/62
64	Rick Barry	vs. Portland	3/26/74
63	Joe Fulks	vs. Indianapolis	2/10/49
	Wilt Chamberlain	vs. Los Angeles	12/14/62
	Wilt Chamberlain	at Philadelphia	11/26/64
62*	Wilt Chamberlain		
61*	Wilt Chamberlain		
60*	Wilt Chamberlain		
59*	Wilt Chamberlain		
	Purvis Short	vs. New Jersey	11/17/84
58*	Wilt Chamberlain		
57*	Wilt Chamberlain		
	Rick Barry	at New York	12/14/65
	Rick Barry	at Cincinnati	10/29/65

PTS.	PLAYER	OPPONENT	DATE
	Purvis Short	vs. San Antonio	1/7/84
56*	Wilt Chamberlain		
55*	Wilt Chamberlain		
	Rick Barry	vs. Philadelphia	1/23/75
	Rick Barry	vs. New York	3/25/78
54*	Wilt Chamberlain		
53*	Wilt Chamberlain		
52*	Rick Barry	vs. Chicago at Fresno, CA	2/16/67
	Joe Barry Carroll	vs. Utah	3/5/83
51*	Wilt Chamberlain		
	Rick Barry	vs. Houston at San Antonio	1/17/73
	Rick Barry	vs. Philadelphia	2/23/74
	Phil Smith	vs. Phoenix	1/8/76
	Phil Smith	vs. Houston	12/11/76
	Rick Barry	vs. Philadelphia	10/29/77
50*	Wilt Chamberlain		
	Neil Johnston	vs. Syracuse at New York	2/16/54
	Rick Barry	at Detroit	1/14/67
	Rick Barry	vs. Boston at Oakland	2/14/67
	Rick Barry	at Cincinnati	12/25/67
	Rick Barry	vs. St. Louis at Phoenix	12/8/66
	Rick Barry	vs. Los Angeles	12/8/73
	Bernard King	vs. Philadelphia	1/3/81

*Wilt Chamberlain scored between 50-62 points in 91 games as a member of the Warriors.

OPPONENTS ALL-TIME TOP SCORING PERFORMANCES

PTS.	PLAYER	OPPONENT	DATE
63	Elgin Baylor	Los Angeles (3OT)	12/6/61
62	Wilt Chamberlain	Philadelphia	3/3/66
58	Fred Brown	Seattle	3/23/74
56	Tom Chambers	Phoenix	2/18/90
52	Elgin Baylor	Los Angeles	12/8/61

PTS.	PLAYER	OPPONENT	DATE
	Elgin Baylor	Los Angeles	12/15/62
51	Bob Pettit	St. Louis	12/6/61
	Elgin Baylor	Los Angeles	12/14/62
	Moses Malone	Houston	3/11/81
50	Richie Guerin	New York	2/25/62

WARRIORS ALL-TIME CAREER LEADERS

POINTS
1.	Wilt Chamberlain	17,783
2.	Rick Barry	16,447
3.	Paul Arizin	16,266
4.	Nate Thurmond	13,191
5.	Chris Mullin	12,727
6.	Jeff Mullins	12,547
7.	Purvis Short	11,894
8.	Neil Johnston	10,023
9.	Joe Barry Carroll	9,996
10.	Joe Fulks	8,003

REBOUNDS
1.	Nate Thurmond	12,771
2.	Wilt Chamberlain	10,768
3.	Larry Smith	6,440
4.	Clyde Lee	6,416
5.	Paul Arizin	6,129
6.	Neil Johnston	5,856
7.	Rick Barry	4,655
8.	Tom Gola	4,528
9.	Joe Grabowski	4,503
10.	Clifford Ray	4,310

STEALS
1.	Chris Mullin	994
2.	Rick Barry	929
3.	Purvis Short	710
4.	Tim Hardaway	659
5.	Sonny Parker	611
6.	Eric Floyd	606
7.	Phil Smith	539
8.	Joe Barry Carrol	531
9.	Larry Smith	516
10.	Lester Conner	463

PERSONAL FOULS
1.	Paul Arizin	2,764
2.	Al Attles	2,417
3.	Larry Smith	2,244
4.	Nate Thurmond	2,065
5.	Jeff Mullins	2,037
6.	Purvis Short	1,964
7.	Tom Gola	1,954
8.	Guy Rodgers	1,940
9.	Rick Barry	1,887
10.	Clifford Ray	1,809

GAMES PLAYED
1.	Nate Thurmond	757
2.	Jeff Mullins	716
3.	Paul Arizin	713
4.	Al Attles	712
5.	Rick Barry	642

6.	Larry Smith	617
7.	Purvis Short	614
8.	Guy Rodgers	587
9.	Clyde Lee	583
10.	Joe Graboski	570

SCORING (minimum 100 games)
1.	Wilt Chamberlain	41.5
2.	Rick Barry	25.6
3.	World Free	23.4
4.	Paul Arizin ·	23.0
5.	Mitch Richmond	22.7
6.	Chris Mullin	22.5
	Bernard King	22.5
8.	Rudy LaRusso	21.3
9.	Tim Hardaway	20.6
10.	Joe Barry Carroll	20.4

ASSISTS
1.	Guy Rodgers	4,855
2.	Rick Barry	3,247
3.	Tim Hardaway	2,988
4.	Jeff Mullins	2,913
5.	Eric Floyd	2,518
6.	Al Attles	2,483
7.	Tom Gola	2,294
8.	Chris Mullin	2,171
9.	Nate Thurmond	2,070
10.	Jack George	1,890

BLOCKED SHOTS
1.	Joe Barry Carroll	837
2.	Manute Bol	583
3.	Robert Parish	549
4.	George Johnson	507
5.	Clifford Ray	465
6.	Larry Smith	384
7.	Chris Mullin	341
8.	Rick Barry	203
9.	Rod Higgins	197
10.	Nate Thurmond	179

DISQUALIFICATIONS
1.	Paul Arizin	101
2.	Tom Gola	74
3.	Al Attles	65
4.	Tom Meschery	53
5.	Joe Barry Carroll	50
5.	Larry Smith	50
7.	Joe Ellis	42
8.	Joe Fulks	41
9.	Guy Rodgers	40
10.	Clifford Ray	37

MINUTES PLAYED
1.	Nate Thurmond	30,729
2.	Paul Arizin	24,897
3.	Rick Barry	24,443
4.	Jeff Mullins	23,495
5.	Guy Rodgers	21,148
6.	Chris Mullin	20,287
7.	Wilt Chamberlain	20,233
8.	Purvis Short	19,230
9.	Neil Johnston	18,298
10.	Larry Smith	18,023

OFFENSIVE REBOUNDS
1.	Larry Smith	2,709
2.	Clifford Ray	1,372
3.	Joe Barry Carroll	1,326
4.	Purvis Short	1,187
5.	Robert Parish	924
6.	Sonny Parker	751
7.	Chris Mullin	731
8.	George Johnson	694
9.	Tyrone Hill	594
10.	Derrek Dickey	563

FIELD GOAL PERCENTAGE
(minimum 1,000 attempts)
1.	Bernard King	577
2.	Larry Smith	539
3.	Clifford Ray	537
4.	Sarunas Marciulionis	528
5.	Victor Alexander	521
	Butch Beard	521
7.	Chris Mullin	517
8.	Charles Dudley	512
9.	Tyrone Hill	509
10.	Wilt Chamberlain	506

FIELD GOALS MADE
1.	Wilt Chamberlain	7,216
2.	Rick Barry	6,466
3.	Paul Arizin	5,628
4.	Jeff Mullins	5,183
5.	Nate Thurmond	5,029
6.	Purvis Short	4,830
7.	Chris Mullin	4,827
8.	Joe Barry Carroll	4,010
9.	Neil Johnston	3,303
10.	Guy Rodgers	3,046

ALL-TIME RECORDS

WARRIORS ALL-TIME CAREER LEADERS

FREE THROWS MADE

1.	Paul Arizin	5,010
2.	Rick Barry	3,515
3.	Neil Johnston	3,417
4.	Wilt Chamberlain	3,351
5.	Nate Thurmond	3,133
6.	Chris Mullin	2,741
7.	Joe Fulks	2,355
8.	Jeff Mullins	2,181
9.	Purvis Short	2,133
10.	Joe Barry Carroll	1,976

FIELD GOALS ATTEMPTED

1.	Rick Barry	14,392
2.	Wilt Chamberlain	14,270
3.	Paul Arizin	13,354
4.	Nate Thurmond	11,836
5.	Jeff Mullins	11,126
6.	Purvis Short	10,091
7.	Chris Mullin	9,339
8.	Joe Fulks	9,338
9.	Joe Barry Carroll	8,263
10.	Guy Rodgers	8,052

THREE-POINT FIELD GOALS MADE

1.	Tim Hardaway	349
2.	Chris Mullin	332
3.	Rod Higgins	261
4.	Eric Floyd	169
5.	Joe Hassett	115
6.	Mitch Richmond	107
7.	Purvis Short	101
8.	Latrell Sprewell	73
9.	Greg Ballard	32
10.	Manute Bol	29

FREE THROWS ATTEMPTED

1.	Paul Arizin	6,189
2.	Wilt Chamberlain	6,037
3.	Nate Thurmond	4,636
4.	Neil Johnston	4,447
5.	Rick Barry	3,921
6.	Chris Mullin	3,154
7.	Joe Fulks	3,075
8.	Joe Barry Carroll	2,672
9.	Jeff Mullins	2,667
10.	Purvis Short	2,608

DEFENSIVE REBOUNDS

1.	Larry Smith	3,731
2.	Clifford Ray	2,938
3.	Joe Barry Carroll	2,742
4.	Robert Parish	1,998
5.	Rick Barry	1,946
6.	Chris Mullin	1,841
7.	Purvis Short	1,789
8.	Jamaal Wilkes	1,418
9.	George Johnson	1,231
	Rod Higgins	1,231

THREE-POINT FIELD GOALS ATTEMPTED

1.	Tim Hardaway	1021
2.	Chris Mullin	962
3.	Rod Higgins	732
4.	Eric Floyd	525
5.	Purvis Short	354
6.	Joe Hassett	339
7.	Mitch Richmond	300
8.	Latrell Sprewell	198
9.	Manute Bol	139
10.	Winston Garland	92

FREE THROW PERCENTAGE
(minimum 500 attempts)

1.	Rick Barry	.896
2.	Chris Mullin	.869
3.	Cazzie Russell	.841
4.	Mitch Richmond	.840
5.	Jim Barnett	.831
	Ron Williams	.831
7.	Rod Higgins	.829
8.	Eric Floyd	.824
9.	Purvis Short	.818
	Jeff Mullins	.818

ALL-TIME HOME ATTENDANCE

YEAR	REGULAR SEASON GAMES	TOTAL	AVG.	OPENING GAME	PLAYOFFS GAMES	TOTAL	AVG.
1946-47	30	129,142	4,305	4,185	5	36,886	7,377
1947-48	24	109,095	4,546	3,578	6	35,777	6,462
1948-49	29	94,847	3,721	4,088	1	3,536	3,536
1949-50	30	63,270	2,109	4,784	1	2,215	2,215
1950-51	32	105,108	3,285	5,603	1	2,667	2,667
1951-52	31	96,578	3,115	8,909	2	4,302	2,151
1952-53	17	56,882	3,346	4,872	*	*	*
1953-54	19	113,088	5,952	6,077	*	*	*
1954-55	21	123,438	5,878	6,101	*	*	*
1955-56	28	164,929	3,890	3,055	6	53,798	8,966
1956-57	31	158,004	5,097	6,152	1	4,525	4,525
1957-58	28	156,988	5,067	6,511	3	22,748	7,583
1958-59	26	153,566	5,906	4,206	*	*	*
1959-60	28	226,412	8,086	9,211	5	56,623	11,324
1960-61	29	196,223	6,766	8,277	2	10,780	5,390
1961-62	29	161,795	5,579	4,688	6	48,274	8,046
1962-63	33	101,218	3,067	5,215	*	*	*
1963-64	39	132,678	3,402	5,106	6	52,345	8,724
1964-65	36	76,963	2,138	3,112	*	*	*
1965-66	26	124,160	4,775	5,836	*	*	*
1966-67	28	216,352	7,727	4,622	8	82,274	10,409
1967-68	41	185,322	4,520	5,609	5	41,635	8,327
1968-69	41	194,683	4,748	8,924	3	33,142	11,047
1969-70	36	189,642	5,268	4,591	*	*	*
1970-71	38	195,935	5,156	2,574	2	15,936	7,968
1971-72	35	200,917	5,740	6,292	2	23,722	11,861
1972-73	41	244,504	5,964	9,926	5	54,598	10,920
1973-74	41	265,095	6,465	6,596	*	*	*
1974-75	41	360,740	8,799	4,402	9	115,451	12,828
1975-76	41	490,846	11,972	12,787	7	90,877	12,982
1976-77	41	479,328	11,691	13,155	5	65,079	13,016
1977-78	41	474,715	11,578	8,871	*	*	*
1978-79	41	427,252	10,421	10,264	*	*	*
1979-80	41	344,483	8,402	7,780	*	*	*
1980-81	41	413,480	10,084	8,624	*	*	*
1981-82	41	401,646	9,796	7,193	*	*	*
1982-83	41	341,243	8,323	7,506	*	*	*
1983-84	41	337,817	8,239	6,550	*	*	*
1984-85	41	300,580	7,331	6,547	*	*	*
1985-86	41	401,279	9,787	6,593	*	*	*
1986-87	41	423,997	10,341	10,584	4	60,100	15,025
1987-88	41	465,348	11,350	13,223	*	*	*
1988-89	41	587,820	14,337	15,025	3	45,075	15,025
1989-90	41	616,025	15,025	15,025	*	*	*
1990-91	41	616,025	15,025	15,025	4	60,100	15,025
1991-92	41	616,025	15,025	15,025	2	30,050	15,025
1992-93	41	616,025	15,025	15,025	*	*	*
TOTALS	1,646	12,951,508	7,868	—	104	1,052,515	10,120

WARRIORS AWARD WINNERS

MOST VALUABLE PLAYER
1959-60   Wilt Chamberlain

ROOKIE OF THE YEAR
1957-58   Woody Sauldsberry
1959-60   Wilt Chamberlain
1965-66   Rick Barry
1974-75   Keith Wilkes
1988-89   Mitch Richmond

ALL-ROOKIE TEAM
1963-64   Nate Thurmond
1965-66   Rick Barry, Fred Hetzel
1974-75   Keith Wilkes
1975-76   Gus Williams
1980-81   Joe Barry Carroll, Larry Smith
1988-89   Mitch Richmond
1989-90   Tim Hardaway
1991-92   Billy Owens
1992-93   Latrell Sprewell, 2nd Team

ALL-STAR GAME PARTICIPANTS
1951   Paul Arizin, Joe Fulks, Andy Phillip
1952   Paul Arizin, Joe Fulks, Andy Phillip
1953   Neil Johnston
1954   Neil Johnston
1955   Paul Arizin, Neil Johnston
1956   Paul Arizin, Jack George, Neil Johnston
1957   Paul Arizin, Jack George, Neil Johnston
1958   Paul Arizin, Neil Johnston
1959   Paul Arizin, Woody Sauldsberry
1960   Paul Arizin*, Wilt Chamberlain, Tom Gola
1961   Paul Arizin, Wilt Chamberlain, Tom Gola
1962   Paul Arizin, Wilt Chamberlain, Tom Gola*
1963   Wilt Chamberlain, Tom Meschery, Guy Rodgers
1964   Wilt Chamberlain, Guy Rodgers
1965   Wilt Chamberlain, Nate Thurmond
1966   Rick Barry, Guy Rodgers
1966   Rick Barry, Guy Rodgers, Nate Thurmond
1967   Rick Barry, Nate Thurmond
1968   Jim King, Rudy LaRusso, Clyde Lee
1969   Rudy LaRusso, Jeff Mullins
1970   Jeff Mullins, Nate Thurmond*
1971   Jerry Lucas, Jeff Mullins
1972   Cazzie Russell
1973   Rick Barry*, Nate Thurmond
1974   Rick Barry, Nate Thurmond
1975   Rick Barry, Al Attles
1976   Rick Barry, Phil Smith, Jamaal Wilkes, Al Attles
1977   Rick Barry, Phil Smith
1978   Rick Barry
1982   Bernard King
1987   Joe Barry Carroll, Eric Floyd
1989   Chris Mullin
1990   Chris Mullin
1991   Tim Hardaway, Chris Mullin
1992   Tim Hardaway, Chris Mullin, Don Nelson
1993   Tim Hardaway, Chris Mullin*
Selected but did not play due to injury

COACH OF THE YEAR
1963-64   Alex Hannum
1991-92   Don Nelson

EXECUTIVE OF THE YEAR
1974-75   Dick Vertlieb

JACK McMAHON AWARD
1989-90   Tim Hardaway
1990-91   Mitch Richmond
1991-92   Sarunas Marciulionis

ALL-DEFENSIVE TEAM
1968-69   Nate Thurmond, 1st Team
           Rudy LaRusso, 2nd Team
1970-71   Nate Thurmond, 1st Team
1971-72   Nate Thurmond, 2nd Team
1972-73   Nate Thurmond, 2nd Team
1973-74   Nate Thurmond, 2nd Team
1975-76   Phil Smith, 2nd Team
           Jamaal Wilkes, 2nd Team
1976-77   Jamaal Wilkes, 2nd Team
1977-78   E.C. Coleman, 2nd Team

ALL-NBA TEAM
1946-47   Joe Fulks, 1st Team
1947-48   Joe Fulks & Howie Dallmar, 1st Team
1948-49   Joe Fulks, 1st Team
1950-51   Joe Fulks, 2nd Team
1951-52   Paul Arizin, 1st Team
           Andy Phillip, 2nd Team
1952-53   Neil Johnston, 1st Team
           Andy Phillip, 2nd Team
1953-54   Neil Johnston, 1st Team
1954-55   Neil Johnston, 1st Team
1955-56   Paul Arizin & Neil Johnston, 1st Team
           Jack George, 2nd Team
1956-57   Paul Arizin, 1st Team
           Neil Johnston, 2nd Team
1957-58   Tom Gola, 2nd Team
1958-59   Paul Arizin, 2nd Team
1959-60   Wilt Chamberlain, 1st Team
1960-61   Wilt Chamberlain, 1st Team
1961-62   Wilt Chamberlain, 1st Team
1962-63   Wilt Chamberlain, 2nd Team
1963-64   Wilt Chamberlain, 1st Team
1965-66   Rick Barry, 1st Team
1966-67   Rick Barry, 1st Team
1972-73   Rick Barry, 2nd Team
1973-74   Rick Barry, 1st Team
1974-75   Rick Barry, 1st Team
1975-76   Rick Barry, 1st Team
           Phil Smith, 2nd Team
1981-82   Bernard King, 2nd Team
1988-89   Chris Mullin , 2nd Team
1989-90   Chris Mullin, 3rd Team
1990-91   Chris Mullin, 2nd Team
1991-92   Chris Mullin, 1st Team
           Tim Hardaway, 2nd Team
1992-93   Tim Hardaway, 3rd Team

WARRIORS TEAM RECORDS

MOST POINTS SCORED

ONE GAME:	169	Philadelphia vs. New York at Hershey, PA	3/2/62
WEST COAST:	162	Golden State at Denver	11/2/90
1ST HALF:	88	Golden State vs. Sacramento	11/2/91
2ND HALF:	90	Philadelphia vs. New York at Hershey, PA	3/2/62
WEST COAST:	87	Golden State vs. Sacramento	3/4/89
1ST QUARTER:	48	Golden State vs. Sacramento	11/2/9
2ND QUARTER:	44	San Francisco vs. Seattle	10/13/67
	44	Golden State vs. Denver	3/18/81
	44	Golden State at Denver	11/2/90
3RD QUARTER:	57 *	Golden State vs. Sacramento	3/4/89
4TH QUARTER:	50	Golden State vs. Los Angeles Clippers	3/7/89
	50	Golden State vs. Portland	3/21/89

FEWEST POINTS SCORED

ONE GAME:	66	Philadelphia at Ft. Wayne	1/2/55
WEST COAST:	74	Golden State at Cleveland	11/21/74
	74	Golden State at Portland	10/21/79
	74	Golden State at Portland	1/1/83
1ST HALF:	25	Golden State vs. Chicago	1/1/74
2ND HALF:	25 *	Golden State vs. Boston	2/14/78
1ST QUARTER:	8	San Francisco at San Diego Rockets	12/2/67
2ND QUARTER:	7	Golden State at Portland	1/1/83
3RD QUARTER:		Unable to Determine	
4TH QUARTER:	9	Golden State vs. Boston	2/14/78
	9	Golden State vs. Portland	4/6/79

FIELD GOALS MADE

ONE GAME:	65	Golden State vs. Indiana	3/19/77
ONE HALF:	36	Golden State vs. Indiana	3/19/77
ONE QUARTER:	23 *	Golden State vs. Sacramento	3/4/89
FEWEST GAME:	25	San Francisco vs. Phoenix	1/3/71

FIELD GOALS ATTEMPTED

ONE GAME:	153 *	Philadelphia vs. Los Angeles (3OT)	2/8/61
WEST COAST:	134	San Francisco vs. Baltimore	1/27/67
ONE HALF:	83 *	Philadelphia vs. Syracuse	11/4/59
WEST COAST:	81	San Francisco vs. Los Angeles	2/2/69
ONE QUARTER:	43	Philadelphia vs. Syracuse	11/4/59
WEST COAST:	38	San Francisco vs. Baltimore	1/27/67
FEWEST GAME:	59	Philadelphia vs. Milwaukee at Albany, NY	3/14/55
WEST COAST:	69	Golden State vs. San Antonio	11/21/81
	69	Golden State at New York	11/20/84
	69	Golden State vs. New Jersey	3/10/88
	69	Golden State at Boston	2/7/93

FIELD GOAL PERCENTAGE

HIGHEST:	.636	Golden State vs. San Antonio (63-99)	3/8/87
LOWEST:	.160	Philadelphia vs. Boston (17-106)	1/22/47
WEST COAST:	.267	San Francisco vs. Boston (28-105)	12/5/64

NBA All-Time Record

WARRIORS TEAM RECORDS

THREE-POINT FIELD GOALS MADE
ONE GAME:	10	Golden State at Portland	1/26/93
ONE HALF:	7	Golden State at San Antonio	2/5/91
	7	Golden State at Portland	1/26/93
ONE QUARTER:	6	Golden State at Portland	1/26/93

THREE-POINT FIELD GOALS MADE, NONE MISSED
ONE GAME:	3	Golden State vs. Seattle	2/ 26/85

THREE-POINT FIELD GOALS ATTEMPTED
ONE GAME:	20	Golden State vs. Indiana (OT)	3/2/89
	20	Golden State vs. Philadelphia	2/16/91
	20	Golden State at Los Angeles Clippers	4/16/93
ONE HALF:	14	Golden State vs. Indiana (OT)	3/2/89
	14	Golden State vs. Philadelphia	2/16/91
ONE QUARTER:	9	Golden State vs. Detroit	3/12/92
	9	Golden State at Los Angeles Clippers	4/16/93
OVERTIME:	6	Golden State vs. Indiana (OT)	3/2/89

THREE-POINT FIELD GOALS ATTEMPTED, NONE MADE
ONE GAME:	10	Golden State vs. New Jersey	11/24/90
	10	Golden State vs. Washington	2/14/93

FREE THROWS MADE
ONE GAME:	55	Golden State vs. Utah	3/29/90
ONE HALF:	36 *	Golden State vs. Utah	3/29/90
ONE QUARTER:	22	Golden State vs. Utah	3/29/90
FEWEST GAME:	4	Golden State vs. Chicago	3/6/77

FREE THROWS ATTEMPTED
ONE GAME:	74	San Francisco vs. New York (2OT)	11/6/64
ONE HALF:	43	Golden State vs. Utah	3/29/90
ONE QUARTER:	28	Philadelphia vs. Cincinnati	11/8/59
WEST COAST:	26	San Francisco at Detroit	2/18/68
FEWEST GAME:	4	Golden State vs. Chicago	3/6/77

FREE THROW PERCENTAGE
HIGHEST:	1.000	Golden State vs. Houston (33-33)	4/11/91
	1.000	Golden State at Buffalo (22-22)	11/19/74
	1.000	Golden State at Philadelphia (17-17)	11/25/77
	1.000	Golden State at Chicago (14-14)	2/12/80
	1.000	Golden State vs. Chicago (4-4)	3/6/77
LOWEST:	.375	San Francisco at Los Angeles (12-32)	3/2/63

REBOUNDS
ONE GAME:	104	Philadelphia vs. Syracuse	11/ 4/59
	104	Philadelphia vs. Cincinnati	11/8/59
WEST COAST:	99	San Francisco vs. Baltimore	11/15/65
ONE HALF:	62	Philadelphia vs. Syracuse	11/9/61
WEST COAST:	51	San Francisco vs. Baltimore	11/15/65
ONE QUARTER:	40	Philadelphia vs. Syracuse	11/9/61
WEST COAST:	28	San Francisco vs. Detroit	11/14/62
	28	San Francisco vs. Baltimore	11/15/65
FEWEST GAME:	22	Golden State at Los Angeles	3/6/85

NBA All-Time Record

OFFENSIVE REBOUNDS

ONE GAME:	35	Golden State vs. Los Angeles	1/21/75
FEWEST GAME:	4	Golden State vs. Milwaukee	3/19/74
	4	Golden State vs. San Antonio	11/21/81
	4	Golden State at Seattle	12/27/85
	4	Golden State at Boston	1/21/90

DEFENSIVE REBOUNDS

ONE GAME:	52	Golden State vs. New Orleans	1 2/3/74
FEWEST GAME:	13	Golden State at San Diego	3/19/81

ASSISTS

ONE GAME:	46	Golden State vs. Denver	11/7/81
ONE HALF:	26	Philadelphia vs. Los Angeles	12/1/60
	26	Golden State vs. Philadelphia	3/1/93
ONE QUARTER:	15	San Francisco vs. Boston	2/18/66
	15	Golden State vs. Sacramento	1/2/91
FEWEST GAME:	11	Golden State vs. Seattle	2/5/82

PERSONAL FOULS

ONE GAME:	42	Philadelphia vs. Fort Wayne at Buffalo	12/15/54
WEST COAST:	41	Golden State at Portland	11/11/84
FEWEST GAME:	10	Golden State vs. Detroit	3/25/86

DISQUALIFICATIONS

ONE GAME:	4	Golden State vs. Philadelphia	12/29/81

STEALS

ONE GAME:	25	Golden State vs. Los Angeles	3/25/75
	25	Golden State vs. San Antonio	2/15/89
FEWEST GAME:	0 *	Golden State at New York	11/24/73

BLOCKED SHOTS

ONE GAME:	18	Golden State vs. New Jersey	2/ 2/90

TURNOVERS

ONE GAME:	37	Golden State at Kansas City	2/ 9/83
FEWEST GAME:	6	Golden State vs. New Orleans	1/14/78
	6	Golden State vs. Portland	3/18/88
	6	Golden State at Dallas	2/7/91

NBA All-Time Record

OPPONENTS TEAM RECORDS

MOST POINTS SCORED

ONE GAME:	163	Syracuse vs. San Francisco	3/10/63
1ST HALF:	87	Phoenix at Golden State	3/23/89
2ND HALF:	91	Los Angeles vs. Golden State	3/19/72
1ST QUARTER:	50	Syracuse at San Francisco	12/16/62
2ND QUARTER:	47	Atlanta at Golden State	11/9/90
3RD QUARTER:	49	Los Angeles vs. Golden State	3/19/72
4TH QUARTER:	51	Dallas at Golden State	1/15/85
OVERTIME:	23	Indiana vs. Golden State	3/31/91

FEWEST POINTS SCORED

ONE GAME:	70	Syracuse at Philadelphia	11/29/54
WEST COAST:	71	Washington vs. Golden State	11/22/75
1ST HALF:	31	Boston vs. San Francisco	12/4/64
2ND HALF:	32	Atlanta vs. Golden State	2/28/82
1ST QUARTER:	9	Houston vs. Golden State	12/21/82
2ND QUARTER:	9	Los Angeles at San Francisco	1/10/64
3RD QUARTER:	10	Atlanta vs. Golden State	2/28/82
4TH QUARTER:	13	Philadelphia at Golden State	1/23/75
OVERTIME:	3	Phoenix at Golden State (2OT)	12/9/81

FIELD GOALS MADE

ONE GAME:	69	Syracuse vs. San Francisco	3/1 0/63
	69	Los Angeles vs. Golden State	3/19/72
ONE HALF:	37	Los Angeles vs. Golden State	3/19/72
ONE QUARTER:	21	Syracuse vs. San Francisco	12/16/62
	21	Dallas at Golden State	1/15/85
FEWEST GAME:	25	Cleveland at San Francisco	11/10/70
	25	Washington vs. Golden State	11/22/75

FIELD GOALS ATTEMPTED

ONE GAME:	150	Boston vs. Philadelphia	3/2/60
WEST COAST:	138	San Diego Rockets vs. San Francisco	11/19/67
ONE HALF:	83 *	Boston at Philadelphia	12/27/60
WEST COAST:	77	Denver vs. Golden State	11/2/90
ONE QUARTER:	44	San Diego Rockets vs. San Francisco	11/19/67
FEWEST GAME:	66	Utah vs. Golden State	12/10/79

FIELD GOAL PERCENTAGE, GAME

HIGHEST:	.705	Chicago at Golden State	12/2/81
LOWEST:	.238	Cleveland at San Francisco (25-105)	11/10/70

THREE-POINT FIELD GOALS MADE

ONE GAME:	16 *	Sacramento vs. Golden State	2/9/89
ONE HALF:	9	Sacramento vs. Golden State	2/9/89
	9	Sacramento vs. Golden State	3/4/89
ONE QUARTER:	6	Indiana at Golden State	3/2/89

THREE-POINT FIELD GOALS MADE, NONE MISSED

ONE GAME:	3	Denver at Golden State	2/22/80

NBA All-Time Record

THREE-POINT FIELD GOALS ATTEMPTED

ONE GAME:	31 *	Sacramento vs. Golden State	2/9/89
ONE HALF:	17	New York at Golden State	1/18/89
	17	Sacramento at Golden State	3/4/89
ONE QUARTER:	12	New York at Golden State	1/18/89

THREE POINT FIELD GOALS ATTEMPTED, NONE MADE

ONE GAME:	14	Cleveland at Golden State (2OT)	11/12/92

FREE THROWS MADE

ONE GAME:	48	Minneapolis at Philadelphia	11/2/57
	48	Philadelphia vs. Golden State	12/29/81
ONE HALF:	34	Philadelphia vs. Golden State	12/29/81
ONE QUARTER:	22	Philadelphia vs. Golden State	12/29/81
FEWEST GAME:	5	Detroit vs. Golden State	11/4/78

FREE THROWS ATTEMPTED

ONE GAME:	64	Minneapolis vs. Philadelphia at Camden, NJ	2/15/57
	64	Minneapolis at Philadelphia	11/2/57
WEST COAST:	61	Los Angeles vs. San Francisco	1/20/68
ONE HALF:	42	Minneapolis vs. Philadelphia at Camden, NJ	2/15/5 7
	42	Philadelphia vs. San Francisco	12/18/65
ONE QUARTER:	27	Philadelphia vs. Golden State	12/29/81
FEWEST GAME:	7	Kansas City vs. Golden State	12/10/77

FREE THROW PERCENTAGE

HIGHEST:	1.000	Dallas vs. Golden State (24-24)	3/26/85
	1.000	Chicago vs. Golden State (22-22)	1/27/81
	1.000	Portland vs. Golden State (21-21)	4/1/77
	1.000	Kansas City-Omaha vs. Golden State (17-17)	12/23/73
	1.000	New Orleans vs. Golden State (16-16)	12/17/78
	1.000	New York vs. Golden State (13-13)	11/24/73
	1.000	Chicago vs. Golden State (13-13)	12/16/75
	1.000	L.A. Clippers at Golden State (8-8)	12/20/88
LOWEST:	.471	Seattle at Golden State (16-34)	10/19/77

REBOUNDS

ONE GAME:	93	New York vs. Philadelphia	1/19/68
WEST COST:	82	Boston vs. San Francisco	3/14/65
	82	San Diego Rockets vs. San Francisco	12/2/67
ONE HALF:	55	San Diego Rockets vs. San Francisco	12/2/69
ONE QUARTER:	31	Philadelphia vs. San Francisco	12/14/68
FEWEST GAME:	21	New York vs. Golden State	2/18/75

OFFENSIVE REBOUNDS

ONE GAME:	37	San Antonio vs. Golden State (OT)	2/28/90
FEWEST GAME:	2	Phoenix at Golden State	3/12/80

DEFENSIVE REBOUNDS

ONE GAME:	49	Boston at Golden State	12/18/73
	49	New York at Golden State	1/12/74
	49	Portland at Golden State	1/24/76
FEWEST GAME:	13 *	New York vs. Golden State	2/18/75

NBA All-Time Record

OPPONENTS TEAM RECORDS

ASSISTS

ONE GAME:	52	Denver at Golden State	4/21/89
ONE HALF:	28	Denver at Golden State	4/21/89
ONE QUARTER:	15	St. Louis at Philadelphia	12/6/61
	15	Los Angeles vs. Golden State	3/19/72
	15	Portland vs. Golden State	3/27/74
	15	L.A. Clippers vs. Golden State (twice in one game)	12/28/89
	15	L.A. Clippers vs. Golden State	12/28/89
FEWEST GAME:	10	Chicago vs. Golden State	1/4/78

PERSONAL FOULS

ONE GAME:	53	Baltimore vs. Philadelphia	11/20/52
WEST COAST:	44	New York vs. San Francisco	11/6/64
FEWEST GAME:	7	Milwaukee vs. Philadelphia at Chicago	11/27/53
WEST COAST:	9	Los Angeles at Golden State	3/28/73
	9	Philadelphia vs. Golden State	2/3/88

DISQUALIFICATIONS

ONE GAME:	5	Pittsburgh at Philadelphia	11/7/46
	5	Rochester at Golden State	10/23/73

STEALS

ONE GAME:	24	Portland vs. Golden State	3/17/84
FEWEST GAME:	1	Milwaukee at Golden State	10/13/73
	1	Los Angeles at Golden State	12/8/73
	1	Chicago vs. Golden State	3/14/78
	1	Portland vs. Golden State	12/25/79

BLOCKED SHOTS

ONE GAME:	20	San Antonio vs. Golden State	2/24/81

TURNOVERS

ONE GAME:	40	San Antonio at Golden State	2/15/89
FEWEST GAME:	6	Chicago at San Francisco	1/3/70
	6	Golden State at Utah	4/13/92

NBA All-Time Record

WARRIORS INDIVIDUAL RECORDS

MOST POINTS
ONE GAME:	100*	Wilt Chamberlain, Philadelphia vs. New York at Hershey, PA	3/2/62
WEST COAST:	73	Wilt Chamberlain, San Francisco at New York	11/16/62
ONE HALF:	59*	Wilt Chamberlain, Philadelphia vs. New York at Hershey, PA	3/2/62
WEST COAST:	45	Wilt Chamberlain, San Francisco at New York	11/16/62
ONE QUARTER:	31	Wilt Chamberlain, Philadelphia vs. New York at Hershey, PA	3/2/62
WEST COAST:	27	Wilt Chamberlain, San Francisco at Cincinnati	2 /7/63

MOST FIELD GOALS MADE
ONE GAME:	36*	Wilt Chamberlain, Philadelphia vs. New York at Hershey, PA	3/2/62
WEST COAST:	30	Rick Barry, Golden State vs. Portland	3/26/74
ONE HALF:	22*	Wilt Chamberlain, Philadelphia vs. New York at Hershey, PA	3/2/62
WEST COAST:	17	Wilt Chamberlain, San Francisco at New York	11/16/62
ONE QUARTER:	12	Wilt Chamberlain, Philadelphia vs. New York at Hershey, PA	3/2/62
WEST COAST:	11	Wilt Chamberlain, San Francisco vs. Syracuse	12 /11/62
		Wilt Chamberlain, San Francisco at Cincinnati	2/7/63

MOST FIELD GOALS MADE, NONE MISSED
ONE GAME:	11	Chris Mullin, Golden State at Miami	12/1/90

MOST CONSECUTIVE FIELD GOALS MADE
OVERALL:	19	Wilt Chamberlain, San Francisco vs. New York at Boston (18)	11/27/63
		and San Francisco at Baltimore (1)	11/29/63
ONE GAME:	18	Wilt Chamberlain, San Francisco vs. New York at Boston	11/27/63

MOST FIELD GOALS ATTEMPTED
ONE GAME:	63*	Wilt Chamberlain, Philadelphia vs. New York at Hershey, PA	3/2/62
WEST COAST:	60	Wilt Chamberlain, San Francisco at Cincinnati (OT)	10/28/62
ONE HALF:	37*	Wilt Chamberlain, Philadelphia vs. New York at Hershey, PA	3/2/62
WEST COAST:	30	Wilt Chamberlain, San Francisco at Cincinnati (OT)	10/28/62
	30	Wilt Chamberlain, San Francisco vs. Syracuse	12/11/62
ONE QUARTER:	21*	Wilt Chamberlain, Philadelphia vs. New York at Hershey, PA	3/2/62
`WEST COAST:	16	Wilt Chamberlain, San Francisco vs. Syracuse	12/11/62

MOST FIELD GOALS ATTEMPTED, NONE MADE
ONE GAME:	17*	Tim Hardaway, Golden State at Minnesota (OT)	12/27/91

MOST THREE POINT FIELD GOALS MADE
ONE GAME:	7	Chris Mullin, Golden State at Phoenix	12/22/92
ONE HALF:	5	Joe Hassett, Golden State vs. Denver	3/28/81
ONE QUARTER:	5	Joe Hassett, Golden State vs. Denver	3/28/81

MOST THREE-POINT FIELD GOALS MADE, NONE MISSED
ONE GAME:	5	Mitch Richmond, Golden State at Sacramento	1/21/89

MOST CONSECUTIVE THREE POINT FIELD GOALS MADE
OVERALL:	7	Rod Higgins, Golden State	1/20/89-1/28/89

MOST THREE-POINT FIELD GOALS ATTEMPTED
ONE GAME:	13	Tim Hardaway, Golden State vs. Seattle	4/25/93
ONE HALF:	8	Joe Hassett, Golden State vs. Denver	3/28/81
ONE QUARTER:	7	Joe Hassett, Golden State vs. Denver	3/28/81

NBA All-Time Record

WARRIORS INDIVIDUAL RECORDS

MOST THREE-POINT FIELD GOALS ATTEMPTED, NONE MADE

ONE GAME:	6	Tim Hardaway, Golden State at Cleveland		3/20/92
	6	Tim Hardaway, Golden State at Washington		2/5/93

MOST FREE THROWS MADE

ONE GAME:	28*	Wilt Chamberlain, Philadelphia vs. New York at Hershey, PA	3/2/62
WEST COAST:	21	Rick Barry, San Francisco at New York	12/14/65
	21	Rick Barry, San Francisco at Baltimore	11/6/66
ONE HALF:	17	Rick Barry, San Francisco at New York	12/6/66
ONE QUARTER:	14*	Rick Barry, San Francisco at New York	12/6/66

MOST FREE THROWS MADE, NONE MISSED

ONE GAME:	18	Rick Barry, Golden State vs. Portland	12/26/74
	18	Rick Barry, Golden State vs. Washington	2/6/75

MOST CONSECUTIVE FREE THROWS MADE

OVERALL:	60	Rick Barry, Golden State	10/22/76-11/16/76

MOST FREE THROWS ATTEMPTED

ONE GAME:	34*	Wilt Chamberlain, Philadelphia vs. St. Louis	2/22/62
WEST COAST:	25	Rick Barry, San Francisco vs. Baltimore	11/6/66
ONE HALF:	20	Nate Thurmond, San Francisco at Philadelphia	1/5/71
ONE QUARTER:	15	Wilt Chamberlain, Philadelphia vs. Syracuse	11/9/61
	15	Wilt Chamberlain, Philadelphia at Cincinnati	2/13/62
	15	Rick Barry, San Francisco at New York	12/6/66

MOST FREE THROWS ATTEMPTED, NONE MADE

ONE GAME:	10*	Wilt Chamberlain, Philadelphia vs. Detroit	11/4/60
WEST COAST:	5	Bernard King, Golden State at Washington	11/18/80

MOST REBOUNDS

ONE GAME:	55*	Wilt Chamberlain, Philadelphia vs. Boston	11/24/60
WEST COAST:	42	Nate Thurmond, San Francisco vs. Detroit	11/9/65
ONE HALF:	31	Wilt Chamberlain, Philadelphia vs. Boston	11/24/60
WEST COAST:	24	Nate Thurmond, San Francisco at Los Angeles	12/20/66
ONE QUARTER:	18*	Nate Thurmond, San Francisco at Baltimore	2/2 8/65

MOST OFFENSIVE REBOUNDS

ONE GAME:	16	Larry Smith, Golden State vs. Denver	3/23/86

MOST DEFENSIVE REBOUNDS

ONE GAME:	25	Robert Parish, Golden State vs. New York	3/30/79

MOST ASSISTS

ONE GAME:	28	Guy Rodgers, San Francisco vs. St. Louis	3/14/63
ONE HALF:	16	Guy Rodgers, San Francisco vs. St. Louis	3/14/63
ONE QUARTER:	12	John Lucas, Golden State vs. Chicago	11/17/78

MOST STEALS

ONE GAME:	9	Rick Barry, Golden State vs. Buffalo	10/29/74
	9	Michael Ray Richardson, Golden State vs. San Antonio	2/5/83

* NBA All-Time Record

MOST BLOCKED SHOTS

ONE GAME:	13	Manute Bol, Golden State vs. New Jersey	2/2/90
ONE HALF:	8	Manute Bol, Golden State vs. New Jersey	2/2/90
ONE QUARTER:	7	Manute Bol, Golden State at Los Angeles Clippers	3/12/90

MOST TURNOVERS

| ONE GAME: | 13 | Chris Mullin, Golden State at Utah | 3/31/88 |

MOST MINUTES PLAYED

| ONE GAME: | 64 | Eric Floyd, Golden State vs. New Jersey (4OT) | 2/1/87 |

OPPONENTS INDIVIDUAL RECORDS

MOST POINTS

ONE GAME:	63	Elgin Baylor, Los Angeles at Philadelphia (3OT)	12/8/61
WEST COAST:	62	Wilt Chamberlain, Philadelphia vs. San Francisco	3/3/66
ONE HALF:	40	Tom Chambers, Phoenix at Golden State	2/18/90
ONE QUARTER:	25	Terry Porter, Portland at Golden State	11/14/92
OVERTIME:	12	Walter Davis, Phoenix vs. Golden State	3/29/84

MOST FIELD GOALS MADE

ONE GAME:	26	Wilt Chamberlain, Philadelphia vs. San Francisco	3/3/66
ONE HALF:	18	Hal Greer, Syracuse vs. Philadelphia at Boston	2/14/59
WEST COAST:	15	Tom Chambers, Phoenix at Golden State	2/18/90
ONE QUARTER:	10	Gus Williams, Seattle at Golden State	11/10/81

MOST FIELD GOALS ATTEMPTED

ONE GAME:	55	Elgin Baylor, Los Angeles at Philadelphia (3OT)	12/8/61
WEST COAST:	40	Mark Aguirre, Dallas vs. Golden State	11/14/81
ONE HALF:	30	Bob Pettit, St. Louis at Philadelphia	12/6/61
WEST COAST:	23	Wilt Chamberlain, Philadelphia vs. San Francisco	3/3/66
ONE QUARTER:	19	Bob Pettit, St. Louis at Philadelphia	12/6/61
WEST COAST:	12	Sidney Wicks, Portland vs. Golden State	3/17/72
	12	Gus Williams, Seattle at Golden State	11/10/81
	12	Mark Aguirre, Dallas vs. Golden State	11/14/81
	12	Michael Jordan, Chicago vs. Golden State	1/18/90
	12	Tom Chambers, Phoenix at Golden State	2/18/90

MOST FIELD GOALS MADE, NONE MISSED

| ONE GAME: | 14 | Bailey Howell, Baltimore vs. San Francisco | 1/3/65 |

MOST FIELD GOALS ATTEMPTED, NONE MADE

| ONE GAME: | 15 | Charlie Tyra, New York at Philadelphia | 11/7/57 |
| WEST COAST: | 11 | Ron Lee, Phoenix vs. Golden State | 4/2/78 |

OPPONENTS INDIVIDUAL RECORDS

MOST THREE-POINT FIELD GOALS MADE
ONE GAME:	7	Ricky Berry, Sacramento vs. Golden State	2/9/89
	7	Michael Jordan, Chicago vs. Golden State	1/18/90
	7	Terry Porter, Portland at Golden State	11/14/92
	7	Danny Ainge, Phoenix at Golden State	2/11/93
ONE HALF:	5	Mark Price, Cleveland at Golden State	3/9/89
	5	Dennis Scott, Orlando vs. Golden State	11/30/90
ONE QUARTER:	5	Mark Price, Cleveland at Golden State	3/9/89

MOST THREE-POINT FIELD GOALS MADE, NONE MISSED
ONE GAME:	7	Terry Porter, Portland at Golden State	11/14/92

MOST THREE POINT FIELD GOALS ATTEMPTED
ONE GAME:	14	Ricky Berry, Sacramento vs. Golden State	2/9/89
ONE HALF:	10	Danny Ainge, Sacramento at Golden State	3/4/89
ONE QUARTER:	7	Mike Newlin, New Jersey vs. Golden State	2/27/80
	7	Danny Ainge, Sacramento at Golden State	3/4/89

MOST THREE-POINT FIELD GOALS ATTEMPTED, NONE MADE
ONE GAME:	7	Mark Price, Cleveland at Golden State (2OT)	11/12/92

MOST FREE THROWS MADE
ONE GAME:	22	Eric Floyd, Houston vs. Golden State (2OT)	2/3/91
	22	Detlef Schrempf, Indiana at Golden State	12/8/92
ONE HALF:	18	Detlef Schrempf, Indiana at Golden State	12/8/92
ONE QUARTER:	11	Eric Floyd, Houston vs. Golden State (2OT)	2/3 /91

MOST FREE THROWS MADE, NONE MISSED
ONE GAME:	17	Dolph Schayes, Syracuse vs. Philadelphia at Camden, NJ	1/23/58
	17	Howard Komives, New York vs. San Francisco	1/5/66

MOST FREE THROWS ATTEMPTED
ONE GAME:	27	Eric Floyd, Houston vs. Golden State (2OT)	2/3/91
ONE HALF:	19	Karl Malone, Utah at Golden State	3/29/90
	19	Detlef Schrempf, Indiana at Golden State	12/8/92
ONE QUARTER:	13	Bill Russell, Boston at Philadelphia	2/9/59
WEST COAST:	12	Wilt Chamberlain, Philadelphia vs. San Francisco	2/4/68
	12	Connie Hawkins, Phoenix vs. San Francisco	1/23/70
	12	Happy Hairston, Detroit vs. Golden State	12/17/75
	12	Eric Floyd, Houston vs. Golden State (2OT)	2/3/91
	12	Larry Smith, San Antonio vs. Golden State	12/28/92

MOST FREE THROWS ATTEMPTED, NONE MADE
ONE GAME:	7	Connie Simmons, Rochester vs. Phila. at New Haven, CT	1/2/56
WEST COAST:	6	Larry Smith, Houston at Golden State	4/11/91

MOST REBOUNDS
ONE GAME:	49	Bill Russell, Boston at Philadelphia	11/16/57
WEST COAST:	38	Bill Russell, Boston at San Francisco	2/21/63
	38	Wilt Chamberlain, Philadelphia vs. San Francisco	3/2/67
ONE HALF:	32 *	Bill Russell, Boston vs. Philadelphia	11/16/57
WEST COAST:	21	Toby Kimball, San Diego Rockets vs. San Francisco	12/2/67
ONE QUARTER:	17	Bill Russell, Boston vs. Philadelphia	11/16/57
WEST COAST:	16	Wilt Chamberlain, Philadelphia vs. San Francisco	3/2/67

NBA All-Time Record

MOST OFFENSIVE REBOUNDS
ONE GAME: 16   Terry Cummings, San Antonio vs. Golden State (OT)   2/28/90

MOST DEFENSIVE REBOUNDS
ONE GAME: 22   Bill Walton, Portland at Golden State   1/24/76

MOST ASSISTS
ONE GAME: 27   Geoff Huston, Cleveland at Golden State   1/27/82
ONE HALF: 16   Lafayette Lever, Denver at Golden State   4/21/89
ONE QUARTER: 11   Isiah Thomas, Detroit vs. Golden State   1/24/85

MOST STEALS
ONE GAME: 9   Archie Clark, Seattle vs. Golden State   11/7/74
                     9   Johnny Moore, San Antonio vs. Golden State   1/8/85

MOST BLOCKED SHOTS
ONE GAME: 13   George Johnson, San Antonio vs. Golden State   2/24/81

MOST TURNOVERS
ONE GAME: 11   Bob Dandridge, Washington at Golden State   2/7/78
                   11   Magic Johnson, L.A. Lakers vs. Golden State   3/30/86

MOST MINUTES PLAYED
ONE GAME: 63   Wilt Chamberlain, Los Angeles vs. San Francisco (3OT)   2/2/69

WARRIORS HIGH/LOW SCORING GAMES

WARRIORS HIGHEST SCORING GAMES

PTS.	DATE	OPPONENT	SCORE
169	3/2/62	New York at Hershey	169-147
162	11/2/90	at Denver	162-158
155	3/4/89	Sacramento	155-143
154	1/7/84	San Antonio	154-133
153	3/28/92	at New Jersey (OT)	153-148
	11/2/91	Sacramento	153-91
152	11/7/81	Denver	152-107
151	11/9/61	Syracuse	151-108
150	12/22/89	Indiana	150-124
	2/1/87	New Jersey (4OT)	150-147
	1/15/86	Utah	150-104
	3/19/77	Indiana	150-91
148	3/31/92	at Sacramento (2OT)	148-136
	3/10/64	at Syracuse	148-163
147	2/27/62	at St. Louis	147-137
	12/8/61	Los Angeles (3OT)	147-151
	1/8/91	Denver	147-125
146	1/16/89	Seattle	146-117
	1/24/67	Baltimore	146-125

WARRIORS LOWEST SCORING GAMES

PTS.	DATE	OPPONENT	SCORE
66	12/26/54	at Fort Wayne	66-89
72	12/29/54	Syracuse	72-70
74	12/25/54	at Minneapolis	74-76
	11/21/74	at Cleveland	74-102
	10/21/79	at Portland	74-91
	1/1/83	at Portland	74-105
77	2/27/55	at Syracuse	77-105
	1/11/69	New York	77-85
	10/14/72	Milwaukee	77-81
78	2/15/55	Rochester at New Haven, CT	78-73
	3/8/55	at Milwaukee	78-75
	3/10/55	at Minneapolis	78-86
	1/4/58	at Detroit	78-81
79	11/16/54	Syracuse	79-73
	12/14/54	at Rochester	79-92
	2/17/55	Rochester at Buffalo	79-72
	12/18/55	at Syracuse	79-99
	12/27/55	at New York	79-80
	3/6/57	at Rochester	79-82
	12/17/67	at St. Louis	79-97
	1/11/83	at New York	79-103

OPPONENTS HIGHEST SCORING GAMES

PTS.	DATE	OPPONENT	SCORE
163	3/10/63	at Syracuse	148-163
162	3/19/72	at Los Angeles	99-162
158	11/2/90	at Denver	162-158
154	3/23/89	Phoenix	154-124
153	3/7/62	at Boston	102-153
152	1/20/68	at Los Angeles	122-152
	2/13/62	at Cincinnati	132-152
151	1/18/62	Cincinnati	133-151
	12/8/61	Los Angeles (3OT)	147-151
150	2/23/91	at Denver	150-145
149	1/15/85	Dallas	104-149
	2/25/62	New York	135-149
	3/1/61	at Syracuse	128-149
148	3/28/92	at New Jersey (OT)	153-148
	1/16/68	at Cincinnati	121-148
	3/11/62	at Syracuse	130-148
	11/18/61	at Syracuse	130-148
147	2/1/87	New Jersey (4OT)	150-147
	12/27/69	at Baltimore	112-147
	3/2/62	New York at Hershey, PA	169-147
146	2/14/71	at Seattle	101-146
	3/5/61	at Boston	129-146

OPPONENTS LOWEST SCORING GAMES

PTS.	DATE	OPPONENT	SCORE
70	12/29/54	Syracuse	72-70
72	2/15/55	Rochester at Buffalo	79-72
73	11/16/54	Syracuse at New York	79-73
	2/17/55	Rochester at New Haven, CT	78-73
	12/15/55	Fort Wayne	80-73
74	11/10/70	Cleveland	109-74
75	3/8/55	at Milwaukee	78-75
	10/15/71	at Boston	97-75
76	12/25/54	at Minneapolis	74-76
77	11/18/54	New York at Syracuse	86-77
	2/28/82	at Atlanta	105-77
78	12/28/54	at New York	84-78
	2/15/56	Fort Wayne at Miami	101-78
	11/22/56	Boston	101-78
	1/5/57	at Rochester	81-78
79	2/12/56	at St. Louis	87-79
	12/31/63	at New York	101-79
	2/4/64	Detroit	118-79
	10/25/80	Dallas	86-79

WARRIORS ALL-TIME WINNING/LOSING STREAKS

MAJOR WINNING STREAKS

STREAK	COACH	DATES	END OF STREAK	
11	Attles	12/29/71-1/22/72	1/24/72	at Chicago (105-110)
10	Attles	12/6/75-12/23/75	12/27/75	vs. Houston (110-113)
	Johnston	12/28/59-1/13/60	1/15/60	vs. Boston (112-124)
9	Nelson	4/11/91-11/6/91	11/8/91	at Philadelphia (116-126)
8	Nelson	2/11/92-2/24/92	2/26/92	at Houston (116-118)
	Nelson	1/9/89-1/21/89	1/23/89	at Cleveland (109-142)
	Attles	1/20/74-2/5/74	2/7/74	vs. Detroit (86-101)
	Sharman	11/17/67-12/1/67	12/2/67	at San Diego (103-127)
	Senesky	2/7/56-2/18/56	2/19/56	at Boston (118-120)
7	Attles	12/28/72-1/9/73	1/11/73	at Kansas City (108-109)
	Sharman	11/6/66-11/21/66	11/22/66	vs. Baltimore at New York (117-125)
	McGuire	1/19/62-1/28/62	1/30/62	at New York (110-116)
6	Nelson	1/2/90-1/13/90	1/15/90	at Indiana (105-144)
	Nelson	12/12/89-12/22/89	12/26/89	at Utah (118-133)
	Karl	11/22/86-12/4/86	12/6/86	vs. Dallas (104-109)
	Attles	10/27/78-11/4/78	11/8/78	vs. Kansas City (97-105)
	Attles	11/1/75-11/15/75	11/16/75	at Seattle (98-102)
	Attles	10/25/74-11/3/74	11/7/74	vs. Seattle (93-104)
	Attles	10/27/72-11/7/72	11/8/72	at Boston (111-128)
	Attles	2/27/72-3/10/72	3/12/72	at Cincinnati (106-117)
	Sharman	10/22/67-11/1/67	11/4/67	at Philadelphia (110-117)
	Hannum	1/7/64-1/17/64	1/18/64	at Baltimore (86-93)
	Senesky	1/30/58-2/5/58	2/7/58	vs. Cincinnati (100-103)

MAJOR LOSING STREAKS

STREAK	COACH	DATES	END OF STREAK	
17	Hannum	12/20/64-1/26/65	1/28/65	vs. Cincinnati (105-95)
16	Bach	12/29/84-1/31/85	2/2/85	vs. New York (114-98)
13	Senesky	2/6/57-3/3/57	3/5/57	vs. Fort Wayne at New York (114-80)
12	Gottlieb	2/17/53-3/5/53	3/6/53	at Rochester (78-69)
11	Hannum	2/12/65-3/3/65	3/4/65	vs. Detroit at Fort Wayne (115-110)
	Feerick	11/13/62-12/9/62	12/11/62	vs. Syracuse (136-124)
	Gottlieb	11/22/52-12/10/52	12/11/52	vs. Rochester (98-86)
10	Gottlieb	1/7/53-2/1/53	2/4/53	vs. Baltimore at Boston (96-88)
	Gottlieb	12/13/52-1/4/53	1/6/53	at Indianapolis (76-71)
9	Gottlieb	12/2/48-12/28/48	12/30/48	vs. St. Louis (74-61)
8	Nelson	1/29/93-2/11/93	2/13/93	at Sacramento (111-110)
	Karl	2/24/88-3/8/88	3/10/88	vs. New Jersey (128-112)
	Bach	1/17/86-1/30/86	2/1/86	vs. Philadelphia (125121)
7	Gregory	3/25/88-4/6/88	4/8/88	vs. Phoenix (112-111)
	Karl	11/13/87-11/24/87	11/27/87	vs. Philadelphia (109-103)
	Attles	3/12/83-3/26/83	3/29/83	vs. Dallas (109-103)
	Attles	11/16/82-11/28/82	11/30/82	vs. Phoenix (110-98)
	Attles	12/7/79-12/21/79	12/22/79	vs. New Jersey (107-101)
	Attles	12/14/73-12/27/73	12/19/73	vs. Los Angeles (102-101)
	Attles	2/22/70-3/4/70	3/6/70	vs. Phoenix (107-97)
	Senesky	11/10/56-11/21/56	11/22/56	vs. Boston (101-78)

WARRIORS ALL-TIME WINNING/ LOSING STREAKS

LARGEST MARGINS OF VICTORY

MARGIN	DATE	OPPONENT	SCORE
62	11/2/91	vs. Sacramento	153-91
59	3/19/77	vs. Indiana	150-91
46	1/15/86	vs. Utah	150-104
45	11/7/81	vs. Denver	152-107
43	11/9/61	vs. Syracuse	151-108
42	1/7/75	vs. New Orleans	136-94
41	4/2/93	at Dallas	134-93
40	3/8/90	vs. Cleveland	145-105
	11/22/75	at Washington	111-71

LARGEST MARGINS OF DEFEAT

MARGIN	DATE	OPPONENT	SCORE
63*	3/19/72	at Los Angeles	99-162
51	3/7/62	at Boston	102-153
49	3/9/69	at Boston	89-138
	2/3/67	at Los Angeles	80-129
48	1/5/69	vs. Boston	86-134
46	12/14/68	at Philadelphia	91-137
45	12/22/87	at Portland	91-136
	1/15/85	vs. Dallas	104-149
	1/8/85	at San Antonio	94-139
	3/2/80	at Philadelphia	99-144
	2/14/71	at Seattle	101-146

NBA All-Time Record

MISCELLANEOUS STATISTICS

CONSECUTIVE GAMES PLAYED

# GAMES	PLAYER	DATES
333	Wilt Chamberlain	2/16/60-3/18/64
321	Phil Smith	3/6/75-2/16/79
306	Eric Floyd	1/19/83-12/12/87
288	Joe Graboski	1954/55-1959/60
286	Neil Johnston	11/1/52-1956/57
234	Tim Hardaway	11/14/89-4/7/92
206	Rod Higgins	3/12/89-12/12/91
198	George T. Johnson	2/19/74-11/13/76
194	Joe Fulks	1947/48-1951/52
190	Chris Mullin	1/29/88-3/18/90
183	Terry Teagle	3/12/85-4/19/87
179	Jamaal Wilkes	10/18/74-11/23/76
	Clifford Ray	10/18/74-11/23/76
178	Clifford Ray	2/3/78-3/2/80

WARRIORS TRIPLE DOUBLE CLUB

PLAYER	#	MOST RECENT
Guy Rodgers	8	1/5/66
Rick Barry	6	11/6/76
Wilt Chamberlain	5	3/10/64
Tim Hardaway	4	1/16/92
Nate Thurmond	2	12/20/67
Jerry Lucas	2	2/24/71
Winston Garland	2	12/20/88
Jeff Mullins	1	2/16/68
Alvin Attles	1	12/6/68
Phil Smith	1	4/6/76
Robert Parish	1	10/29/78
Purvis Short	1	2/22/81
Mickey Johnson	1	3/10/83
Chris Mullin	1	1/9/89

WARRIORS 40-40 CLUB

PLAYER	#	MOST RECENT
Wilt Chamberlain	2	11/22/64

WARRIORS 30-30 CLUB

PLAYER	#	MOST RECENT
Wilt Chamberlain	26	2/30/64
Nate Thurmond	2	1/19/69
Robert Parish	1	3/30/79

OPPONENTS 30-30 CLUB

PLAYER	#	MOST RECENT
Wilt Chamberlain	4	2/27/68

OPPONENTS 25-25 CLUB

PLAYER	#	MOST RECENT
Wilt Chamberlain	6	4/18/67
Jerry Lucas	2	1/29/67
Sidney Wicks	2	3/17/72
Bob Pettit	1	1/20/63
Bill Russell	1	2/21/63
Bill Bridges	1	4/5/67
Happy Hairston	1	12/28/68
Elvin Hayes	1	2/14/70
Bob McAdoo	1	3/13/75
Bill Walton	1	1/24/76

OPPONENTS TRIPLE DOUBLE CLUB

PLAYER	#	MOST RECENT
Oscar Robertson	15	3/1/68
Magic Johnson	9	4/13/90
Wilt Chamberlain	6	2/13/68
Jerry West	3	11/19/65
Bill Russell	3	3/9/69
Walt Frazier	3	1/7/70

Sidney Wicks	2	11/17/72
Norm Van Lier	2	2/11/73
Alvan Adams	2	12/21/85
Lafayette Lever	2	4/21/89
Hakeem Olajuwon	2	3/3/90
Michael Jordan	2	1/15/93
Elgin Baylor	1	11/7/62
K.C. Jones	1	1/2/63
Dave DeBusschere	1	3/5/63
Guy Rodgers	1	10/18/66
Lenny Wilkens	1	12/7/68
Connie Hawkins	1	12/1/72
Bob Lanier	1	3/12/74
Kareem Abdul-Jabbar	1	3/5/76
Bill Walton	1	2/3/78
Campy Russell	1	3/7/79
Jack Sikma	1	2/14/84
Johnny Moore	1	1/8/85
Artis Gilmore	1	2/4/85
Larry Bird	1	2/19/86
Kevin Johnson	1	3/16/88
Lester Conner	1	2/2/89
Darrell Walker	1	2/5/90
Alvin Robertson	1	12/26/90
Gary Payton	1	12/21/91
Ron Harper	1	4/17/92
Micheal Williams	1	12/19/92
Mark Jackson	1	2/26/93
Kevin Gamble	1	3/16/93
Dikembe Mutombo	1	3/25/93

MISCELLANEOUS INDIVIDUAL RECORDS

CONSECUTIVE GAMES 50 OR MORE POINTS
7* Wilt Chamberlain 12/16/61-12/29/61

MOST COMPLETE GAME, SEASON
79* Wilt Chamberlain 1961-62

CONSECUTIVE COMPLETE GAMES
47* Wilt Chamberlain 1/5/62-3/14/62

CONSECUTIVE GAMES 50 OR MORE POINTS
7* Wilt Chamberlain 12/16/61-12/29/61

CONSECUTIVE GAMES 40 OR MORE POINTS
14* Wilt Chamberlain 12/8/61-12/30/61
14* Wilt Chamberlain 1/11/62-2/1/62

CONSECUTIVE GAMES 30 OR MORE POINTS
65* Wilt Chamberlain 11/4/61-2/22/62

CONSECUTIVE GAMES 20 OR MORE POINTS
126* Wilt Chamberlain 10/19/61-1/19/63

CONSECUTIVE FREE THROWS MADE
60 Rick Barry 10/22/76-11/16/76

MISCELLANEOUS TEAM RECORDS

CONSECUTIVE GAMES WON
11 Golden State 12/29/71-1/22/72

CONSECUTIVE GAMES WON, HOME
15 Golden State 12/13/89-2/15/90

CONSECUTIVE GAMES WON, ROAD
7 San Francisco 1/19/69-2/11/69

CONSECUTIVE GAMES WON, START
9 Phildelphia 10/22/60-11/11/61

CONSECUTIVE GAMES WON, END
6 Philadelphia 3/8/51-3/17/51

CONSECUTIVE GAMES LOST
17 San Francisco 12/20/64-1/26/65

CONSECUTIVE GAMES LOST, HOME
12 San Francisco 2/13/65-10/15/65

CONSECUTIVE GAMES LOST, ROAD
17 Golden State 11/6/87-1/18/88

CONSECUTIVE GAMES LOST, START
4 San Francisco 10/17/64-10/23/64
   San Francisco / Golden State 10/26/84-11/1/84

CONSECUTIVE GAMES LOST, END
6 Golden State 4/13/89-4/22/89

CONSECUTIVE OVERTIME GAMES
3* San Francisco 10/26/62-10/28/62

CONSECUTIVE OVERTIME GAMES LOST
10* Golden State 10/13/79-3/15/81

CONSECUTIVE OVERTIME LOSSES, SEASON
8* Golden State 1979-80

CONSECUTIVE GAMES 100+ PTS., SEASON
66 Philadelphia 11/4/61-2/22/62

CONSECUTIVE GAMES 100+ PTS., OVERALL
74 San Francisco 2/12/66-2/2/67

NBA All-Time Record

171

WARRIORS ALL-TIME ROSTER

MAHDI ABDUL-RAHMAN
Ht. 6'3" Wt. 185   UCLA '64   Born Apr. 15, 1942

TOM ABERNETHY
Ht. 6'7" Wt. 220   Indiana '76   Born May 6, 1954

CHUCK ALEKSINAS
Ht. 6'11" Wt. 260   Connecticut '82   Born Feb. 26, 1959

STEVE ALFORD
Ht. 6'2" Wt. 185   Indiana '87   Born Nov. 23, 1964

BOB ALLEN
Ht. 6'9" Wt. 205   Marshall '68   Born July 17, 1946

PAUL ARIZIN
Ht. 6'4" Wt. 200   Villanova '50   Born Apr. 9, 1928

ROBERT ARMSTRONG
Ht. 6'8" Wt. 230   Michigan State '56   Born June 17, 1933

VINCENT ASKEW
Ht. 6'6" Wt. 210   Memphis State '88   Born Feb. 28, 1966

AL ATTLES
Ht. 6'0" Wt. 185   North Carolina '60   Born Nov. 7, 1936

GREG BALLARD
Ht. 6'7" Wt. 215   Oregon '77   Born Jan. 29, 1955

JIM BARNETT
Ht. 6'4" Wt. 175   Oregon '66   Born July 7, 1944

RICK BARRY
Ht. 6'7" Wt. 220   Miami '65   Born Mar. 28, 1944

VIC BARTOLOME
Ht. 7'0" Wt. 230   Oregon State '70   Born Sept. 29, 1948

KENNY BATTLE
Ht. 6'6" Wt. 210   Illinois '89   Born Oct. 10, 1964

BUTCH BEARD
Ht. 6'3" Wt. 185   Louisville '69   Born May 4, 1947

ERNEST BECK
Ht. 6'4" Wt. 190   Pennsylvania '53   Born Dec. 11, 1931

HENRY BENDERS
Ht. 6'6" Wt. 185   Long Island

GALE BISHOP
Ht. 6'3" Wt. 195   Washington State '48   June 4, 1922

UWE BLAB
Ht. 7'1" Wt. 250   Indiana '85   Born Mar. 26, 1962

NELSON BOBB
Ht. 6'0" Wt. 170   Temple '49   Born Feb. 25, 1924

MANUTE BOL
Ht. 7'7" Wt. 225   U. of Bridgeport '88 Born Oct. 6, 1962

DAVE "JAKE" BORNHEIMER
Ht. 6'5" Wt. 205   Muhlenberg '48   Born June 29, 1927

COSTIC BORSAVAGE
Ht. 6'1" Wt. 200   Temple '50   Born July 25, 1924

STEVE BRACEY
Ht. 6'1" Wt. 175   Tulsa '72   Born Aug. 1, 1950

MIKE BRATZ
Ht. 6'2" Wt. 185   Stanford '77   Born Oct. 17, 1955

THOMAS BRENNAN
Ht. 6'3" Wt. 195   Villanova '54   Born Aug. 6, 1930

RON BREWER
Ht. 6'4" Wt. 185   Arkansas '78   Born Sept. 16, 1955

BILL BRIDGES
Ht. 6'6" Wt. 235   Kansas '61   Born Apr. 4, 1939

RICKEY BROWN
Ht. 6'10" Wt. 235   Mississippi St. '80   Born Aug. 20, 1958

STAN BROWN
Ht. 6'3" Wt. 200   Born June 27, 1929

WALTER BUDKO
Ht. 6'5" Wt. 220   Columbia '48   Born June 30, 1925

STEVE BURTT
Ht. 6'2" Wt. 185   Iona '84   Born Nov. 5, 1962

JOE BARRY CARROLL
Ht. 7'1" Wt. 255   Purdue '80   Born July 24, 1958

WILT CHAMBERLAIN
Ht. 7'1" Wt. 275   Kansas '58   Born Aug. 21, 1936

PHIL CHENIER
Ht. 6'3" Wt. 180   California '71   Born Oct. 30, 1950

E. C. COLEMAN
Ht. 6'8" Wt. 225   Houston Baptist '73 Born Sept. 25, 1950

DON COLLINS
Ht. 6'6" Wt. 190   Washington St. '80   Born Nov. 28, 1958

ED CONLIN
Ht. 6'6" Wt. 200   Fordham '55   Born Sept. 2, 1933

LESTER CONNER
Ht. 6'4" Wt. 185   Oregon State '82   Born Sept. 17, 1959

WAYNE COOPER
Ht. 6'10" Wt. 220   New Orleans '78   Born Nov. 16,1956

LARRY COSTELLO
Ht. 6'1" Wt. 188   Niagara '54   Born July 2, 1931

JOHN COUGHRAN
Ht. 6'8" Wt. 230   California '73   Born Sept. 12, 1951

JOE COURTNEY
Ht. 6'8" Wt. 240   Southern Miss.'92   Born Oct. 17, 1969

WESLEY COX
Ht. 6'6" Wt. 215   Louisville '77   Born Jan. 27, 1955

RON CREVIER
Ht. 7'0" Wt. 235   Boston College '83   Born Apr. 8, 1958

RUSSELL CROSS
Ht. 6'9" Wt. 240   Purdue '83   Born Sept. 5, 1961

FRANCIS CROSSIN
Ht. 6'1" Wt. 165   Pennsylvania '47   Born June 4, 1924

ED DAHLER
Ht. 6'5" Wt. 190   Duquesne '50   Born Jan. 31, 1926

HOWIE DALLMAR
Ht. 6'4" Wt. 202   Stanford '46   Born May 24, 1922

DWIGHT DAVIS
Ht. 6'8" Wt. 220   Houston '72   Born Oct. 28, 1949

WALTER DAVIS
Ht. 6'8" Wt. 205   Texas A & M '52   Born Jan. 5, 1931

GEORGE DEMPSEY
Ht. 6'3" Wt. 192   King's (DE) '51   Born July 19, 1929

DERREK DICKEY
Ht. 6'7" Wt. 210   Cincinnati '73   Born Oct. 26, 1951

CONNIE DIERKING
Ht. 6'10" Wt. 222   Cincinnati '58   Born Oct. 2, 1936

CHARLES DUDLEY
Ht. 6'2" Wt. 180   Washington '72   Born Mar. 5, 1950

TERRY DUEROD
Ht. 6'2" Wt. 180   Univ. of Detroit '79   Born July 29, 1956

PAT DUNN
Ht. 6'2" Wt. 180   Utah State '53   Born Mar. 17, 1931

PAT DURHAM
Ht. 6'7" Wt. 215   Colorado State '89   Born Mar. 10, 1967

MARIO ELIE
Ht. 6'5" Wt. 210   American Int'l. '85   Born Nov. 26, 1963

JOE ELLIS
Ht. 6'6" Wt. 175   San Francisco '66   Born May 3, 1944

CHRIS ENGLER
Ht. 7'0" Wt. 248   Wyoming '82   Born Mar. 1, 1959

RAY EPPS
Ht. 6'6" Wt. 195   Norfolk State '77   Born Aug. 20, 1956

KEITH ERICKSON
Ht. 6'5" Wt. 200   UCLA '65   Born Apr. 19, 1944

PHIL FARBMAN
Ht. 6'1" Wt. 190   CCNY '46   Born Apr. 3, 1924

DAVID FEDOR
Ht. 6'6" Wt. 192   Florida State '62   Born Dec. 10, 1940

DAVE FEITL
Ht. 7'0" Wt. 240   Texas-El Paso '86   Born June 8, 1962

DANIEL FINN
Ht. 6'1" Wt. 185   St. John's (NY) '51   Born May 27, 1928

JEROME FLEISHMAN
Ht. 6'2" Wt. 190   NY University '44   Born Feb. 14, 1922

ERIC "SLEEPY" FLOYD
Ht. 6'3" Wt. 175   Georgetown '82   Born Mar. 6, 1960

LEVI FONTAINE
Ht. 6'4" Wt. 190   Maryland State '70   Born Nov. 1, 1948

TELLIS FRANK
Ht. 6'10" Wt. 240   West. Kentucky '87   Born Apr. 26, 1965

WILBERT FRAZIER
Ht. 6'7" Wt. 210   Grambling '65   Born Aug. 24, 1942

WARRIORS ALL-TIME ROSTER

WORLD B. FREE
Ht. 6'2" Wt. 185   Guilford College '75   Born Dec. 9, 1953

JOE FULKS
Ht. 6'5" Wt. 190   Murray State '46   Born Oct. 26, 1921

MICHAEL GALE
Ht. 6'4" Wt. 190   Elizabeth City St. '71 Born July 18, 1950

DAVE GAMBEE
Ht. 6'6" Wt. 215   Oregon State '58   Born Apr. 16, 1937

VERN GARDNER
Ht. 6'5" Wt. 205   Utah '50   Born May 14, 1925

WINSTON GARLAND
Ht. 6'2" Wt. 175   SW Missouri St. '87   Born Dec. 19, 1964

JACK GEORGE
Ht. 6'3" Wt. 190   LaSalle '53   Born Nov. 13, 1928

THOMAS GOLA
Ht. 6'6" Wt. 205   LaSalle '55   Born Jan. 13, 1933

AL GOUKAS
Ht. 6'5"   St. Joseph's

MATT GOUKAS, SR.
Ht. 6'3" Wt. 195   St. Joseph's   Born Nov. 11, 1915

JOSEPH GRABOSKI
Ht. 6'8" Wt. 230   Born Jan. 15, 1930

ORLANDO GRAHAM
Ht. 6'9" Wt. 220   Auburn-Mont. '88   Born May 5, 1965

RICKEY GREEN
Ht. 6'1" Wt. 170   Michigan '77   Born Aug. 18, 1954

NORM GREKIN
Ht. 6'5" Wt. 180   LaSalle '53   Born June 22, 1930

DAVE GUNTHER
Ht. 6'7" Wt. 220   Iowa '62   Born July 22, 1937

CHARLES HALBERT
Ht. 6'9" Wt. 225   W. Texas State '42   Born Feb. 27, 1919

STEVE HARRIS
Ht. 6'5" Wt. 195   Tulsa '85   Born Oct. 15, 1963

JOSEPH HASSETT
Ht. 6'5" Wt. 185   Providence '77   Born Sept. 11, 1955

VERN HATTON
Ht. 6'3" Wt. 195   Kentucky '58   Born Jan. 13, 1936

ROBERT "BUBBLES" HAWKINS
Ht. 6'4" Wt. 190   Illinois State '76   Born June 30, 1954

KEVIN HENDERSON
Ht. 6'4" Wt. 195   Cal-St. Fullerton '86 Born Mar. 22, 1964

LAWRENCE HENNESSY
Ht. 6'3" Wt. 220   Villanova '55   Born May 20, 1929

FRED HETZEL
Ht. 6'8" Wt. 230   Davidson '65   Born July 21, 1942

ROD HIGGINS
Ht. 6'7" Wt. 205   Fresno State '82   Born Jan. 31, 1960

SEAN HIGGINS
Ht. 6'8" Wt. 210   Michigan '90   Born Dec. 30, 1968

WAYNE HIGHTOWER
Ht. 6'8" Wt. 192   Kansas '62   Born Jan. 14, 1940

GARY HILL
Ht. 6'4" Wt. 185   Oklahoma City '63   Born Oct. 7, 1941

TYRONE HILL
Ht. 6'9" Wt. 243   Xavier '90   Born Mar. 17, 1968

ARTHUR HILLHOUSE
Ht. 6'7" Wt. 230   Long Island '38   Born June 12, 1916

DARNELL HILLMAN
Ht. 6'9" Wt. 215   San Jose State '70   Born Aug. 28, 1949

LEW HITCH
Ht. 6'9" Wt. 215   Kansas State '51   Born July 16, 1929

PAUL HOFFMAN
Ht. 6'2" Wt. 205   Purdue '47   Born May 5, 1925

DAVE HOPPEN
Ht. 6'11" Wt. 235   Nebraska '86   Born Mar. 13, 1964

GEOFF HUSTON
Ht. 6'2" Wt. 175   Texas Tech '79   Born Nov. 8, 1957

JAREN JACKSON
Ht. 6'4" Wt. 190   Georgetown '89   Born Oct. 27, 1967

LES JEPSEN
Ht. 7'0" Wt. 245   Iowa '90   Born June 24, 1967

ANDY JOHNSON
Ht. 6'5" Wt. 215   Portland '54   Born Nov. 8, 1931

CHARLES JOHNSON
Ht. 6'0" Wt. 170   California '71   Born Mar. 31, 1949

GEORGE JOHNSON
Ht. 6'11" Wt. 205   Dillard '70   Born Dec. 18, 1948

LYNBERT "CHEESE" JOHNSON
Ht. 6'6" Wt. 195   Wichita State '79   Born Sept. 7, 1957

MARQUES JOHNSON
Ht. 6'7" Wt. 235   UCLA '77   Born Feb. 8, 1956

STEVE JOHNSON
Ht. 6'10" Wt. 240   Oregon State '81   Born Nov. 3, 1957

WALLACE "MICKEY" JOHNSON
Ht. 6'9" Wt. 190   Aurora College '74   Born Aug. 31, 1952

NEIL JOHNSTON
Ht. 6'8" Wt. 215   Ohio State '49   Born Feb. 4, 1929

RYAN "NICK" JONES
Ht. 6'2" Wt. 190   Oregon '67   Born Mar. 28, 1945

SHELTON JONES
Ht. 6'8" Wt. 210   St. John's '88   Born Apr. 6, 1966

RALPH KAPLOWITZ
Ht. 6'2" Wt. 170   N.Y. University '46   Born May 18, 1919

MIKE KEARNS
Ht. 6'2" Wt. 178   Princeton '51   Born June 18, 1929

FRANK KENDRICK
Ht. 6'6" Wt. 200   Purdue '74   Born Nov. 11, 1951

BILL KENNEDY
Ht. 5'11" Wt. 180   Temple '60   Born May 17, 1938

LARRY KENON
Ht. 6'9" Wt. 215   Memphis State '73   Born Dec. 13, 1952

BERNARD KING
Ht. 6'7" Wt. 205   Tennessee '77   Born Dec. 4, 1956

JAMES KING
Ht. 6'2" Wt. 175   Tulsa '63   Born Feb. 7, 1941

BART KOFOED
Ht. 6'4" Wt. 210   Kearney State '87   Born Mar. 24, 1964

HERBERT "BUD" KOPER
Ht. 6'6" Wt. 210   Oklahoma City '64   Born Aug. 9, 1942

BARRY KRAMER
Ht. 6'4" Wt. 200   N.Y. University '64   Born Nov. 10, 1942

FRANK KUDELKA
Ht. 6'2" Wt. 193   St. Mary's (CA) '52   Born June 25, 1925

FRED LA COUR
Ht. 6'5" Wt. 210   San Francisco '60   Born Feb. 7, 1938

YORK LARESE
Ht. 6'4" Wt. 183   North Carolina '61   Born July 18, 1938

RUDY LA RUSSO
Ht. 6'7" Wt. 220   Dartmouth '59   Born Nov. 11, 1937

DAVE LATTIN
Ht. 6'7" Wt. 230   Texas Western '67   Born Dec. 23, 1943

HAL LEAR
Ht. 6'0" Wt. 163   Temple '56   Born Jan. 31,1935

CLYDE LEE
Ht. 6'10" Wt. 230   Vanderbilt '66   Born Mar. 14, 1944

GEORGE LEE
Ht. 6'4" Wt. 200   Michigan '60   Born Nov. 23,1936

BOB LEWIS
Ht. 6'3" Wt. 185   North Carolina '67   Born Mar. 20, 1945

FRED LEWIS
Ht. 6'2" Wt. 195   Eastern Kentucky '47   Born Jan. 6, 1921

ALTON LISTER
Ht. 7'0" Wt. 245   Arizona State '81   Born Oct. 1, 1958

RON LIVINGSTONE
Ht. 6'10" Wt. 220   St. Mary's (CA) '49   Born Oct. 9, 1925

LEWIS LLOYD
Ht. 6'6" Wt. 215   Drake '81   Born Feb. 22, 1959

DON LOFGRAN
Ht. 6'6" Wt. 200   San Francisco '50   Born Nov. 18, 1928

JERRY LUCAS
Ht. 6'3" Wt. 235   Ohio State '62   Born Mar. 30, 1940

JOHN LUCAS
Ht. 6'3" Wt. 185   Maryland '76   Born Oct. 31, 1953

WARRIORS ALL-TIME ROSTER

TOM "TED" LUCKENBILL
Ht. 6'6" Wt. 205   Houston '61   Born July 27, 1939

PACE MANNION
Ht. 6'7" Wt. 190   Utah '83   Born Sept. 22, 1960

RICKEY MARSH
Ht. 6'3" Wt. 200   Manhattan '77   Born Mar. 10, 1954

TONY MASSENBURG
Ht. 6'9" Wt. 220   Maryland '90   Born July 31, 1967

WILLIAM MAYFIELD
Ht. 6'7" Wt. 205   Iowa '80   Born Oct. 17, 1957

JACK McCLOSKEY
Ht. 6'2" Wt. 192   Pennsylvania '48

BEN McDONALD
Ht. 6'8" Wt. 225   Cal-Irvine '84   Born July 20, 1962

HANK McDOWELL
Ht. 6'9" Wt. 215   Memphis State '81   Born Nov. 13, 1959

McCOY McLEMORE
Ht. 6'7" Wt. 230   Drake '64   Born Apr. 3, 1942

BOB McNEIL
Ht. 6'1" Wt. 180   St. Joseph's (PA) '60 Born Oct. 22, 1938

LARRY McNEILL
Ht. 6'9" Wt. 195   Marquette '74   Born Jan. 31, 1951

JOHN MENGELT
Ht. 6'2" Wt. 195   Auburn '71   Born Oct. 16, 1971

TOM MESCHERY
Ht. 6'6" Wt. 215   St. Mary's (CA) '61 Born Oct. 26, 1938

EDWARD MIKAN
Ht. 6'8" Wt. 230   DePaul '50   Born Oct. 20, 1925

DIRK MINNIEFIELD
Ht. 6'3" Wt. 180   Kentucky '83   Born Jan. 17, 1961

BILL MLKVY
Ht. 6'4" Wt. 190   Temple '52   Born Jan. 19,1931

LEO MOGUS
Ht. 6'4" Wt. 190   Youngstown '49   Born Apr. 13,1921

PAUL MOKESKI
Ht. 7'0" Wt. 255   Kansas '79   Born Jan. 3, 1957

HOWARD MONTGOMERY
Ht. 6'6" Wt. 220   Pan American '63   Born Aug. 22, 1940

JAMES MOONEY
Ht. 6'5" Wt. 212   Villanova '52   Born July 8, 1930

JACK MOORE
Ht. 6'5" Wt. 182   LaSalle '54   Born Sept. 24, 1932

ELMORE MORGANTHALER
Ht. 6'9" Wt. 230   Boston College '50   Born Aug. 3, 1922

PERRY MOSS
Ht. 6'2" Wt. 185   Northeastern '82   Born Nov. 11, 1958

JEFF MULLINS
Ht. 6'4" Wt. 200   Duke '64   Born Mar. 18, 1942

JOHN MURPHY
Ht. 6'2" Wt. 175   Born Sept. 13, 1924

KEN MURRAY
Ht. 6'2" Wt. 195   St. Bonaventure '50 Born Apr. 20, 1928

ANGELO MUSI
Ht. 5'9" Wt. 145   Temple '46   Born July 25, 1918

CHARLES "COTTON" NASH
Ht. 6'5" Wt. 225   Kentucky '64   Born July 24, 1942

WILLIE NAULLS
Ht. 6'6" Wt. 225   UCLA '56   Born Oct. 7, 1934

ED NEALY
Ht. 6'7" Wt. 240   Kansas State '82   Born Feb. 19, 1960

PAUL NEUMANN
Ht. 6'1" Wt. 175   Stanford '59   Born Jan. 30, 1938

JIM NOLAN
Ht. 6'8" Wt. 210   Georgia Tech '49   Born June 9, 1927

MIKE NOVAK
Ht. 6'9" Wt. 220   Loyola (IL) '49   Born Apr. 23, 1915

BOB O'BRIEN
Ht. 6'4" Wt. 190   Pepperdine '48   Born Jan. 26, 1927

RALPH OGDEN
Ht. 6'5" Wt. 205   Santa Clara '70   Born Jan. 25, 1948

ENOCH "BUD" OLSEN
Ht. 6'8" Wt. 230   Louisville '62   Born July 25, 1940

CLAUDE OVERTON
Ht. 6'2" Wt. 195   E. Cent. Okla. '50   Born Dec. 16, 1927

EASY PARHAM
Ht. 6'3" Wt. 200   Texas Wesleyan '50 Born Dec. 27, 1921

ROBERT PARISH
Ht. 7'0" Wt. 230   Centenary '76   Born Aug. 30, 1953

ROBERT "SONNY" PARKER
Ht. 6'6" Wt. 200   Texas A & M '76   Born Mar. 22, 1955

CHARLIE PARSLEY
Ht. 6'2" Wt. 175   Western Kentucky '48

JOHN PAYAK
Ht. 6'4" Wt. 174   Bowling Green '49   Born Nov. 20, 1926

MEL PAYTON
Ht. 6'4" Wt. 185   Tulane '51   Born July 16, 1926

JIM PETERSEN
Ht. 6'10" Wt. 235   Minnesota '84   Born Feb. 22, 1962

JAMES PHELAN
Ht. 6'1" Wt. 175   LaSalle '51   Born Mar. 19,1929

ANDREW "ANDY" PHILLIP
Ht. 6'3" Wt. 200   Illinois '47   Born Mar. 7, 1922

GARY PHILLIPS
Ht. 6'3" Wt. 189   Houston '61   Born Dec. 7, 1939

GARY PLUMMER
Ht. 6'9" Wt. 215   Boston Univ. '84   Born Feb. 21, 1962

RALPH POLSON
Ht. 6'8" Wt. 205   Whitworth '53   Born in 1930

BOB PORTMAN
Ht. 6'5" Wt. 200   Creighton '69   Born Mar. 22, 1947

PAUL PRESSEY
Ht. 6'5" Wt. 205   Tulsa '82   Born Dec. 24, 1958

KEVIN PRITCHARD
Ht. 6'3" Wt. 185   Kansas '90   Born July 18, 1967

ROY PUGH
Ht. 6'6" Wt. 210   Southern Methodist '48   Born in 1923

FRANK RADOVICH
Ht. 6'8" Wt. 235   Indiana '60   Born Mar. 3, 1938

MOE RADOVICH
Ht. 6'0" Wt. 160   Wyoming '52   Born May 5, 1929

RAY RADZISZEWSKI
Ht. 6'5" Wt. 210   St. Joseph's (PA) '57   Born Mar. 1, 1935

CLIFFORD RAY
Ht. 6'11" Wt. 235   Oklahoma '71   Born Jan. 21, 1949

BILLY REID
Ht. 6'5" Wt. 195   San Francisco '80   Born Sept. 10, 1957

MICHEAL RAY RICHARDSON
Ht. 6'5" Wt. 190   Montana '78   Born Apr. 11, 1955

MITCH RICHMOND
Ht. 6'5" Wt. 215   Kansas State '88   Born June 30, 1965

TONY ROBERTSON
Ht. 6'4" Wt. 195   West Virginia '77   Born Jan. 1, 1956

LARRY ROBINSON
Ht. 6'5" Wt. 176   Centenary '90   Born Jan. 11, 1968

JACK ROCKER
Ht. 6'5" Wt. 186   California '48   Born Aug. 12, 1922

GUY RODGERS
Ht. 6'0" Wt. 185   Temple '58   Born Sept. 1, 1935

MARSHALL ROGERS
Ht. 6'1" Wt. 190   Pan American '76   Born Aug. 27, 1953

PHIL ROLLINS
Louisville '56   Born Jan. 19, 1934

LORENZO ROMAR
Ht. 6'1" Wt. 175   Washington '80   Born Nov. 13, 1958

ALEXANDER ROSENBERGER
Ht. 5'10" Wt. 165   St. Joseph's (PA)   Born Apr. 7, 1918

LENNIE ROSENBLUTH
Ht. 6'4" Wt. 200   North Carolina '57   Born Jan. 22, 1933

JOHN RUDOMETKIN
Ht. 6'6" Wt. 205   USC '62   Born June 6, 1940

JOE RUKLICK
Ht. 6'9" Wt. 220   Northwestern '59   Born Aug. 3, 1938

JERRY RULLO
Ht. 5'10" Wt. 165   Temple '46   Born June 23, 1923

WARRIORS ALL-TIME ROSTER

CAZZIE RUSSELL
Ht. 6'5" Wt. 220   Michigan '66   Born June 7, 1944

KENNETH SAILORS
Ht. 5'10" Wt. 176   Wyoming '47   Born June 14, 1922

RALPH SAMPSON
Ht. 7'4" Wt. 235   Virginia '83   Born July 7, 1960

WOODY SAULDSBERRY
Ht. 6'7" Wt. 200   Texas Southern '57   Born July 11, 1934

BOB SCHAFER
Ht. 6'3" Wt. 195   Villanova '55

DALE SCHLUETER
Ht. 6'10" Wt. 235   Colorado State '67   Born Nov. 12, 1945

KENNY SEARS
Ht. 6'9" Wt. 195   Santa Clara '55   Born Aug. 17, 1933

GEORGE SENESKY
Ht. 6'2" Wt. 200   St. Joseph's (PA) '46

JOHN SHASKY
Ht. 6'11" Wt. 240   Minnesota '86   Born July 21, 1964

FRED SHEFFIELD
Ht. 6'2" Wt. 165   Utah '47   Born Nov. 5, 1923

PURVIS SHORT
Ht. 6'7" Wt. 215   Jackson State '78   Born July 2, 1957

GENE SHUE
Ht. 6'2" Wt. 175   Maryland '54   Born Dec. 18, 1931

ADRIAN SMITH
Ht. 6'1" Wt. 185   Kentucky '58   Born Oct. 5, 1936

CLINTON SMITH
Ht. 6'6" Wt. 210   Cleveland State '86 Born Jan. 19, 1964

DEREK SMITH
Ht. 6'7" Wt. 215   Louisville '82   Born Nov. 1, 1961

LARRY SMITH
Ht. 6'8" Wt. 235   Alcorn State '80   Born Jan. 18, 1958

OTIS SMITH
Ht. 6'5" Wt. 210   Jacksonville '86   Born Jan. 30, 1964

PHIL SMITH
Ht. 6'4" Wt. 187   San Francisco '74   Born Apr. 22, 1952

GUY SPARROW
Ht. 6'6" Wt. 218   Detroit '55   Born Nov. 2, 1932

JOHN STARKS
Ht. 6'3" Wt. 180   Oklahoma St. '88   Born Aug. 10, 1965

JOHN STROEDER
Ht. 6'10" Wt. 260   Montana '80   Born July 24, 1958

LEONARD TAYLOR
Ht. 6'8" Wt. 225   California '89   Born May 2, 1966

TERRY TEAGLE
Ht. 6'5" Wt. 195   Baylor '82   Born Apr. 10, 1960

PETER THIBEAUX
Ht. 6'7" Wt. 200   St. Mary's (CA) '83 Born Oct. 3, 1961

NATE THURMOND
Ht. 6'11" Wt. 235   Bowling Green '63   Born July 25, 1941

DARREN TILLIS
Ht. 6'11" Wt. 215   Cleveland State '82 Born Feb. 23, 1960

IRV TORGOFF
Ht. 6'2" Wt. 192   Long Island '47   Born Mar. 6, 1917

RAYMOND TOWNSEND
Ht. 6'3" Wt. 175   UCLA '78   Born Dec. 20, 1955

BILL TURNER
Ht. 6'7" Wt. 225   Akron '67   Born Feb. 18, 1944

KELVIN UPSHAW
Ht. 6'2" Wt. 180   Utah '86   Born Jan. 24, 1963

PETER VERHOEVEN
Ht. 6'9" Wt. 215   Fresno State '81   Born Feb. 15, 1959

MARK WADE
Ht. 6'0" Wt. 175   U.N.L.V. '87   Born Oct. 15, 1965

JIM WALSH
Ht. 6'4" Wt. 195   Stanford   Born Aug. 29, 1931

PAUL WALTHER
Ht. 6'2" Wt. 160   Tennessee '53   Born in 1927

BOB WARLICK
Ht. 6'5" Wt. 205   Denver '65   Born Mar. 20, 1941

CHRIS WASHBURN
Ht. 6'11" Wt. 255   N. Carolina St. '86 Born May 13, 1965

WARRIORS DRAFT CHOICES

ROUND	PICK	PLAYER	SCHOOL
1947			
1		Francis Crossin	Pennsylvania
1948			
1		Phil Farbman	C.C.N.Y.
1949			
1		Vern Gardner	Utah
2		Jim Nolan	Georgia Tech
1950			
1	3	Paul Arizin	Villanova
2	15	Ed Dahler	Duquesne
3	27	Buddy Cate	Western Kentucky
4	39	Paul Senesky	St. Joseph's (PA)
5	51	Ike Borsavage	Temple
6	63	Dick Dallmer	Cincinnati
7	75	Charles Northrup	Siena
8	87	Brooks Ricca	Villanova
9	99	Joel Kaufman	N.Y.U.
10	111	Bernie Adams	Princeton
11	123	Leo Wolfe	Villanova
12	135	Ed Montgomery	Tennessee
1951			
1	9	Don Sunderlage	Illinois
2	19	Mel Payton	Tulane
3	29	Bob Schloss	Georgia
4	39	Jud Milhon	Ohio Wesleyan
5	49	Mike Kearns	Princeton
6	59	Bob Swails	Indiana Central
7	69	George Dempsey	King's College (PA)
8	79	Jim Phelan	LaSalle
9	89	Hugh Faulkner	Pepperdine
10	99	Paul Gerwin	Cornell
1952			
1	*	Bill Mlkvy	Temple
2		Walter Davis	Texas A&M
		Tom Brennan	Villanova
		Bob Brown	Louisville
		Burr Carlson	Connecticut
		Newt Jones	LaSalle
		Nick Kladis	Loyola (IL)
		Moe Radovich	Wyoming
		Dick Retherford	Baldwin-Wallace
		Don Scanlon	Pennsylvania
		Glenn Smith	Utah
		Ben Stewart	Villanova

Territorial Choice (order of selection unknown)

ROUND	PICK	PLAYER	SCHOOL
1953			
1	1	Ernie Beck	Pennsylvania
2	10	Larry Hennessy	Villanova
3	19	Norm Grekin	LaSalle
4	28	Fred Ihle	LaSalle
5	37	Eddie Solomon	West Virginia Tech
6	46	Don Eby	U.S.C.
7	55	Bob Marske	South Dakota
8	64	Bill Dodd	Colgate
9	73	Bob Sassone	St. Bonaventure
10	81	Toar Hester	Centenary
11	88	John Doogan	St. Joseph's (PA)
12	95	Charles Duffley	St. Anselem's
1954			
1	3	Gene Shue	Maryland
2	12	Larry Costello	Niagra
3	21	Ben Peters	St. Benedict
4	30	Chuck Noble	Louisville
5	39	Rudy D'Emilio	Duke
6	48	Len Winograd	Brandeis
7	57	Bob Brady	San Diego State
8	66	Bob Hodges	East Carolina
9	75	Vince Leta	Wyoming
10	83	Bill Sullivan	Notre Dame
11	92	Frank O'Hara	LaSalle
12	95	John Glinski	
13	96	John Holup	George Washington
1955			
1	*	Tom Gola	LaSalle
		Jack Devine	Villanova
		Walt Devlin	George Washington
		Al Didriksen	Temple
		Jerry Koch	St. Louis
		Lester Lane	Oklahoma
		Bob Schafer	Villanova
		Harry Silcox	Temple
		George Swyers	West Virginia Tech
		Ed Wiener	Tennessee
1956			
1	8	Hal Lear	Temple
2	16	Phil Rollins	Louisville
3	24	Bevo Francis	Rio Grande
4	32	Phil Wheeler	Cincinnati
5	40	Joe Belmont	Duke
6	48	Mickey Winograd	Duquesne
7	56	John Fannon	Notre Dame
8	63	Max Anderson	Oregon
9	70	Ron Clark	Springfield

WARRIORS DRAFT CHOICES

ROUND	PICK	PLAYER	SCHOOL
1957			
1	6	Len Rosenbluth	North Carolina
2	14	Jack Sullivan	Mount St. Mary's
3	22	Angelo Lombardo	Manhattan
4	30	Ray Radziszewski	St. Joseph's (PA)
5	38	Jim Radcliffe	Lafayette
6	46	Alonza Lewis	LaSalle
7	53	Max Jamisson	Kentucky
8	60	Woody Sauldsberry	Texas Southern
9	67	Steve Hamilton	Morehead State
10	73	Jerry Calvert	Kentucky
Supplemental Draft			
1	1	Jerry Gibson	
1958			
1	5	Guy Rodgers	Temple
2	13	Lloyd Sharrar	West Virginia
3	21	Frank Howard	Ohio State
4	29	Temple Tucker	Rice
5	37	Don Ohl	Illinois
6	45	Bucky Allen	Duke
7	53	Jay Norman	Temple
8	61	Tom Brennan	Villanova
9	68	Nick Davis	Maryland
10	73	Larry Hedden	Michigan State
1959			
1	*	Wilt Chamberlain	Kansas
2	11	Joe Ruklick	Northwestern
3	19	Jim Hockaday	Memphis State
4	27	Ron Stevenson	Texas Christian
5	35	Bill Telasky	Geo. Washington
6	43	Joe Spratt	St. Joseph's (PA)
7	50	Joe Ryan	Villanova
8	56	Dave Gunther	Iowa
9	62	Carl Belz	Princeton
10	68	Tony Sellari	Lenoir Rhyne
11	74	Phil Warren	Northwestern

Was originally selected in 1955 out of high school as a territorial choice eligible in 1959.

ROUND	PICK	PLAYER	SCHOOL
1960			
1	7	Al Bunge	Maryland
2	15	Bill Kennedy	Temple
3	23	Bob Mealy	Manhattan
4	31	Charley Sharp	Southwest Texas
5	39	Alvin Attles	North Carolina A&T
6	47	Jim Brangan	Princeton
7	55	Bob Clarke	St. Joseph's (PA)
8	63	George Raveling	Villanova

ROUND	PICK	PLAYER	SCHOOL
1961			
1	7	Tom Meschery	St. Mary's (CA)
2	16	Ted Luckenbill	Houston
3	30	Jack Egan	St. Joseph's (PA)
4	39	John Tidwell	Michigan
5	48	Bruce Spraggins	Virginia Union
6	57	Dick Goldberg	Mississippi South.
7	66	Charles McNeil	Maryland
8	75	Larry Swift	N.E. Missouri St.
9		No Selection	
10	90	Leo Hill	Los Angeles State
Supplemental Draft			
1	6	Corky Whitrow	Georgetown (KY)
1962			
1	5	Wayne Hightower	Kansas
2	14	Hubie White	Villanova
3	23	Dave Fedor	Florida State
4	32	Garry Roggenburk	Dayton
5	41	Jack Jackson	Virginia Union
6	50	Jim Hudock	North Carolina
7	59	Howard Montgomery	Pan American
8	67	Bill Kirvin	Xavier
9	76	Tom Kiefer	St. Louis
Supplemental Draft			
1	6	Ken McComb	North Carolina
2	11	Donnie Walsh	North Carolina
3	14	Charles Warren	Oregon
1963			
1	3	Nate Thurmond	Bowling Green
2	12	Gary Hill	Oklahoma City
3	21	Steve Gray	St. Mary's (CA)
4	30	Dave Downey	Illinois
5	39	Don Turner	Southwest Kansas
6	48	Gene Shields	Santa Clara
7	57	Don Clemetson	Stanford
Supplemental Draft			
1	3	Harry Dennell	Pepperdine
2	8	Chuck White	Idaho
1964			
1	7	Barry Kramer	N.Y. University
2	16	Bud Koper	Oklahoma City
3	25	McCoy McLemore	Drake
4	34	Gene Elmore	South. Methodist
5	43	Roger Suttner	Kansas State
6	52	Ray Carey	Missouri
7	61	Dave Lee	U. San Francisco
8	70	Bob Garibaldi	Santa Clara
9	77	Camden Wall	California
10	84	Jeff Cartwright	Chapman College

ROUND	PICK	PLAYER	SCHOOL
1965			
1	2	Fred Hetzel	Davidson
1	4	Rick Barry	Miami (Fla.)
2	13	Wilbur Frazier	Grambling
3	22	Keith Erickson	U.C.L.A.
4	31	Warren Rustand	Arizona
5	40	Eddie Jackson	Oklahoma City
6	49	Jim Jarvis	Oregon State
7	58	Dan Wolters	California
8	67	Willie Cotton	Central Oklahoma
1966			
1	3	Clyde Lee	Vanderbilt
2	13	Joe Ellis	U. San Francisco
3	23	Steve Chubin	Rhode Island
4	33	Steve Vacendak	Duke
5	43	Tom Kerwin	Centenary
6	53	Jim Pitts	Northwestern
7	63	Lon Hughey	Fresno State
8	73	Ken Washington	U.C.L.A.
1967			
1	10	Dave Lattin	Texas Western
2		No Selection	
3	27	Bill Turner	Akron
4	39	Bob Lewis	North Carolina
5	51	Mike Lynn	U.C.L.A.
6	63	Dale Schlueter	Colorado State
7	75	Sonny Bustion	Colorado State
8	87	Bob Krulisch	Pacific
9	98	Richard Dean	Syracuse
10	109	Joe Galbo	San Francisco St.
11	119	Bill Morgan	New Mexico
12	130	David Fox	Pacific
1968			
1	9	Ron Williams	West Virginia
2		No Selection	
3	29	Don Sidle	Oklahoma
4	43	Edgar Lacey	U.C.L.A.
5	57	Jim Eakins	Brigham Young
6	71	Bob Allen	Marshall
7	85	Dave Reasor	West Virginia
8	99	Walt Piatkowski	Bowling Green
9	113	Art Wilmore	U. San Francisco
10	127	Bob Heaney	Santa Clara
11	140	Jerry Chandler	Nevada Southern
12	153	Bob Wolfe	California

ROUND	PICK	PLAYER	SCHOOL
1969			
1	7	Bob Portman	Creighton
2	22	Ed Siudet	Holy Cross
3	36	Tom Hagan	Vanderbilt
4	50	Lee Lafayette	Michigan State
5	64	Willie Weiss	Drake
6	78	Dan Obravak	Dayton
7	92	Pat Foley	Pacific
8	106	Steve Rippe	Santa Barbara
9	120	Greg Reed	Sacramento State
10	134	Dick Chapman	San Francisco St.
11	148	Rich Holmberg	St. Mary's (CA)
12	161	Joe Callahan	San Francisco St.
1970			
1	3	*Traded to Detroit for Dave Gambee*	
2	19	*Traded to Cincinnati for Adrian Smith*	
3	36	Earl Higgins	Eastern Michigan
4	53	Ralph Ogden	Santa Clara
5	70	Levi Fontaine	Maryland State
6	87	Vic Bartolome	Oregon State
7	104	Joe Bergman	Creighton
8	121	Jeff Sewell	Marquette
9	138	Lou Small	Nevada
10	155	Coby Dietrick	San Jose State
1971			
1	8	Darnell Hilman	San Jose State
2	25	*Traded to Portland for Jim Barnett*	
3	42	*Traded to Portland for Jim Barnett*	
4	59	Greg Gary	St. Bonaventure
5	76	Odis Allison	U.N.L.V.
6	93	Charles Johnson	California
7	110	Ken May	Dayton
8	127	Jim Haderlein	Loyola (CA)
9	143	Clarence Smith	Villanova
10	159	Bill Drosdiak	Oregon
Supplemental Draft			
1	3	Cyril Baptiste	Creighton
1972			
1		*Forfeited by selection in 1971 supplementary draft*	
2	26	*Traded to Portland for Jim Barnett*	
3	43	Bill Chamberlain	North Carolina
4	60	John Tschogl	Cal-Santa Barbara
5	76	Charles Dudley	Washington
6	93	Henry Bacon	Louisville
7	110	Bill Franklin	Purdue
8	126	John Burks	U. San Francisco
9	141	Bill Duey	California

WARRIORS DRAFT CHOICES

ROUND	PICK	PLAYER	SCHOOL
1973			
1	11	Kevin Joyce	South Carolina
2	29	Derrick Dickey	Cincinnati
3	46	Jim Retseck	Auburn
4	63	Ron King	Florida State
5	80	Nate Stephens	Long Beach State
6	97	Bob Lauriski	Utah State
7	114	Steve Smith	Loyola (CA)
8	131	Jeff Dawson	Illinois
9	146	Everett Fopma	Idaho State
10	160	Fred Lavoroni	Santa Clara
1974			
1	11	Keith Wilkes	U.C.L.A.
2	29	Phil Smith	U. San Francisco
3	47	Frank Kendrick	Purdue
4	65	Willie Biles	Tulsa
5	83	Steve Erickson	Oregon
6	101	John Errecart	Pacific
7	119	Brady Allen	California
8	137	Clarence Allen	Cal-Santa Barbara
9	155	Carl Meier	California
10	172	Marvin Buckley	Nevada-Reno
1975			
1	15	Joe Bryant	LaSalle
2	20	Gus Williams	U.S.C.
3	40	Otis Johnson	Stetson
3	51	Robert Hawkins	Illinois State
4	69	Billy Taylor	LaSalle
5	87	Larry Pounds	Washington
6	105	Tony Styles	U. San Francisco
7	123	Stan Boyer	Wyoming
8	141	Mike Rozenski	St. Mary's (CA)
9	157	Scott Trobbe	Stanford
10	171	Maurice Harper	St. Mary's
1976			
1	8	Robert Parish	Centenary
1	17	Sonny Parker	Texas A&M
2	34	Marshall Rogers	Pan American
3	—	Skip Wise	Clemson
4	68	Jeff Fosnes	Vanderbilt
5	86	Carl Bird	California
6	91	Duane Barnett	Stanford
6	104	Gene Cunningham	Norfolk State
7	122	Jesse Campbell	Mercyhurst
8	140	Stan Boskovich	West Virginia
9	158	Howard Smith	U. San Francisco
10	176	Ken Smith	San Diego State

ROUND	PICK	PLAYER	SCHOOL
1977			
1	16	Rickey Green	Michigan
1	18	Wesley Cox	Louisville
2	38	Ricky Love	Alabama-Huntsville
3	60	Marlon Redmond	U. San Francisco
4	82	Roy Smith	Kentucky State
4	87	Leartha Scott	Wisconsin-Parkside
5	104	Ray Epps	Norfolk State
6	126	Jack Phelan	St. Francis (PA)
7	146	Jerry Thurston	Mercer
8	165	Ricky Marsh	Manhattan
1978			
1	5	Purvis Short	Jackson State
1	22	Raymond Townsend	U.C.L.A.
2	40	Wayne Cooper	New Orleans
3	56	Steve Neff	Bethany Nazarene
4	77	Derrick Jackson	Georgetown
5	101	Bubba Wilson	Western Carolina
6	122	Buzz Hartnett	U. San Diego
7	142	Rick Bernard	St. Mary's (CA)
8	163	Tony Searcy	Appalachian State
9	179	Bobby Humbles	Bradley
10	193	Mike Muff	Murray State
1979			
1	9	*Traded to Boston for JoJo White*	
2	28	Danny Salisbury	Pan American
3	54	Lynbert Johnson	Wichita State
4	75	Ron Ripley	Wisc.-Green Bay
4	82	Jerry Sichting	Purdue
5	96	George Lett	Centenary
6	118	Jim Mitchem	DePaul
7	137	Ren Watson	Virginia CW
8	155	Mario Butler	Briarcliff
9	175	Gene Ransom	California
101	92	Kevin Heenan	Cal-Fullerton
1980			
1	1	Joe Barry Carroll	Purdue
1	13	Rickey Brown	Mississippi State
2	24	Larry Smith	Alcorn State
2	25	Jeff Ruland	Iona
3	49	John Virgil	North Carolina
4	71	Robert Scott	Alabama
5	95	Don Carfino	U.S.C.
6	117	Neil Bresnahan	Illinois
7	141	Lorenzo Romar	Washington
8	162	Kurt Kanaskie	LaSalle
9	182	Billy Reid	U. San Francisco
10	200	Tim Higgins	Kearney State

ROUND	PICK	PLAYER	SCHOOL
1981			
1	10	*Traded to Portland for 1978 1st Round Pick*	
2	33	Sam Williams	Arizona State
3	56	Carlton Neverson	Pittsburgh
4	76	Lewis Lloyd	Drake
4	80	Terry Adolph	West Texas State
5	102	Hank McDowell	Memphis State
6	126	Carter Scott	Ohio State
7	148	Robbie Dotsy	Arizona
8	171	Yasutaka Okayama	U. of Osaka (Japan)
9	192	Doug Murrey	San Jose State
10	213	Barry Brooks	U.S.C.
1982			
1	14	Lester Conner	Oregon State
2	35	Derek Smith	Louisville
2	38	Wayne Sappleton	Loyola (IL)
3	60	Chris Engler	Wyoming
4	83	Ken Stancell	Virginia CW
5	106	Albert Irving	Alcorn State
6	129	David Vann	St. Mary's (CA)
7	152	Matt Waldron	Pacific
8	175	Mark King	Florida Southern
9	198	Nick Morken	Tenn.-Chattanooga
10	219	Randy Whieldon	Cal-Irvine
1983			
1	6	Russell Cross	Purdue
2	43	Pace Mannion	Utah
3	53	Michael Holton	U.C.L.A.
4	77	Peter Thibeaux	St. Mary's (CA)
5	99	Greg Hines	Hampton Institute
6	123	Tom Heywood	Weber State
7	145	Peter Williams	Utah
8	169	Doug Harris	Central Washington
9	190	Greg Goorjian	Loyola-Marymount
10	212	Michael Zeno	Long Beach State

ROUND	PICK	PLAYER	SCHOOL
1984			
1	8	*Traded to LA Clippers for World Free*	
2	30	Steve Burtt	Iona
2	31	Jay Murphy	Boston College
2	35	Othell Wilson	Virginia
2	45	Gary Plummer	Boston University
3	55	Lewis Jackson	Alabama State
4	77	*Traded to Chicago for Mike Bratz*	
5	101	Steve Bartek	Doane College (NE)
5	110	Scott McCollum	Pepperdine
6	123	Tony Martin	Wyoming
7	147	Cliff Higgins	Cal-State Northridge
8	169	Paul Brozovich	U.N.L.V.
9	192	Mitch Arnold	Fresno State
10	213	Tim Bell	Cal-Riverside
1985			
1	7	Chris Mullin	St. John's
2	42	Bobby Lee Hurt	Alabama
3	49	Brad Wright	U.C.L.A.
4	71	Luster Goodwin	Texas-El Paso
5	95	Greg Cavener	Missouri
6	117	Gerald Crosby	Georgia
7	141	Eric Boyd	North Carolina A&T
1986			
1	3	Chris Washburn	N. Carolina State
2	29	*Traded to Cleveland for Darren Tillis*	
3	51	Mike Williams	Bradley
3	59	Wendell Alexis	Syracuse
4	75	Dan Bingenheimer	Missouri
5	97	Clinton Smith	Cleveland State
6	121	Bobby Lee Hurt	Alabama
7	143	Steve Kenilvort	Santa Clara
1987			
1	14	Tellis Frank	West. Kentucky
2	36	*Traded to Washington for Greg Ballard*	
3	58	Darryl Johnson	Michigan State
4	83	Bennie Bolton	N. Carolina State
5	105	Terry Williams	South. Methodist
6	152	Ronnie Leggette	West Virginia St
1988			
1	5	Mitch Richmond	Kansas State
2	41	Keith Smart	Indiana
1989			
1	14	Tim Hardaway	Texas-El Paso

ROUND	PICK	PLAYER	SCHOOL
1990			
1	11	Tyrone Hill	Xavier
2	28	Les Jepsen	Iowa
2	34	Kevin Pritchard	Kansas
1991			
1	16	Chris Gatling	Old Dominion
1	17	Victor Alexander	Iowa State
1	25	Shaun Vandiver	Colorado
2	43	Lamont Strothers	Christopher Newport
		Traded to Portland for 1995 and 1999 2nd Round Picks	
1992			
1	24	Latrell Sprewell	Alabama
2	43	Predrag Danilovic	Partizan Belgrade
2	50	Matt Fish	NC-Wilmington
1993			
1	3	Anfernee Hardaway	Memphis State
		Traded to Orlando with three future first round picks for Chris Webber	
2	34	Darnell Mee	Western Kentucky
		Traded to Denver for Josh Grant and a 1994 second round pick	

INDEX

COMMITMENT TO THE COMMUNITY

The Golden State Warriors strive to be winners both on and off the court. Their goal is to make a difference in the Bay Area communities. They consider that goal achieved each time they witness the smiles and high spirits of kids and adults alike, who come in contact with the team through their numerous and varied community programs.

What is not so apparent at times is the reciprocal nature of their outreach. Their players and coaches receive just as much as they give. Tim Hardaway proudly displays in his home the mementos given him by organizations he has helped. Drawings of the players, sent by young fans, can be found on the locker room bulletin board. Byron Houston beams when he talks about playing one-on-three with school kids from Hayward.

This is a team with heart…

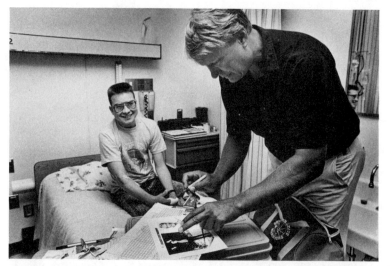

TOP: *Tim Hardaway shares some basketball tips with a tiny friend at a clinic benefitting Big Brothers/Big Sisters of Santa Clara. Photo by Daniel J. Murphy.*
BOTTOM: *Coach Nelson signs an autograph for a happy young fan at Children's Hospital Oakland. Photo by Sam Forencich.*

ABOVE: Tim Hardaway addresses a group of junior high school students during National NBA Stay in School Day. Photo by Martha Jane Stanton.

LEFT: A Junior Warriors Basketball Club member practices his shot at the annual clinic. Photo by Sam Forencich.

Chuck Gill, a member of the Warriors' wheelchair basketball team, the Road Warriors, dribbles down court. Photo by Sam Forencich.

Chris Mullin relaxes with friends from the United Way's Fund for Families, Children and Youth. Photo by Sam Forencich.

SPORTS COLLECTOR'S EDITION SERIES

Get ALL the insider information on the best Bay Area teams!

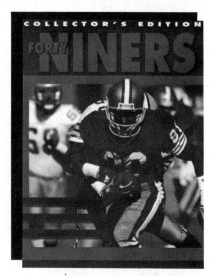

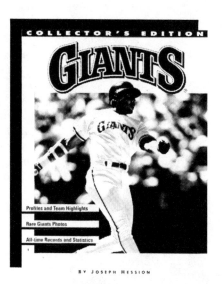

Forty Niners: Collector's Edition

by Joseph Hession—foreword by George Seifert

Giants: Collector's Edition

by Joseph Hession—foreword by Dusty Baker

These two great Collector's Editions feature the outstanding histories of two of the most colorful and exciting franchises in sports—and they're right here in the Bay Area!

You'll get the fascinating stories of great wins and heartbreaking losses, hundreds of vintage black-and-white and color photos, behind-the-scenes information, plus features on all the superstars.

These handsome Collector's Editions make outstanding gifts for your friends, relatives, co-workers and clients.

SPECIAL OFFER! Normally $19.95 each— Get both for $34.95!* Call 1-800-FOGHORN today!

*Offer expires 12/94. CA residents must add 8.5% sales tax to book prices. All orders must add $3 shipping for the first book, plus 50¢ for each additional book. To order, call 1-800-FOGHORN or send check/money order to: Foghorn Press, 555 De Haro Street, San Francisco, CA 94107.

Foghorn Press books are also available wherever great sports books are sold.